# PEDAGOGY IN HIGHER EDUCATION

What can Cultural Historical Activity Theory (CHAT) contribute to the solution of the problems facing higher education today? This edited volume brings together the work of an international group of scholars and researchers to address this important question. Drawing on contemporary interpretations of CHAT, the contributors take on a wide scope of issues, ranging from pedagogy to administration and from teacher preparation to university outreach. An introduction presents the key principles of CHAT. Subsequent chapters address such issues as effective ways of teaching large undergraduate classes, providing support for struggling writers or for students with disabilities, opening up opportunities for students from historically underserved communities, preparing students for the professions, and building bridges between higher education and the wider community. Readers with an interest in higher education will encounter ideas in these chapters that will prompt them to rethink their role in preparing today's students for tomorrow's challenges.

Gordon Wells is Professor of Education Emeritus at the University of California, Santa Cruz. As an educator, his particular interest is in fostering dialogic inquiry as an approach to learning and teaching at all levels, based on the work of Vygotsky and other sociocultural theorists.

Anne Edwards is a professor of education at the University of Oxford, where she co-convenes the Oxford Centre for Sociocultural and Activity Theory Research. She has written extensively on cultural historical approaches to learning in the workplace and in formal education settings.

# Pedagogy in Higher Education

## A Cultural Historical Approach

Edited by

**GORDON WELLS**

*University of California, Santa Cruz*

**ANNE EDWARDS**

*University of Oxford*

CAMBRIDGE
UNIVERSITY PRESS

# CAMBRIDGE
## UNIVERSITY PRESS

University Printing House, Cambridge CB2 8BS, United Kingdom

Cambridge University Press is part of the University of Cambridge.

It furthers the University's mission by disseminating knowledge in the pursuit of education, learning and research at the highest international levels of excellence.

www.cambridge.org
Information on this title: www.cambridge.org/9781107565944

First published 2013
First paperback edition 2015

*A catalogue record for this publication is available from the British Library*

*Library of Congress Cataloguing in Publication data*
Pedagogy in higher education : a cultural historical approach / [edited by] Gordon Wells, Anne Edwards.
pages    cm
Includes bibliographical references and index.
ISBN 978-1-107-01465-7 (hardback)
1. Critical pedagogy.    2. Education, Higher – Philosophy.    I. Wells, Gordon, 1935–
LC196.P453    2013
370.11′5–dc23          2013012172

ISBN 978-1-107-01465-7 Hardback
ISBN 978-1-107-56594-4 Paperback

# Contents

# Author Biographies

**Glenn Auld** is a senior lecturer working in education, teaching in the areas of language and literacy at Deakin University in Melbourne, Australia. His research interests include indigenous literacies with new media and literacies in higher education. Glenn was the inaugural winner of the Betty Watts Award for research in indigenous education from the Australian Association of Researchers in Education. He is currently exploring preservice teachers' placement experiences in a remote indigenous community.

**Tamara Ball** is a postdoctoral educational researcher working with the Institute for Science and Engineer Educators (ISEE) and the Sustainable Engineering and Ecological Design (SEED) collaborative at the University of California, Santa Cruz. She is interested in understanding how curricular and cocurricular innovations can support meaningful campus-community connections in higher education and improve learning outcomes. Her research focuses on educational designs that emphasize student initiative and agency through inquiry or problem-based learning and scientific argumentation. Her work is broadly informed by Cultural Historical Activity Theory. Dr. Ball has worked as a research Fellow with several National Science Foundation Centers for Learning and Teaching.

**Michael Cole** is a professor of communication, psychology, and human development at the University of California, San Diego. He is currently the director of the Laboratory of Comparative Human Cognition, where broad study of the role of culture in development is a central theme. He was one of the editors of Vygotsky's *Mind in Society* (1978) and author of *Cultural Psychology: A Once and Future Discipline*, published by Belknap Press of Harvard University Press (1996). He was also the originator of The Fifth Dimension, a model of university-community partnership that now exists in many countries.

**Anne Edwards** is the director of the Department of Education at the University of Oxford and with Viv Ellis convenes the Oxford Centre for Sociocultural and Activity Theory Research (OSAT). She is also a visiting professor at the University of Oslo. She has worked in the area of professional learning, using a CHAT perspective, for the last twenty years. Her most recent research and publications focus on the relational aspects of expertise in interprofessional collaborations on complex problems. She is also one of the founding editors of *Learning, Culture and Social Interaction*, a new journal published by Elsevier.

**Viv Ellis** is professor and head of Education at Brunel University in London, UK, and Professor II at Bergen University College in Norway. Prior to Brunel, he was a university lecturer in the Department of Education at the University of Oxford and co-convenor of the Oxford Centre for Sociocultural and Activity Theory Research. With Jane McNicholl, he is author of *Transforming Teacher Education: Reconfiguring the Academic Work* (Bloomsbury, 2014).

**Noah Finkelstein** is a professor in the Department of Physics at the University of Colorado, Boulder, and conducts research in physics education. He serves as a director of the Physics Education Research (PER) group at Colorado and is also a director of the Integrating STEM Education initiative (iSTEM) to establish a national-scale center for STEM learning. Finkelstein's research focuses on studying the conditions that support students' interest and ability in physics – developing models of context. These research projects range from the specifics of students learning particular concepts, to the departmental and institutional scales of sustainable educational transformation.

**Russell Francis** is a postdoctoral research Fellow with the Linnaeus Centre for Research on Learning, Interaction and Mediated Communication in Contemporary Society (LinCS) at the Department of Education, Communication and Learning, University of Gothenburg. His work explores the implications of media change for learning, cognition, and education.

**Jan Georgeson** graduated from Oxford University (1980, experimental psychology) and worked on research projects examining reading and visual perception. She took a PGCE at Bristol Polytechnic in 1984 and taught children with special educational needs in secondary, primary, and preschool settings. She completed a doctorate in educational disadvantage and special educational needs at Birmingham University in 2006 and then joined the Improving Disabled Student Learning in Higher Education project of the Teaching and Learning Research Programme. Since then she has been involved in projects supporting schools to collect data about disabled pupils and investigating interprofessional working by early years practitioners.

**Anton Havnes** is a professor at the Centre for the Study of Professions at Oslo and Akershus University College for Applied Sciences. His main interests of research are learning and assessment in higher education, professional education, workplace learning, and educational development in higher education.

**Geoff Hayward** is the head of the School of Education at the University of Leeds. Previously he worked in the Department of Education at the University of Oxford where he was the director of research; the associate director of the ESRC Research Centre for Skills, Knowledge and Organisational Performance (SKOPE); and a director of the Nuffield 14–19 Review of Education and Training. His research interests include vocational education and training policy and practice, higher education–business interaction, and sociocultural theory.

**Lisa Hunter** is the director of the Institute for Scientist and Engineer Educators at the University of California, Santa Cruz, and the director of the Akamai Workforce Initiative at the University of Hawaii. She develops, manages, and evaluates education programs aimed at increasing the diversity of science, technology, engineering, and mathematics (STEM). Her work focuses on inquiry, diversity, and equity and how they are related. Her projects are primarily aimed at promoting changes in higher education at the undergraduate and graduate levels.

**Ioanna Kinti** is currently a visiting lecturer in the Department of Public Policy and Business Administration at University of Cyprus and an associate research Fellow with the ESRC Research Centre for Skills, Knowledge and Organisational Performance (SKOPE) at the Department of Education, University of Oxford, where she received her doctorate in 2008. A member of the Oxford Centre for Sociocultural and Activity Theory Research (OSAT) group at the Department of Education during her doctorate and postdoctorate years, Ioanna is now focusing her research and teaching on knowledge, learning, and collaborative expertise within and between organizations.

**Jorge Larreamendy-Joerns** is an associate professor and chair of the Department of Psychology at Universidad de los Andes (Colombia). His empirical work inquires, from a sociocultural perspective, about science learning in formal and informal settings and issues such as learning and identity. He has been a visiting professor at the Learning Research and Development Center

(University of Pittsburgh). Currently, his teaching focuses on research methods (particularly discourse analysis and ethnography) at the graduate level.

**Natalie Lundsteen** is a higher education researcher and consultant. She received her doctorate from the University of Oxford and is currently a research associate in the Oxford Centre for Sociocultural and Activity Theory Research (OSAT) in the Department of Education at the University of Oxford and a research associate in the Centre for Skills, Knowledge and Organisational Performance (SKOPE) at the University of Oxford and Cardiff University. Her current research projects focus on the development of expertise in practices, student development theory, and university student transition experiences.

**Monica E. Nilsson** is an assistant professor of education in the Department of Child and Youth Studies at the University of Stockholm, Sweden. She received her PhD in education from the University of Helsinki, Finland, in 2003. Dr. Nilsson's research focuses on early childhood education and on higher education.

**Honorine Nocon** (PhD, University of California, San Diego) is an associate professor of linguistically diverse education at the University of Colorado, Denver, and the associate dean for Teaching and Learning in the School of Education and Human Development. Nocon uses qualitative methods and a sociocultural historical lens in her research on the development of language, culture, and content knowledge in contexts in which people from diverse culture groups interact. An ethnographer of formal and informal learning contexts, Nocon is an affiliate scholar with the Laboratory of Comparative Human Cognition at the University of California, San Diego.

**David R. Russell** is a professor of English in the rhetoric and professional communication area at Iowa State University. He has published widely on writing in the disciplines and professions, international writing instruction, and computer-supported collaborative learning. All are theorized with Cultural Historical Activity Theory and genre theory. His book, *Writing in the Academic Disciplines: A Curricular History*, examines the history of American writing instruction since 1870. He coedited a special issue of *Mind, Culture, and Activity* on writing research, *Writing Selves/Writing Societies: Research from Activity Perspectives*, and *Writing and Learning in Cross-National Perspective: Transitions from Secondary to Higher Education*.

**Holli A. Tonyan** (PhD) is an assistant professor of psychology at California State University, Northridge. After completing undergraduate studies in psychology at Carleton College, she completed graduate psychological studies in education at the University of California, Los Angeles, where she studied links between and among the ecologies of home, child care, and peers as contexts for development. During a postdoctoral fellowship in psychology at the University of California, Santa Cruz, she studied Cultural Historical Activity Theory. She was a lecturer of early childhood education at Monash University in Melbourne, Australia, before taking her current position.

**Chandra Turpen** is a research associate at the University of Maryland, College Park. She completed her PhD in physics at the University of Colorado at Boulder, specializing in physics education research. Chandra's work involves designing and researching contexts for learning within higher education. In her research, Chandra draws from the perspectives of anthropology, cultural psychology, and the learning sciences. Through in situ studies of classroom and institutional practice, Chandra focuses on the role of culture in science learning and educational change. Chandra pursues projects that have high potential for leveraging sustainable change in undergraduate STEM programs and makes these struggles for change a direct focus of her research efforts.

**Gordon Wells** is a professor of education at the University of California, Santa Cruz. His particular interests are fostering dialogic inquiry as an approach to learning and teaching at all levels, based on the work of Vygotsky and other sociocultural theorists. Previously, he was the director of the Bristol Study of Language Development (1969–84) and a professor at the Ontario Institute for Studies in Education/University of Toronto (1984–2000), where he was involved in a collaborative action research project, "Developing Inquiring Communities in Education" (DICEP), funded by the Spencer Foundation. Previous books he has authored include *The Meaning Makers* (second edition), Multilingual Matters (2009); *Dialogic Inquiry*, (Cambridge University Press 1999); and *Action, Talk and Text: Learning and Teaching through Inquiry* (Teachers College Press 2001).

**Deborah Downing Wilson** is a research associate in the Laboratory of Comparative Human Cognition and a lecturer at the University of California, San Diego. Her research, writing, and teaching explore the intersection of education, culture, and communication, with a focus on the social and intellectual development of university students. Her ethnographic research is conducted among undergraduates engaged in academic activities in intercultural settings, both on and off the university campus. She is particularly interested in experiential learning, in facilitating the transition from student life to engaged citizenship, and in promoting the smooth deployment of university-acquired knowledge in the larger social arena.

# Introduction: The Changing Face of Higher Education

## Gordon Wells and Anne Edwards

Higher education, initially small universities gathered around respected teachers, has always had two purposes: first, to provide an advanced education in the disciplines that support the existing order by maintaining existing knowledge and passing this knowledge on to succeeding generations; second, to offer opportunities for research, debate, and the extension of knowledge. There is a third purpose, which, although not so explicit, has become increasingly important, namely to provide a forum for the articulation and critique of the values of societies that proclaim themselves to be democratic. These – sometimes competing – roles of universities as guardians of established knowledge and as creators of new understandings through challenging existing beliefs have been central to their contributions to society. For example, in the late Middle Ages and the Renaissance, alongside educating those who sustained the two pillars of a stable society, universities were pivotal in the rediscovery of the intellectual achievements of Greece and Rome and, based on them, in the creation of new knowledge and values, particularly in the sciences.

To a considerable degree, contemporary higher education is still assumed to have the first two functions of creating and stabilizing knowledge, which have allowed institutions of higher education to both shape and respond to the educational demands of the societies of which they are a part. However, in the past two centuries, there have been several specific changes in the ways higher education has been expected to perform its functions for the benefit of the larger society.

First, the Industrial Revolution provoked an emphasis on the knowledge involved in the practical application of new discoveries, particularly in the sciences. This led initially to the creation of new disciplines such as engineering, medicine, and, more recently, computer science and applied psychology to meet the need for workers with the specialized knowledge and skills necessary for the development of a modern, technology-based society.

Second is the enormous expansion of higher education in the past fifty years to enable all those who meet the required entry criteria to benefit from advanced education, with specialization in their chosen field. In addition, higher education now also caters for older students who wish either to improve their qualifications or to develop a personal interest through more systematic study. However, while this expansion has widened the demographic range of the student population, it has come at considerable cost, both in the increased size of classes and reduced opportunities for individual tutoring, and in the fees borne by students or their families, which place a particularly onerous burden on students from minority or impoverished backgrounds. At the same time, to meet the growing demand for postsecondary education, additional tertiary institutions, such as community colleges, have been created, which means higher education is no longer solely the responsibility of universities.

The third major change is the increasing dependence of many public universities on alternative sources of funding to overcome shortfalls in state support for their teaching functions. The result is that universities are being forced to operate like businesses, with faculty pressured to seek large grants, to devote time to research and publication, and to engage in entrepreneurial activities, all at the expense of a commitment to teaching at a time when increasing participation rates are making additional demands on faculty teaching responsibilities.

All three changes have arisen through challenges presented by society to the original functions and boundaries of higher education. By responding to these demands, higher education has played – and continues to play – an important role both in the development of individual citizens through their formal education and – albeit less directly – in their contributions to the directions taken by society as a whole. The enduring tension between the roles of universities as guardians and creators/exploiters of knowledge has therefore meant that higher education has changed considerably in the past century or so in response to the changes in the social, political, and technological contexts in which it is embedded and to which it has substantively contributed. However, it does not follow that these changes, in themselves, constitute improvements. Indeed changes in societal demands continue to present challenges for the sector, challenges that we suggest call for a renewed emphasis on the pedagogies of higher education. The question of how best to meet these demands is the focus of this collection of chapters. But before going into further detail about the individual chapters, we first wish to outline what we consider some of the most important challenges facing higher education today.

## Challenges Facing Higher Education in the Twenty-First Century

### *Equity of Participation*

As already mentioned, as a result of expansion, there is now much wider participation in higher education than even half a century ago. In many countries, there is at least partial state financial support for students whose families cannot afford to pay the fees and other necessary expenses, and this has made it possible for many more academically successful students from lower-class backgrounds to gain the benefits of attending college or university. However, several categories of young people are still largely excluded: those with disabilities that make it difficult for them to study in the same ways and at the same pace as their age peers; the children of immigrants whose home language is different from the language of instruction; children of families who live in impoverished neighborhoods, particularly found in large urban areas; and children from minority groups that have traditionally been socially excluded.

While many colleges and universities engage in outreach activities that attempt to better prepare students from these groups to qualify for admission, their efforts are only partially successful in overcoming the barriers they face. In a democratic society, every young person should have an equal opportunity to become prepared to meet the criteria for entry into higher education. At present, however, opportunities are not equal, because the schools students attend differ greatly in the quality of education they provide, and, within these schools, the additional support minority students need is often not available. It seems clear, therefore, that if all segments of society are to have the opportunity to benefit equally from higher education, outreach needs to go beyond the upper level of secondary schools to contribute to the improvement of public education more generally.

### *Theories of Learning*

The expansion of higher education came at a time when theories of learning and teaching were undergoing major changes. In the early part of the twentieth century, behaviorism was the accepted paradigm, with its emphasis on association and reinforcement as the key concepts. This theory had little influence on the way small seminar classes and tutorials were conducted in colleges and universities. But when classes began to increase in size (currently some introductory courses are taught to a thousand or more students), the old ways of teaching became unmanageable and, for want of a better alternative, teaching reverted to "delivering the curriculum," with an emphasis on lectures and textbooks, and with learning assessed by exams mainly concerned to test whether students can correctly remember what has been taught.

Furthermore, all new learning is now recognized as building on the learner's previous experiences and what he or she currently understands.

In the meantime, many of the behaviorist assumptions about human development, learning, and teaching have been challenged by theoretical and empirical research, which has led to a very different conception of the ways they are interrelated.

First is the active nature of learning. Far from being overwhelmed by a confusing barrage of sensory input, from the beginning the newborn infant actively works on constructing meaning of the events in which he or she is involved. Theorists vary in how far they attribute the meanings that are made – the concepts or schemata that are constructed – to the innate organization of the mind and brain, but all are agreed that the infant's learning is dependent on acting in the world and gaining information through feedback that allows "hypotheses" to be tested and, when necessary, revised.

Second is the recognition that learning is not solely an individual achievement. A considerable amount of learning occurs through taking part in activities undertaken jointly with others, in which more expert participants model and provide assistance in mastering the knowledge and skills that need to be learned. And third, learning is no longer seen as a purely cognitive process, because it involves the learner's social relationships with other participants as well as his or her emotions and motivation with respect to what has to be learned.

These new theories of learning, which are now supported by a wide range of technology-enhanced pedagogical tools, call for a different kind of teaching from the traditional lecture and test approach. Not only do students need to play a more active part in the construction of knowledge, but they also need to engage collaboratively with their peers in this process. Furthermore, in addition to the necessary focus on the core concepts of the discipline into which they are being apprenticed, students should be encouraged to explore the social and political implications of what they are learning through projects that foster their creativity and self-direction in planning and carrying out practical investigations and interventions beyond their role as students. Thus, higher education should be not only a preparation for a career but also a basis for lifelong learning as an informed and engaged contributor to the wider society.

### Blurring the Boundaries of Higher Education

These goals, and the forms of active learning that support them, have also led to a questioning of simple relationships between acquiring knowledge in universities and applying that knowledge in the fields of practice. Simple knowledge transfer is no longer taken for granted; instead the alternative notion of progressive transitions has led to a new focus on the learning trajectories of students as they move between sites of higher education and the workplace. This focus on student learning across diverse sites has required universities, particularly in the area of professional preparation, to develop pedagogic partnerships with a wide range of workplaces. At the same time, the relationships between academic researchers and research users have placed new emphases on the co-configuration of new knowledge in partnerships that span the boundaries between universities and other institutions in the wider society.

While these developments ensure a stronger link between universities and the societies in which they are situated, these societies now recognize that they in turn are embedded within transnational, indeed global, economic and social systems. Globalization and the social mobility it requires present new challenges to national systems of standardized accreditation, and these challenges are leading universities to think of their teaching as well as their research in international terms.

### Education as Business

In many countries, state support for higher education in recent decades has failed to keep pace with the increasing numbers of students eligible for admission. In addition to increasing class sizes, as already mentioned, institutions of higher education have had to find other ways to balance their budgets. This has led to a considerable increase in the search for alternative sources of funding. Particularly in universities, the securing of large research grants from industry, as well as from national research councils, has become a major activity in which all faculty members are encouraged to participate. Indeed, one of the criteria by which these institutions are judged is the total amount of external funding they are able to obtain.

An inevitable consequence of this business orientation is that securing grants and carrying out the research for which the grants were obtained becomes the first priority for many faculty members. They therefore have less time to devote to their role as educators. True, research grants allow the most able graduate students to be employed as research assistants and to benefit from the stipends involved; however, this reduces the likelihood of these students gaining the apprenticeship into university teaching that is possible when they are employed as teaching assistants in large courses. The long-term effect of treating institutions of higher education as businesses is that improving the quality of undergraduate education through adoption of the methods derived from contemporary theories of learning and teaching is likely to have a low priority. The challenge for institutions of higher education, therefore, is to achieve a better balance between keeping afloat in hard times and continuing to fulfill their major responsibility of providing the best possible education for their students.

## Preparing Students for the Professions

As has long been the case, higher education plays a major role in preparing those who plan to enter the professions. In this way, it has a strong influence on the kinds of knowledge that shape the various professions and organize the world of business and industry, though, as we have observed, new partnerships mean this knowledge is now developed in closer relationship with the fields in which it is used. Crucially, this responsibility is not confined to ensuring that graduates from professional programs are fully abreast of the latest theories and technologies in their fields. Equally important is that they have given serious and sustained thought to the roles the professions serve in society and to the values that guide the performance of those roles. This is particularly important in the preparation of future educators, because it is on them that many aspects of the future of society as a whole depends.

So far, we have considered how universities and other institutions of higher education have, over time, faced a series of potential contradictions between their espoused purposes and societal demands and on how they have attempted to resolve those contradictions. However, responses to the new challenges posed by globalization, global warming, and the ongoing financial crisis have shown even more starkly that the problems outlined here have not been adequately resolved and, indeed, that they are now more pressing than ever.

The editors of this volume and the contributing authors share the belief that analytic tools developed in the tradition of Cultural Historical Activity Theory (CHAT) may contribute to meeting these challenges in ways that are in accord with the key purposes of higher education just outlined. In the next section, therefore, we offer a brief overview of the development of the key principles of this theory for those who may not be familiar with it.

## The Contribution of Cultural Historical Activity Theory (CHAT)

Although relatively new to the English-speaking world, Cultural Historical Activity Theory originated in Russia in the 1920s and 1930s in the work of Lev Vygotsky and his colleagues, Alexander Luria and Alexei Leontiev. Suppressed by the Soviet government for several decades, the work was continued after Vygotsky's death by Luria and Leontiev, and gradually became publicly available again in the late 1950s with the first translation into English of Vygotsky's major text, which appeared in 1962 under the title *Thought and Language* and included a foreword by Jerome Bruner. Since then, works by all three intellectuals in the original group have been published in many languages in addition to English, and scholars from around the world have continued to develop the theory.

Reacting to the prevailing psychological theories of the early twentieth century, Vygotsky and his colleagues set out to develop an alternative that would center on the explanation of human consciousness, with the aim of creating a theory that would provide a basis for improving the human condition. Central to this project was Vygotsky's important initial insight that, unlike other species, which act directly on the objects of importance to them, humans make use of artifacts to mediate their actions. The most obvious of these artifacts are material tools, but Vygotsky recognized that "signs" – language, diagrams, and so forth – also function in an analogous way to mediate mental activity. Furthermore, he argued that, over the course of phylogenetic development and the historical development of individual cultures, human beings had increasingly come to use these different artifacts to regulate their own material actions and mental processes – "from the outside in" – and thus to gain greater control over the world around them. This concept of "double stimulation" – creating an artifact to mediate action – played an important role in the group's early experiments and in Luria's later work in neuropsychology. In more recent times, recognition of the self-direction made possible by these mediational means has provided the basis for the development of a theory of human "agency" (Stetsenko & Arievitch , 2004).

Much of Vygotsky's own research focused on the role of semiotic (i.e., sign-based) mediation in human development. Unlike those who see conceptual development as largely building on innate foundations, Vygotsky distinguished between natural and cultural development, arguing the two are intertwined from the beginning, with biological inheritance given specific form by the child's participation in a particular culture. This led him to emphasize the importance of history for understanding development: not only do individuals develop over time, but so do cultures and the families, communities, and institutions that constitute them. Hence the name "cultural-historical" for the theory Vygotsky and his colleagues originated.

Leontiev summarized Vygotsky's thinking about the development of higher psychological, or mental, functions:

The tool mediates activity and thus connects humans not only with the world of objects but also with other people. Because of this, humans' activity *assimilates the experience of humankind.* This means that humans' mental processes (their "higher psychological functions") acquire a structure necessarily tied to the sociohistorically formed means and methods transmitted to them by others in the process of cooperative labor and social interaction. But it is impossible to transmit the means and methods needed to carry out a process in any way other than a social form – in the form of an action or external speech. In other words, higher psychological processes unique to humans can be acquired only through interaction with others, that is, through interpsychological processes that only later will begin to be carried out independently by the individual. (1981, pp. 55–56, emphases in the original)

During his brief professional life, Vygotsky had a continuing interest in the role of semiotic mediation in the developing relationship between speaking, thinking, and concept development. From his research and in reaction to Piaget's early work on "egocentric speech," Vygotsky proposed a sequence in which children's speech development starts as an integral aspect of their social interaction with other speakers; then, around three to four years of age, they begin to vocalize their speech – even when alone – as an "egocentric" accompaniment to, or director of, their own actions; finally, this externalized speech for self loses its external aspect and becomes what Vygotsky called "inner speech," the medium for solo thinking and problem solving. Through this sequence of development, children gradually take over the ways of thinking already established in their culture, transforming them into a personal medium for reasoning, problem solving, and reflection through the dialogue of inner speech.

In his last book, *Thinking and Speech*, Vygotsky turned his attention to the role of semiotic mediation in the early school years, when children begin to encounter and gradually master what he called "scientific concepts" – or what is nowadays called "academic language." It was in this context, too, that he developed most fully the metaphor of "the zone of proximal development" (zpd). Because he believed that learning leads development, he argued that "learning is only good when it proceeds ahead of development," and so, when a teacher works in a student's zpd by assisting him or her with a task he or she cannot manage alone, the student's learning "awakens and rouses to life those functions which are in a stage of maturing" (1987, p. 212). While Vygotsky envisaged the assistance being given by an expert other, some scholars have proposed that development can also be advanced by other participants in a collaborative activity in which no member is an expert but all learn with and from each other (Wells, 1999). Expanding this line of thinking further, it becomes clear that all knowledge is created, as well as appropriated by individuals, in the discourse among people working together in a specific situation to create or improve an artifact or to solve a problem of importance to the group.

Whereas Vygotsky tended to focus on interpersonal interaction and the relationship between speaking and thinking, Leontiev was more concerned with the context of activity in which tool use as well as symbolic interaction occurred. However, both were in agreement that "cooperative, goal-directed, artifact-mediated activity" was the basic unit of analysis. In the years following Vygotsky's death in 1934, Leontiev went on to give greater precision to the concept of activity by proposing an analysis involving three levels or strata: activity, action, and operation. From one perspective, these categories can be treated as a hierarchy, with an activity carried out through an action or sequence of actions, each consisting of one or more operations. However, as Leontiev formulated the relationship between the three strata, it is clear he also thought of them as different perspectives on the same event: "When a concrete process – external or internal – unfolds before us, from the point of view of its motive, it is human activity, but in its subordination to a goal, it is an action or chain of actions" and "the action has special qualities, its own special 'components,' especially the means by which it is carried out … actions are concerned with goals and operations with conditions" (1981, pp. 61, 63).

Another way of distinguishing among the three perspectives is according to their relative scope. Activities are driven by motives to meet basic human needs and, as such, are not individual in origin but are collective endeavors that are socially and historically developed within a particular culture. Actions, on the other hand, are specific instantiations of an activity and are situated in a particular time and place with goals appropriate to the occasion. Furthermore, because each occasion involves particular participants and available resources, the operations by means of which an action is carried out will depend on these aspects of the situation.

By putting forward this tri-stratal theory of human activity, Leontiev clarified the relationship between individuals' actions and the larger activity systems in which those actions are carried out. First, a particular activity can be enacted in many different ways and, similarly, the same action may play a part in different activity systems. Second, over time, what started as an action may take on the characteristics of an activity system in its own right, as is the case with the development of formal education. Third, an action that initially required thoughtful attention to goal and operational means can become so routinized that it is spontaneously recruited as an operation within a more encompassing action. An example might be a child who first has to deliberately carry out a calculation involving multiplication with pencil and paper but, having memorized the multiplication tables, can do the calculation in his or her head.

Artifacts
Tools and
Practices

Subject                              Object ⟶ Outcome

Values
Rules &                                              Division
Conventions            Community                    of Labor

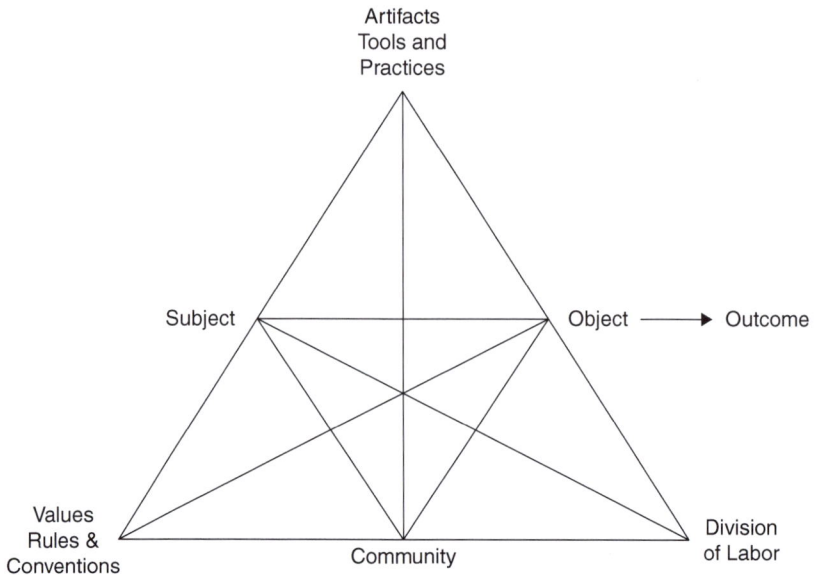

FIGURE 1.1.  Engeström's (1987) representation of an activity system.

Like Vygotsky's theory of semiotic mediation and intellectual development, Leontiev's activity theory has been expanded and put to use in a
variety of research contexts. Particularly influential has been Engeström's
(1987) representation of an activity system in terms of nested mediational
triangles, which show the ways a subject's action on an object with the aid
of mediating artifacts is related to the community activity system in which
it occurs, with its division of labor and its values, rules, and norms (see
Figure 1.1). This conceptual tool has played a key role in the various projects conducted in the field of developmental work research.

   Another important addition to the toolkit is Lave and Wenger's (1991)
conceptualization of learning as an inherent aspect of participation in a
community of practice (CoP), as newcomers gradually move from being
legitimate peripheral participants to knowledgeably skilled old-timers.
Of particular importance from their perspective is the recognition that
learning through participation does not require formal instruction; also
that identity is formed and developed in the process of moving from the
periphery toward the center of the community of practice.

   Once full recognition is given both to the cultural-historical nature of development and to the complex ways individuals become reciprocally related to
increasingly larger groups and to society at large, it becomes necessary to
be explicit about which of the possible levels of analysis is/are appropriate

for a particular research investigation and about how they are related to each other in terms of foreground and background. Rogoff (2003) proposes thinking in terms of different focuses – personal, interpersonal, and cultural-institutional – all three of which are simultaneously relevant in seeking to understand any event. Depending on their purpose, researchers foreground one of these focuses, but, she argues, they should not ignore how the others, presently backgrounded, throw light on what is at the focus of their current attention. Cole (1996) makes a related point in discussing the ways "context" has been conceptualized. Typically, what is not at the focus of the researcher's attention is treated as "that which surrounds"; but this leads to analyses in terms of unidirectional "influences" on what is in focus. Instead, he suggests thinking of context as the "interweaving" of all the elements involved: (a) persons in their relationships to each other and to the artifacts that mediate their interactions with each other and the object of their activity; (b) the beliefs, norms, and values of the activity systems and institutions in which these actions and interactions take place; and (c) the dimension of time, on which the inventions and achievements of previous generations are incorporated and adapted in present activity to create an imagined future.

A final point to be emphasized, whether thinking in terms of activity systems or communities of practice, is that individual persons participate in multiple activities and practices and contribute to any one of these in the light of what they have learned from participation in others; at the same time, their unique contributions play a part in shaping the ongoing development of those same activity systems, communities, and institutions. Furthermore, in the course of their participation, they are forming and transforming their own knowledge, skills, values, and identities, and thus their potential for further development.

In the preceding section, we offered a brief account of some of the most important ideas that have contributed to the development of Cultural Historical Activity Theory. They have emerged as the outcomes of the actions and interactions of scholars and researchers in many disciplines, and, as with many outcomes of activity, they have, in turn, been put to use as tools – mediating artifacts – in further activities. Next, we describe how the authors of the chapters in this volume have made use of some of these tools in attempts to meet the challenges outlined in the opening section of the chapter.

## OVERVIEW OF CHAPTERS

The following chapters are arranged in two main parts, each with further subdivisions. The first part includes contributions concerned with learning and

teaching in higher education and with the resources that support that responsibility; the second includes those concerned with relations between institutions of higher education and the professions for which they prepare their
students, with a subsection devoted to the preparation and further development of teachers and administrators in K-12 schools.

### Part One

*Pedagogy: Teaching Undergraduates*
Teaching has always been a major responsibility of higher education, but, for the
reasons set out earlier in this chapter, it is not currently carried out as effectively
as it should be. The authors of the chapters in this section are concerned about
the current predominance of large, lecture-based classes and report on ways
they are trying to offer alternative approaches based on CHAT principles.

Attempting to organize classes at the undergraduate level so that students engage
in genuine educational activity is the focus of the chapter by Deborah Downing
Wilson and Michael Cole. Their concern is with creating activities in which the
acquisition of knowledge is the motive of students' behavior. Two case studies, taken
from different courses, each designed with CHAT principles in mind, show how
these principles helped make goal formation a routine part of educational activity
and enabled connections between goal formation and identity development.

The third chapter, by Chandra Turpen and Noah Finkelstein, uses activity
theory to analyze two attempts at changing modes of teaching in a university
physics department. The first was the introduction of "peer instruction," in classes taught by different professors, as a means to engage students as producers
rather than as consumers of scientific knowledge. The use of "tutorials" in section meetings was the focus of the second attempt, again with different teachers. In both cases it is shown that, when a new approach is adopted by different
individuals, it may be realized by different activity systems, leading to different
learning opportunities.

Gordon Wells, in the fourth chapter, describes a large introductory class on
theories of education, which he endeavored to teach by enacting as well as presenting CHAT principles. The organization of the course and the reasons for
adopting its specific features are described and students' reflective comments
illustrate their experiences of the course and the transformations that occurred,
for some, in their conceptions of learning and of teaching.

*Resources for Learning*
In his chapter, David Russell reviews North American research on writing
in higher education that draws on CHAT, and argues that writing (often in

conjunction with other media) is profoundly important, mediating learning and underpinning assessment. This research has helped to support student learning through attention to students' writing and to teachers using writing as a teaching tool. It has also led to researchers tracing how writing mediates practices in higher education, including the transition to workplaces, the selection and sorting of students, and the uses of technology.

The main focus in Anton Havnes's chapter is the pedagogical aspects of assessment. Emphasizing the historical development of assessment and the competing interests involved in driving and obstructing its development as a pedagogical resource, he outlines a theoretical rationale for assessment from a CHAT perspective. This rationale includes a multilayered analysis of: (a) learning, instruction, and assessment practices and institutional development and change; (b) individual actions by students and teachers and historically mediated social practices; and (c) the relational demands on students, teachers, and policy makers.

Russell Francis similarly tackles the multilayered contexts in which learners find themselves. Reviewing the role of social and participatory media in public and private life, he suggests that, to understand their implications for higher education, it is necessary to explore the disjuncture between emergent self-directed learning practices supported by students' expanding access to new media and e-learning technologies owned, regulated, and managed by centralized services. He brings Engeström's (1987) version of activity theory to bear on vignettes from a two-year study of university students to reveal how highly resourceful practitioners are becoming adept at negotiating personalized learning trajectories through this hybrid media ecology.

### Equity of Access

With support from the National Science Foundation, many U.S. universities are attempting to increase access to careers in science and engineering for members of traditionally underrepresented groups through intensive programs of preparation for university study. Tamara Ball and Lisa Hunter describe one such program that involved a summer internship in a science lab supported by a carefully designed mentoring program, the aim of which was to help the interns develop the skills necessary to engage in scientific argumentation. In their study, they used CHAT principles to analyze video-recorded interactions to identify the material, interpersonal, and institutional features of the learning environments in both parts of the program that supported or constrained the development of interns' ability to participate effectively in scientific argumentation.

Equity of access demands that students with disabilities are provided with appropriate forms of support to enable them to participate in courses of study on equal terms with their peers, In her chapter, Jan Georgeson draws on data from a national study that followed a cohort of disabled students through their undergraduate courses at different UK universities to explore how CHAT can contribute to an understanding of how students declaring a disability are served by the different support systems they encounter. She argues that students positioned at the boundaries of disability are particularly likely to be involved in working through contradictions within these systems, and that this can affect the development of both their own identities and staff members' understanding of disability provision.


## Part Two

### Higher Education and the Professions

As undergraduates prepare for life after graduation, a wide range of possible professions vies for their services. It is critical, therefore, that universities provide opportunities for them to investigate the roles the various professions serve in society and the values that underpin their activities while, at the same time, equipping them with the necessary knowledge and skills to qualify them for selection in their chosen fields. Encouraging them to undertake internships or other forms of professional experience prior to making their choice is one important way to help them make informed decisions about their future careers.

In the first chapter in this section, Natalie Lundsteen and Anne Edwards report on a five-year study of how students following a variety of undergraduate programs experience three-month placements in an investment bank. They use CHAT concepts to examine how interns navigate the landscape of the banks; the implicit and explicit mediation in play; the kinds of consequential transitions that occur; the relational support offered; and their experiences of the investment bank as a social situation for their own development as potential investment bankers or as people who decide banking is not for them.

Jorge Larreamendy-Joerns's chapter also focuses on a form of internship, but one that forms the culmination of an undergraduate program leading to qualification as a psychologist. The context for his chapter is an institutional change taking place in many Latin American universities involving a reduction in the length of undergraduate programs, which significantly affected the learning trajectories of the students he studied. As he found from his analysis of interviews with them, their supervised practicum was a critical moment in their identity formation, for they were learning not only the craft of professional psychology, but also how much they did not know and needed to learn and become – learning to be ready even when you are not.

The chapter by Ioanna Kinti and Geoff Hayward is concerned with how research training programs prepare graduate students to become researchers in the social sciences. Becoming a researcher, they suggest, involves: (a) learning to negotiate expertise and identity in debates with knowledgeable others; and (b) developing collaborative working skills to foster work across disciplinary and professional boundaries, while also learning to share such skills with peers and younger researchers. However, from a CHAT perspective, they argue, the generic and transferable skills approach widely used in research training does not really address the capabilities young researchers need to engage effectively with knowledge creation at discipline, practice, and organizational boundaries.

*Teacher Education*
Of all the professions, teacher education could be considered the closest to the central activities of higher education, since the quality of teaching in schools is critical for the education of children who aspire to engage successfully in postsecondary education. However, Viv Ellis makes two broader claims: first, that "teacher education is almost uniquely situated as an activity of the public university that has a democratizing function"; and second, that the practices involved constitute a democratic and powerful mode of knowledge production, which grows out of hybrid practices and involves different kinds of knowledge, different forms of professional and practitioner expertise, and dialogue between researchers, research subjects, and research users. In his chapter, Ellis develops these claims by distinguishing the different kinds of knowledge involved and, as an illustration, discusses the use of the tools of Engeström's (2007) developmental work research methodology in a school-university partnership designed to create new spaces for learning.

When university-based teachers work with practitioners to support their learning, they aim at an interplay between the field of practice and useful concepts, through evidence-based conversations. These conversations can ratchet up conceptualizations of the field and allow informed scrutiny of everyday responses to problems of practice. Holli Tonyan and Glenn Auld discuss the challenges of attempting this kind of pedagogy when working in a setting in which familiarity with the local field is lacking. They outline how CHAT tools helped them build a basis of common knowledge in a course for early years professionals in Singapore and how that became a springboard for a more engaged pedagogy.

Starting from the premise that schools and universities must attempt to align pedagogic practices with contemporary learning theory as well as with contemporary societal needs, Honorine Nocon and Monica Nilsson discuss several projects based on the "Fifth Dimension" model in which they have participated as university researchers working in partnerships with schools and other educational institutions and, in particular, two cases that involved the university training of future teachers. In such contexts, they argue, while a pedagogic model based on CHAT principles is very relevant, it is prudent to adopt an approach of "gentle participation."

## Conclusion

In describing the projects in which they are engaged, the authors of the chapters in this volume do not claim to have completely solved the problems they are tackling, still less to have addressed all the challenges currently facing higher education. However, because CHAT attempts to explain the transformations that occur in individuals, in institutions, and in the associated artifacts and procedures that mediate the activities in which they are all involved, the conceptual tools it offers have the potential to enable researchers and practitioners to make visible and to systematically address the problems looming for higher education and public education in general. We hope the studies described here encourage engagement with the resources CHAT offers researchers and practitioners in the field of higher education.

## References

Cole, M. (1996). *Cultural Psychology: A once and future discipline*. Cambridge, MA: The Bellknap Press of Harvard University Press.

Engeström, Y. (1987). *Learning by Expanding: An activity-theoretical approach to developmental research*. Helsinki: Orienta-Konsultit.

   (2007). Putting Vygotsky to Work: The change laboratory as an application of double stimulation. In H. Daniels, M. Cole, and J.V. Wertsch (Eds.), *The Cambridge Companion to Vygotsky* (pp. 363–82). New York: Cambridge University Press.

Lave, J. and Wenger, E. (1991). *Situated Learning: Legitimate peripheral participation*. New York: Cambridge University Press.

Leontiev, A. N. (1981). The problem of activity in psychology. In J. V. Wertsch (Ed.), *The Concept of Activity in Soviet Psychology* (pp. 37–71). Armonk, NY: Sharpe.

Rogoff, B. (2003). *The Cultural Nature of Human Development*. New York: Oxford University Press.

Stetsenko, A. and Arievitch, I. (2004). The self in cultural-historical activity theory: Reclaiming the unity of social and individual dimensions of human development. *Theory and Psychology*, **14** (4), 475–503.

Vygotsky, L. S. (1987). Thinking and speech. (N. Minick, trans.). In R. W. Rieber and A. S. Carton (Eds.), *The Collected Works of L. S. Vygotsky, volume 1: Problems of General Psychology* (pp. 39–285). New York: Plenum.

Wells, G. (1999). *Dialogic Inquiry: Towards a sociocultural practice and theory of education*. Cambridge: Cambridge University Press.

# 2

# Goal Formation and Identity Formation
# in Higher Education

## Deborah Downing Wilson and Michael Cole

In this chapter we describe a form of education we have been developing for upper division students who are primarily, but not entirely, social science majors at the University of California, San Diego (UCSD). As data we offer two individual case studies drawn from two different courses. Each course was designed with CHAT principles in mind although they differed markedly in the particularities of their organization as a result of the institutional niches within which they were located.

In offering these cases we hope to achieve two goals. First, we want to highlight the usefulness of CHAT in guiding the design of courses that make goal formation a routine part of educational activity. Second, we want to contribute to recent efforts to bring together the writings of CHAT theorists on the organization of developmental education with writings about identity formation. These two topics come together in a particularly interesting way when considering CHAT and *higher* education because going to college coincides with the period of life referred to as late adolescence and emerging adulthood, which has been a central focus of developmentalist scholars studying identity formation.

In recent decades, a number of proposals have been made for ways to integrate the line of CHAT theories derived from Vygotsky with those emanating from the work associated with Erik Erikson (e.g., Holland & Lachicotte, 2007; Penuel & Wertsch, 1995). The research reported here was carried out as part of this "integrationist" project.

In seeking to corral the complex mixes of issues that arise when pursuing such an "integrationist" approach, our strategy of exposition is the following: first, we examine the role of goal formation in the constitution of educational activity from a CHAT perspective and the challenge of designing courses that maximize goal formation in formal systems of higher education. Next, we summarize key recent writings that bring together CHAT theorizing about goal formation with relevant literature on identity development, particularly as it applies to the developmental challenges associated with the transition to adulthood. We follow these theoretical considerations with our case studies. We hope to provide enough detail about each example to convey how we sought to make goal formation central to students' coursework experiences and how, through processes of self-documentation, students made available for our analysis the interweaving of identity formation and cognitive development in educational activity.

### Educational Activity and Goal Formation

In the early 1980s, Vasilli Davydov, best known in the United States for his experimental curriculum in mathematics education, visited UCSD. He ended one of his lectures with a laugh, declaring: "You will never see educational activity in a regular school." He was referring to K-12 education, but the issue he had in mind applies equally to higher education.

Yrjo Engeström explained the issues Davydov was referring to in these terms:

The essential peculiarity of school-going as the activity of pupils is the strange "reversal" of object and instrument. In school-going, text takes the role of the object. This object is molded by pupils in a curious manner: the outcome of their activity is above all the same text reproduced and modified orally or in written form (summarized, classified, organized, recombined, and applied in a strictly predetermined manner to solve well-structured, "closed" problems). (Engeström, 1987, pp. 100–101)

Many readers will recognize the close affinity between these views and those of John Dewey (1916 and passim). A common design strategy of those who seek to ensure students are, in fact, allowed to pursue goals of their own choosing as a part of educational activity has been to find ways to connect schooling with its social context so that, in Dewey's words, learning in school has "social meaning."

At our university, the vast majority of students are evaluated primarily on the basis of their ability to respond to short answer or multiple choice questions, covering materials in which all of the answers have been figured out ahead of time. The most utilitarian goal under such circumstances is routinely to get good grades on the tests (e.g., the texts are the object of activity, and the motives for acting are restricted to success in school going – the mastery of received knowledge). Our solution to this problem, in CHAT terms, is to organize college instruction so that a variety of "leading activities" that are a part of each student's life world (most prominently, affiliation, play, and peer interaction) are made a routine part of the instructional process.[1]

## Identity Formation and the "College-Going Age"

The "college-going age" is a particularly advantageous point at which to bring together an analysis of identity formation and goal formation. For many decades, Erik Erikson has been a focal figure for those who seek to understand the transition from childhood to adulthood. He called this transition process "identity formation," during which young people must sort through and make sense of their childhood identities. According to Erikson, college-aged students must reconcile a variety of social pressures (for example, choice of occupation, intimate relationships, political and religious beliefs) as they develop from a state of exploration of the choices life presents to commitments that reconcile the inevitable contradictions that arise as one or another of life's circumstances has to be dealt with. He characterizes this reconciliation process as follows:

The wholeness to be achieved at this stage I have called a *sense of inner identity*. The young person, in order to experience wholeness, must feel a progressive continuity between that which he has come to be during the long years of childhood and that which he promises to become in the anticipated future; between that which he concedes himself to be and that which he perceives others to see in him and to expect of him. Individually speaking, identity includes, but is more than, the sum of all the successive identifications of those earlier years when the child wanted to be, and often was forced to become, like the people he depended on. (1968, p. 87)

Erikson's work is an attractive starting point for bringing together identity theory and CHAT because, as Holland and Lachicotte (2007) note, he accorded cultural and historical factors an essential role in identity formation. Moreover, one can find in his writing the idea of a symmetrical relation between sociocultural-historical factors and biologically individually unique factors,

[1]  Within a CHAT framework, the study of human ontogeny, when speaking of developmental "stages" one must take account not only of broad changes in mental function, but changes in kinds of activity a child of a given age is likely to engage in. According to Leontiev, "In studying the development of the child psyche, we must therefore start by analyzing the child's activity, as this activity is built up in the concrete conditions of its life.... Life or activity as a whole is not built up mechanically, however, from separate types of activity. Some types of activity are the leading ones at a given stage and are of greatest significance for the individual's subsequent development, and other are less important. We can say accordingly that each stage of psychic development is characterized by a definite relation of the child to reality that is the leading one at that stage and by a definite, leading type of activity" (1981, p. 395).

which marks identity formation as double sided and mutually constitutive. To support his ideas, Erikson drew on a variety of materials, including biographical accounts of such historical icons as Luther and Gandhi, and explorations of cultural variations, including his work among Native Americans.

However, those seeking to integrate Erikson and Vygotsky confront at least two difficulties. Developmental psychologists have proposed a variety of methods to assess where individuals are located on the Eriksonian developmental path, with a special eye on youth whose mental health may be considered at risk. At the same time, they have sought to provide evidence of identity formation with respect to specific issues including gender identity, ethnic identity, and so on (See Grotevant, 2001; Lightfoot, Cole, & Cole, 2009; Marcia, 2002). The methods used in these cases (interviews, questionnaires, etc.) have the unfortunate consequence of representing the social context of the individual almost entirely by their "social address," making the actual process of identity formation unavailable for analysis.

Aware of these difficulties, CHAT researchers have sought to provide a more adequate theory of adolescent/emerging adult development by incorporating a complementary account of the sociocultural environment, especially the social relations within which identity formation takes place. This commitment to conceiving of identity formation as a double-sided process highlights a second issue CHAT theorists must deal with – the source of the data for conclusions about identity formation.

CHAT theorists interested in integrating ideas about identity formation into their account of human development have followed Penuel and Wertsch's admonitions that:

1. researchers must "study identity in local activity settings where participants are actively engaged in forming their identities" and
2. it is also necessary to "examine the cultural and historical resources for identity formation as empowering and constraining tools for identity formation" (1995, p. 83).

These considerations have been incorporated into the work of Holland and Lachicotte, whose research program is closely related to our own. First, they argue for the study of identity formation as a part of the wide variety of activities people have chosen to engage in – activities important to their everyday lives. Second, they argue that George Herbert Mead's sociological approach to the self enables researchers to focus on "everyday encounters," with people generalized as social "types." From this perspective, "people form a sense of themselves – identities – in relation to ways of inhabiting roles, positions, and cultural imaginaries that matter to them" (2007, p. 103). Holland and

Lachicotte give examples of such varied roles as a skater, a theoretically sophisticated anthropologist, and a moderate republican. We attempt in the examples examined in this chapter to show how this perspective can be introduced into higher education.

A second challenge to research interested in integrating the ideas of identity and CHAT is that Erikson and Vygotsky (as well as Piaget) display a common tendency to overestimate the logical coherence they attribute to the "wholeness" or the "coherence" of fully formed adult identity. This tendency is on clear display in the following, almost unreadable passage:

> In psychological terms, identity formation employs a process of simultaneous reflection and observation, a process taking place on all levels of mental functioning, by which the individual judges himself in the light of what he perceives to be the way in which others judge him in comparison to themselves and to a typology significant to them; while he judges their ways of judging him in the light of how he perceives himself in comparison to them and to types that have become relevant to him. (Erikson, 1968, pp. 22–23)

The difficulty with this line of thought is that empirical research over the past several decades has led developmentalists to reject the idea of "structures of the whole" with respect to either cognitive processes or identity formation during the adolescent years. For example, Kuhn and Franklin's handbook chapter summarizing cognitive development during adolescence is unequivocal in rejecting the idea of a time in human life when thought is entirely coherent. Although the emergence of a formal operational stage remains a centerpiece of developmental textbooks, they write, "no contemporary scholarly review of research evidence endorses the emergence of a discrete new cognitive structure at adolescence that closely resembles Inhelder and Piaget's description of formal operations" (2006, p. 954).

A particular appeal of Holland and Lachicotte's approach, in light of the shortcomings of attributing identity formation to a hypothetical "system of the whole," is that they seek the origins of identity formation, not in Vygotsky or Piaget's ideas about true concepts or logical thought in adolescence, but in the domain of rule-based games characteristic of middle childhood. For Vygotsky, rule-based games are an activity in which children "acquire the ability to become part of a conceptual world beyond their immediate surroundings in order to become actors who submit to the premises of the game and treat events of the game as *real*. Their desires and motivations become related to a 'fictitious I,' to their roles in the game and its rules" (1978, pp. 112–13).

Holland and Lachicotte argue that in the transition from childhood to adulthood this ability/proclivity to engage the world fictitiously reaches beyond games to characterize their participation in "figured worlds" or "cultural worlds." Such worlds, they write, "refer to socially and culturally constructed realms of interpretation and performance in which particular characters and actors ... are recognized" (2007, p. 115). Identity is performed as actors work to synchronize thoughts and behaviors, internalizing and personalizing society's goals and norms, transforming themselves and their figured worlds in the process. "As a higher-order psychological function, identities constitute a relatively organized complex of thoughts, feelings, memories, and experiences that a person can, more or less, durably evoke as a platform for action and response" (2007, p. 116).

With these ideas in mind, we now turn to our attempt to trace the intertwining of goal formation and identity formation as undergraduates engage in courses deliberately designed to promote goal formation as central to learning that drives developmental change. We begin with the initial focus of our design – to arrange for goal formation as a central part of the educational process. The evidence that emerged from this effort suggests that arranging for goal formation in the ways we did also laid bare the connectedness of educational activity and identity formation. That part of the story unfolds when we get to the case studies.

## Designing for Goal Formation

Both of the two courses we describe in this chapter are designed to promote the processes of *educational activity*. Practically speaking, this requires the students to engage in the process of goal formation as a routine matter in fulfilling the course requirements. In both courses we apply three strategies to arrange for goal formation to occur.

1. Create educational activities that destabilize ordinary classroom practice.
2. Provide multiple sources of motivation by "mixing" leading activities (e.g., affiliation, play, learning, peer relations, work).
3. Ensure reflective practices are a routine, instrumental aspect of their coursework.

With these guideposts in mind, we now turn to the classes and an illustrative case study that takes place within each of them.

## The Practicum Class

LCHC's practicum courses have their roots in the Fifth Dimension and still bear many of the trademark characteristics of that model (see Cole and the Distributed Literacy Consortium, 2000). Canonically, students participate twice a week in an after school program located in community settings, such as schools, libraries, boys' and girls' clubs, community centers, and churches. Each quarter the activities and curricula are differently nuanced depending on the location and population of the site and the interests of the various instructors and researchers, but they always center around issues of learning, development, class, ethnicity, gender, and technology.

Naturally, the undergraduates come into the course with goals of their own, the most salient being to earn a good grade in a course that meets a requirement for graduation. Using that goal as a starting point, the course is structured so that, to get a good grade, the students must identify a research question of personal interest that arises from their daily interactions in the community setting. Because these are real-life situations, new goals must be repeatedly formulated in response to real and unpredictable complications; for the same reason, the students' actions have real consequences. Goal formation becomes a matter of simple survival.

Reflection is also a routine, instrumental feature of the course. In addition to the site visits, the students meet twice a week on campus in seminar-style class sessions. Here they discuss readings chosen for their relevance to the practicum program, recount practicum experiences they believe relevant, and discuss how these experiences relate to the assigned readings. Following each site visit the students write "ethnographic field notes," which they post to a searchable class database, where they are read and commented on by the course instructors, other researchers at the site, and their peers in the class. In addition to a narrative account of their interactions, these notes include a final "reflection section," where the students add comments about their interpretations of the days' events and link them to other events at the site and to the class readings.

At the end of the term, the undergraduates prepare two final papers. The first is a report of the results of their research project. The second is a "final reflection paper" in which they are asked to review their field notes in sequential order and then create an account of their own learning and development in the program.

### Practicum Case Study – Jason

When he entered the practicum class, Jason was a college senior who had entered UCSD as a business major but switched to communication in his junior year. He had waited until the last moment to fulfill his "research methods" requirement and was now enrolled in "The Design of Social Learning Environments" course because it was the only option that fit his schedule.

Jason (like all of the students in this class) understood his task was to engage kids in an after school program in computer-based learning games and to help them with their various homework assignments.

Jason's Chinese-American father was an executive in a large firm with offices in California and Hong Kong. Jason had attended a public (English-speaking) elementary school in the United States while his father was completing his graduate studies, and then an (English- and Chinese-speaking) high school in Hong Kong when his father's job took them there. Jason was completing his undergraduate work at UCSD and applying to MBA programs in California.

The practicum site for Jason's class was a Catholic mission in a working-class Mexican barrio. As a rule, a dozen or more children ranging in age from five to fifteen, five to six undergraduates, a local "site coordinator," and the professor or a teaching assistant gathered in a small facility with two rooms and an outdoor grassy area located on the grounds of a Head Start center at the mission. There they played computer games, completed homework assignments, and engaged in outdoor activities of various kinds four afternoons a week (see Vasquez, 2002 for a full description of the site and the activities).

During the first week of classes, students were introduced to the community site and its activities. They also wrote their first field notes. In what follows, we use accounts derived from these field notes to trace the processes of central concern in this chapter. (Excerpts from student field notes are included in *italic font*. Except as noted, they are presented chronologically.)

### Week 1

Given the topic of the course and the aims of our research, we were concerned to read the field notes Jason submitted after his first site visit.

*There is a big difference in the work ethics of the Chinese and Mexican families. The Mexican parents don't place the same emphasis on education as the Chinese. They think it's fine if their kids drop out of school and get menial jobs because that way they can start to bring money into the family at a younger age. In Hong Kong the children are forced to study hard and stay in school because the parents know that in the long run the kids will be better off.*

We responded indirectly to these initial sentiments by rearranging the order of the reading assignments, selecting an essay for the week on socioeconomic and cultural differences in parenting and on their presumed influence on schooling and child development. As was our regular practice, we close-read the crucial passages in class and organized discussion groups where the students explored these subjects in some depth. In the class discussion following the initial site visit, Jason was outspoken in his opinions. He insisted his desire was to teach the children about the Chinese work ethic and the Chinese emphasis on education as the proper way to better one's life. Other undergraduates attempted to convince him that the Mexican families' situation might not be comparable to his own, but for Jason the situation was clear cut: Mexican immigrant families simply do not value education, and until they do they will be trapped in poverty. The undergraduates' task, as he saw it, was to open their eyes to this fact.

As we mentioned earlier, the students were asked to shape a research question and create a research plan to guide their participation during the quarter. At the time Jason was enrolled in the program, there was considerable local media coverage and a heated public debate over the proposed tightening of immigration practices at the San Diego/Tijuana border. Jason immediately decided to build his research paper around the local families' understanding of the politics of immigration. He drew up a collection of interview questions, a schedule for data collection, and a plan for slipping his questions unobtrusively into conversations with the older kids while assisting them with their homework. Jason was all business. By contrast, his classmates, following the normal practices in the course, took several weeks to sort things out and come up with their research questions.

On his second day at the mission Jason was observed using his questionnaire to interview Natalie, a girl attending middle school, as he helped her with an online writing assignment. His field notes included a detailed account of Natalie's homework progress, but made no mention of their conversations around the immigration issue.

### Weeks 2-3

When Jason arrived on his third day at the mission, second grader Miguel ambushed him and claimed him as his "buddy for the day." If Jason had planned to collect more interview data that day, Miguel's antics ensured it did not happen, and Jason's third set of field notes made no mention of his research project. Instead he talked about his new little buddy at the mission, referring to the two of them as *"together in our outsiderness."*

*Miguel and I both came from families where English isn't the first language. I have encountered the difficulties in learning English, especially the spelling and pronunciation. So, I shared with Miguel some methods that I have adopted when I first learned English, and it was very satisfying to see that Miguel had made some significant improvement after my advice. I think this class should include some readings on bilingual education and on English as a second language, so that we are better equipped to help the kids.*[2]

After his next visit, by which time he had read the assigned article on social class and child rearing by Annette Lareau (2002), Jason's field notes contained the following comments:

*I think Miguel's mom is intimated by the UCSD professors, and maybe even a little by the undergraduates as well. Lareau states that this is normal for low income parents. I think she is embarrassed about her English, or maybe she is just very thankful for our help. I'm not sure.*

From our own observations, we knew Miguel's mother, Rosario, to be a small, pretty, energetic woman who took a fierce interest in her children's academic progress. She had been bringing them to the mission for academic assistance for just over a year. She spoke little English, but it was her habit to help out with snacks and in other small ways as she monitored the situation to see that her children did not get distracted before they completed their homework.

By week 3, Jason and Miguel were spending their afternoons together and Jason displayed a growing awareness that Miguel's mother was in fact interested in her children's education; the beliefs he had articulated so clearly in the first week of class were being tested, as the following field note comments reveal.

*Miguel's mom is acutely aware that she can't help her kids with their homework and she insists that the only thing they are allowed to do with us is homework. When the other kids are outside playing, Miguel has to sit at the homework table. I take him outside to kick a ball around because I think he needs a little break and she doesn't really say anything to us, but I can tell she doesn't want us to be out there too long. She always brings us food to thank us for helping out. It's a little strange, but nice of her I guess.*

### Week 4

In the fourth week of that term, a child's seemingly minor homework assignment rocked the class, Jason most of all. On this particular day, Jason, Jessica (a fellow undergraduate in the class), and several children were all sitting at a table discussing an art project Miguel was working on. Jason was sitting

---

[2] Ironically, Jason's comments following his initial visit to the site (and the resulting reorganization of the reading list) had caused us to hold back the literature on bilingual education, which was accompanied by a presentation of strategies we have found effective when working with Spanish-speaking children. We would introduce them in the following weeks.

next to Miguel and across the table from Miguel's little sister, Juanita. Rosario was observing from her place at the counter, where she was preparing snacks for the undergraduates and children. Below is Jessica's account of this day's homework session:

*On his second assignment Miguel was to draw a map of his bedroom from a bird's eye view. Miguel did not at first get it, but after discussing the assignment for a bit Miguel began to better understand, and as he drew he described to us what was in his room. At first we couldn't understand why he kept drawing curtains in the middle of the space. I thought he was trying to be funny and I just wanted him to get the assignment done. We soon learned that Miguel shared a room with his little sister Juanita, his parents, his grandma and his older cousin. Sharing one room with five other people! I kept thinking that Miguel was just confused and that all those people were really not all in a single room, but he kept saying it and I finally knew. He explained that they had curtains between the beds and that he and his sister would try and sneak out of their bunk beds to be able to see the television, hidden behind the curtain in his parents' portioned area of the room.*

On campus the next day, Jessica and Jason were eager to discuss the event with the rest of the class. Jason kept repeating that this new information put Miguel's mother's "*obsession with homework in a whole new light.*" While he had been aware that no one at Miguel's home could help him with any assignments requiring English, he now understood that the task was further complicated by a lack of space – there simply was no place at home for Miguel to study. In his field notes, Jason described the map-making events much as Jessica had. But in the reflection section of his notes, he compared the situation confronting Miguel and his mother with his own family experience.

*I'm starting to see a major difference between my mother who doesn't speak English and the parents at LCM. My mother has a college degree in China. She knew all of the concepts that I was learning in school. She could explain them to me in Chinese and then I would translate them into English. Some of these parents don't have an education in any language. That is why they bring their children here to us. On one hand I can see why people complain that they (the Mexican immigrants) are a burden to American society. On the other hand if I was in their situation I would be trying to get all of the help I could to help my children get ahead.*

Miguel's bedroom map was the focal topic of conversation among the students that week; at week's end they remained unsettled and overwhelmed by the newly revealed chasm between themselves and the children in their care. Jason's responses in class were typical of the other undergraduates – concerned and uncertain about what if anything he or the class could do to ameliorate the situation.

**Week 5**

When Jason next went to the mission he took with him a set of photographs to show Miguel. They were photos of high-rise apartment buildings in Hong Kong. Each building seemed to be a little city in its own right. Laundry was hanging from every window on the crowded upper floors. The common spaces in the buildings were teeming with meat and vegetable sellers, roaming vendors hawking prepared foods, clothing items, and houseware. Jason showed the pictures to Miguel and told him about extended families that live in single rooms high up in the buildings, who sometimes go for days without ever setting foot on the ground below. It was obvious that Jason had spent a good part of his weekend locating and printing the collection of photographs – photographs that now served as common ground linking Miguel's crowded living conditions to those of people from Jason's far away homeland.

Miguel took great pleasure in this new information, and repeatedly told animated (and heavily embellished) stories about life in Hong Kong to anyone who would listen. A new calm seemed to settle over Jason. It also appeared to us, on the basis of Jason's participation in class and at the mission, that his attitudes toward Miguel, Miguel's mother, Spanish-speaking minorities, and education in general, were growing more complex. His field notes from the following session provide further evidence of this rethinking process.

*I never paid much attention to the lives of other Chinese in America. My father was educated here and then went back to Hong Kong to work, but some of his friends stayed here and their families have always lived here and I think they are all doing fine with plenty of money and everything. I'm thinking that the chances for education are what makes everything different. I know that there are poor Chinese families who came here with nothing and could not go to school because they had to work day and night and now they are still living in poor conditions and just getting by. Now I think it's wrong to say that they are lazy. In fact they probably work harder than anyone, harder than the educated ones.*

**Jason's Final Reflections**

We skip now to the end of the course. Jason never completed the immigration-focused interview project he began with. Instead, he chose to collaborate with two classmates to make a short video production about the after school program. In fact, he made no mention of his original research plans at all until his final reflection paper, based on his rereading the field notes he had written from day one onward. In this paper, he reported that during his first interview with Natalie he learned she and her two younger stepbrothers had been coming to the mission for several years. When he asked her what she knew about the immigration issue Natalie broke into tears (an event no one else had noticed, or at least, no one had recorded in their field notes). Then she told him her stepfather, who did odd jobs for the mission during the afternoons, was in the country legally, but her mother was not. Her younger brothers, born in San Diego to a legal immigrant, were safe, but should Natalie's mother be deported, Natalie, born in Mexico, would have to leave as well. Jason wrote:

*Her step dad is trying to adopt her, just in case, but that takes money, which they don't have much of. Natalie lives in fear. She says she wants to go wherever her mom goes, but her mom wants her to stay here because her educational opportunities are better. I think her dad would also need her help with the two little boys. Natalie will be the one caught in the middle.*

That was the first and last data-collecting interview Jason conducted. Nothing in his notes explains his decision, but through his conversations in class we surmised his brief glimpse of the immigration situation through Natalie's eyes shattered his preconceived hypothesis, and at that time he had no idea how to regroup around the issue. As the quarter progressed, and through his relationship with Miguel, we believe Jason began that regrouping process.

In his final reflection paper, Jason referred to the practicum course as the "hardest and best experience of my life" and then proceeded to write, not about himself or his development as he had been asked to do, but about his concerns for the children at the mission. Just as he had on day one, at the end of his time with us Jason was still expounding on the importance of education, but unlike his earlier rants, this reflection is nuanced, complex, and heartfelt.

*A few days ago, during a class discussion, we talked about how some kids were dealing with learning two languages at the same time. And it was actually one of the things that have always been in my mind. I worked with Miguel a lot, and several times when I was driving back to home from LCM, I would be "worried" about Miguel's learning.... It has been on my mind constantly since the class began. One day, the younger kids, when they are at my age, I am sure that they will have mastered English, but my concern is their situation right now.... I now see that my parents, being educated and having a better understanding of the world, would never let me give up, but these kids' parents, being uneducated and not understanding the world, don't know how to support their children in this. It's not that I worked any harder. These kids work hard. It's that I had a vision of what an educated person looked like and my parents understood what the steps were to get there. Who is going to take this role for these children?*

## Jason after Graduation

The evidence provided so far indicates Jason's experience in the practicum class profoundly shifted his ideas about social class, language, and ethnicity, going beyond what he learned about the children and families at the site to include himself. But, as this same evidence testifies, Jason had resolved neither his uncertainties about how to understand the situation of Mexican immigrant children nor any of the major tasks of identity formation common in the literature on adolescent identity formation.

He had shifted his major, but not his career choice. True to the path his father had laid out for him, Jason attended business school and earned an MA in communication management. He then accepted an internship with a large firm in Hong Kong. However, in his latest correspondence Jason tells us he is now employed by the YMCA in California. He did not share with us his reasons for leaving Hong Kong, but he now organizes community outreach programs aimed at improving educational possibilities for underrepresented youth from a largely Chinese neighborhood.

## Jason's Developmental Pathway: The Interweaving of Goal Formation and Identity

In this section we pause to summarize several key moments in which the interplay of goal formation and identity formation are particularly visible. Jason entered the class with one goal in mind, to earn a passing grade in a course required for graduation. He identified himself as a "good student" and, in keeping with that identity, he immediately prioritized the requirements listed on the syllabus and set about accomplishing them as efficiently as possible. He was engaged in school-going activity. The first goal he set for himself was to design and carry out a research project about a local immigration controversy, but this was quickly derailed when his questioning revealed far more about his subjects' family lives than he was prepared to deal with. Before he was able to find his way back on track with that project, Miguel grabbed Jason's leg – and never let go. Once again Jason was thrown off center, finding himself poorly equipped to understand and meet the needs of his new little buddy. Jason's friendship with Miguel brought affiliation and peer interaction as sources of motivation into what had been school-going activity. In the process of becoming friends with Miguel, Jason formulated a new goal – finding common ground around issues of ethnicity, socioeconomic status, parental education, and attitudes toward academics.

Jason's somewhat romantic invocation of ethnicity was clear in his depiction of himself and Miguel as "together in our outsiderness." As the relationship developed, the additional discrepancies he experienced between his preconceived ideas about Mexican families and what he saw in Miguel's mom motivated him to reflect on his own upbringing. The goals that emerged from this conflict were more complex, and the steps he took to meet them – the experiences he organized for himself and Miguel – had considerable impact on the way Jason saw himself and his place in the world. In his case we see the Eriksonian process of rethinking prior beliefs and roles in an attempt to make sense of his experiences and clarify the roles he played in them. Not until after he left UCSD did the impact of these experiences on identity development become clear.

## Using a Social Simulation as Context for Experiential Learning

The upper division course "Cross-cultural Communication" is intended to address questions related to the ways cultures are created and common understandings among individuals are achieved. In the class we highlight here, we arranged for the students to become enculturated within a simulated society they helped create, and then to experience being an outsider in a foreign culture created by their classmates. Through class discussions and field notes the students analyzed their experiences in light of the scholarly writings and other sources of knowledge about cultural practices that were strategically introduced as the class progressed.

The simulation[3] allowed us to retain many of the elements of real-life tasks, particularly unscripted interactions among the participants, unpredictable responses, and artifacts and relationships the students would have to learn to deal with effectively over time. It also permitted us to introduce play, affiliation, and learning into what might otherwise have been a normal school-going activity.

Participants in the cultural simulation were divided into two groups. Both groups learned a different set of cultural norms to govern their interactions. Once the groups were established, members joined the other group for short periods of time in an effort to learn about its values, customs, and norms without directly asking questions – much as we are forced to learn when

[3] The cultural simulation we implemented is an adaptation of the Bafa Bafa game (Shirts, 1977) which has been widely and successfully used for three decades as a tool for teaching cross-cultural sensitivity in a variety of institutional settings (Sullivan & Duplaga, 1996). The idea behind Bafa Bafa is to give participants an opportunity to experience cultural border crossing in a safe space, and to collectively reflect on and unpack their experience without the prejudices and constraints real-life border crossing often includes.

we travel to a foreign country. Because the two cultures in the simulation were vastly different (Alpha culture was geared toward community spirit and sharing, Beta culture was focused on personal achievement), there was ample potential for misunderstanding. During the simulation, both groups developed hypotheses about the other culture that were tested when the two groups came together in the end to talk about their experiences. We allowed the two cultures to evolve over the first several weeks of the academic term, giving the students an opportunity to come to a deep and nuanced understanding of cultural processes, as well as the time to reflect on and write about their experiences in weekly field notes.[4]

### Simulation Case Study: Jade

Our presentation of Jade's case roughly follows the chronology traced out for Jason. However, the crucial events in the narrative are different. What remains common is the interweaving of goal and identity formation, although the patterns woven by Jason and Jade are unique.

On the first day of the quarter, Jade[5] was assigned to participate as part of the "Beta Cartel," a banking/trading culture. Class was conducted like a business meeting where traders were treated with professional courtesy, issued name tags, and seated around a large conference table. They learned that members of the Beta culture valued honesty, accountability, fair competition, and personal achievement. A successful Betan was consistent, persistent, and able to drive a hard bargain. Students would also discover that time management was an important element of Beta success, as the more transactions accomplished during a single trading session, the more opportunities a Betan would have for increasing his or her wealth, as well as the wealth of the team and the larger cartel.

The "work" of the Beta culture was to participate in a card game where the players traded among themselves to create sets of cards that could be redeemed at the bank for $100 per set. Trading involved striking deals with other players that would be beneficial to both. The Betans were not told that, in the decks distributed among the group, certain necessary cards were extremely scarce.

---

[4]   Both of the cultures submitted their field notes to a separate database. The students had access to the notes of all the students in their own group, but not to those written by members of the other culture.

[5]   Jade's father, an American soldier of Korean descent, met Jade's mother while he was stationed in Seoul. When Jade's father was reassigned, she and her mother remained in Korea in her mother's family home. When Jade was ten the family settled in San Diego, although each summer Jade was sent to her grandmother in Seoul to perfect her Korean language skills and to remember how to "think in Korean."

As the game progressed they would discover the visiting foreigners were rich in these valuable resources.

Participants were divided into four five-person trading teams. At the end of every trading session the banker would tally the day's transactions and display the accumulated totals on progressive line graphs, demonstrating the relative success of the individuals and the teams and the increasing wealth of the larger Beta culture. Jade's notes from day one were typical of those submitted by her classmates:

*This class took me totally by surprise! I walked into what I thought would be a more traditional learning environment where books would be our primary source of material; however I am very refreshed by the hands on approach that will be guiding our experience. We will become immersed in, and actually be, the culture that we will be studying. . . . I am definitely looking forward to this new and unconventional approach, but I am still leery about how completely different this is to what I have been used to during my 14 years of schooling.*

The second week was devoted to practicing being members of the assigned groups – to begin to learn the ropes and in doing so to create their own cultures. Members of the Beta culture learned there would be rewards at the end of the simulation for the most successful traders. Thus motivated, they industriously engaged in learning the rules of exchange and the secret Beta trading language, which included words for colors and numbers, as well as hand and body gestures. We were more than a little surprised at how unself-conscious the students seemed about using the language and body gestures proper trading required. Jade's comments from week two offer an insider's view:

*I observed the class for a minute or two, and it was interesting to listen to the gibberish that everyone was speaking. At times, it even sounded like adults speaking baby babble. The elbows up with the flailing of the arms to say "No" was so silly to watch, but everyone was doing it and had smiles on their faces.*

Once the players had mastered the rules and the trading language, they received $200 in seed money and the bank opened for business. Suddenly the speed with which a trade could be accomplished became a key factor. As completed sets of cards were compiled students would run to the banker's desk and clamor for their cash. The politeness of earlier days all but vanished. Trading that had been animated and conscientious now became frenzied.

At this point Jade reported "feeling sad" because she knew her (male) teammates were frustrated with her tentative participation in the trading sessions.

*They tried to be nice but they kept saying that each one of us should work to add to the team's money totals and then they would look at me to make sure that I understood. I did understand but it was hard for me to speak out in an American way.*

In the first few days of the simulation Jade spent a lot of time trading with a fellow Korean teammate, JiHee. This was more comfortable for the girls but did little to increase their wealth or their perceived value to their trading team. In Jade's notes (from week three) we see the simulation caused her to question her interactions with JiHee, not knowing whether to attribute JiHee's kindness to team affiliation, friendship, or the fact that they were both Korean.

*During my very first trade with one of my group members, JiHee, she offered to give me the card I needed for whatever card I didn't need in exchange, even though she knew that I didn't have any card she really needed. For the first time I felt some kind of group mentality. Then I assumed that it was because we seemed to share the same value of serving others and avoiding unnecessary competitions for the sake of social harmony, but now I wonder. Did I assume we were thinking the same because she gave me what I needed, because we were on the same team, or because she just looked like me because she is Korean like me?*

Aaron, another Korean teammate, wrote in his field notes about frustration in trying to communicate smoothly with Jade, claiming she was "meek and distant." Because Jade had access to Aaron's notes, we were concerned his criticism might cause her to retreat from the simulation, but she proved more resilient than her gentle demeanor suggested:

*I felt betrayed then* [after reading Aaron's field notes] *as my expectations and the connections I thought I shared appeared to be dislocated on the cultural map. It occurred to me that we had figured out how to play the game, but now we were learning why the game was "worth doing." For the first time the game really meant something outside of the money we could earn. I wanted to think like a Betan, not like a Korean or even a college student. I decided that what it meant to be fair within the Beta culture was all that really mattered.*

Jade told us there was never a moment in the simulation when she was not aware of her "Korean-ness." In week five she wrote:

*I was born in South Korea, where people value social harmony and being considerate and thoughtful in understanding each other's needs and wants even without words, more than being aggressive, direct and fast in getting what you want. I felt from the beginning that Beta culture was conflicting with my native culture. This simulation has been a genuine cultural struggle of my own.*

At the outset we assured all of the students they were not compelled to do anything in the simulation that felt wrong to them; they could simply say no without penalty. Jade chose to take part in all of the activities, and she used her field notes as a tool for working through her thoughts and feelings about her position as a Korean woman trying to survive in a highly competitive (albeit simulated) Western business environment. About halfway through the simulation, we invited Jade to office hours to ensure she was holding up and not feeling pressured into doing anything that ran contrary to her beliefs. She assured us she was fine, and her next set of field notes contained the following affirmation:

*In this class I'm doing things I have never done before. I never really pushed myself to try the ways of American girls, although sometimes I would wish I could. Now I know what it feels like to be more aggressive and sometimes even loud. I don't think this will ever be the way I am, but I am happy to say that I have tried it.*

Shortly thereafter Jade and her trading group traveled to the territory occupied by the Other/Alpha culture.[6] Their instructions were to try and learn as much as possible through participation in the other culture's activities, but not to ask direct questions about the other culture's rules or norms. They would then report their findings back to the Beta culture to augment the group's developing understanding of the Others/Alphans. Jade sat quietly while Lauren, one of her teammates, blatantly broke all of the rules of engagement, taking advantage of a member of the other culture who had missed some of the early classes when the rules had been explained. Aggressively, systematically, Lauren fired direct questions at Brianna, who disclosed protected insider information about all areas of Alpha life.

When we learned that almost all of the secret details about Alpha life had been leaked to the Betans, our first reaction was dismay. The entire simulation was grounded in the premise that the two cultures would be opaque to each other. We feared the simulation, as well as our plans for the class, had been spoiled. While we were scrambling to recuperate the simulation, we received the following e-mail correspondence from Jade:

*Dear Mrs. Wilson, You told us in the first week that if we had something private to say in our field notes we should send them to a different email address. I would like for you to keep my notes of this day private. Can you please tell me where to send them?*

---

[6]   While the Beta culture was all about business and individual achievement, the Alpha culture was communal. It was a benevolent matriarchy where the wealth was shared, and all of the activities were aimed at promoting harmony and close relationships.

Jade had been at the game table where the leak occurred. She was also in the stairwell (en route between the two camps immediately following the incident) when Lauren excitedly shared her illicitly acquired knowledge with her team. As it became clear to them just how extensive the leak had been, the team huddled on the landing between floors and cooked up a plan. They reasoned that if they kept secret parts of the information they had gathered from the other Betans, and distorted some of the bits they did report, their team would have a distinct trading advantage over their fellow traders in all future cross-cultural interactions. Jade was writing to me now (and later came to office hours) to confess she had not been brave enough to oppose her teammates on the stairs, especially since the plan had won immediate approval from the team's two male members. Instead Jade had remained silent (and miserable) while Lauren and Aaron delivered their doctored account of the visit to their fellow Betans.

In the days that followed we watched a tough and determined Jade emerge. The "meek and distant" woman her teammate described in the first days of the simulation morphed into a formidable opponent on the trading floor. Jade's notes revealed the dramatic changes in thinking and in her behavior on the trading floor:

*From this cross-cultural incident, my cultural identity was shaken and refocused to develop a more competitive and capitalistic self. I stopped "wasting" time greeting or saying "thank you." I stopped giving away the cards the other person needed, unless the other trader had something beneficial to offer for me. I moved quickly and arranged my cards strategically. I located people I needed to go to get certain kinds of cards on my mental map, and I didn't hesitate to move or interrupt when I needed to. For example, when I didn't need the cards that are difficult to get, such as 3s and 5s, I stayed away from the traffic going to Alpha members even though I knew they might need to trade with me. When I needed those rare numbers at the moment, I immediately jumped in and grabbed their attention.*

But at home, writing her reflections after each trading session, Jade was still working to reconcile her new identity as a successful Betan trader with her Korean heritage:

*I took advantage of my cultural knowledge and experience, and gave them a card I didn't need without considering whether it would be beneficial to them or not. As I was doing so, my native cultural self automatically found a conflict with my own virtues of helping others and made me feel guilty about doing such a thing. My conscious mind immediately came up with the justification of the fact that even if I give them something that would bring them closer to making a set, they wouldn't know how to cash them in, so it didn't matter. And there I was, changed, and defending my new cultural identity like Alvar Nunez.*[7]

Jade and Aaron reported in their final reflections that, because of the rigid gender roles they were accustomed to, the simulation had been a lot easier on Aaron than it had been on Jade. But Jade found a convenient loophole. The cultural pressure she felt for high scholastic performance was not gender specific. The imperative to do well in the class far outweighed any discomfort she might feel at pushing the boundaries of polite behavior. Her eventual willingness to step outside her comfort zone and fully participate in the highly competitive trading was remarkable. Once she gave herself permission to fully participate in the aggressive game, her insider's position in the trading culture provided her with an outsider's perspective on her own South Korean heritage.

*At the same time as I "naturally" resisted to absorb Beta's cultural values because of my native culture, I was rationally preoccupied by following Beta values of making trade efficiently and making maximum profits because I felt pressured to do well in trading as I assumed it would be reflected in my class grade, since my native culture valued education highly. In this process, I became uncomfortable with my own values and began the re-evaluation process of my own culture. Some of the parts were not compatible with the others. I was expected to be quiet and polite, but I was also expected to do whatever was necessary to be successful in school.*

Once each of the participants had had the chance to visit the other culture, the two groups convened as a single class to unpack the events of the simulation in light of the theories about cultural processes they had been reading. Members of the Beta culture opened the discussions with a short presentation on what they had learned or surmised about the Alpha culture during the simulation. The Alphans responded with a more comprehensive presentation about "how it really was." During both presentations members of the class were encouraged to interrupt with questions or comments. The idea was for the integrated group to have an open, and hopefully fun and informative, dialog of discovery about the simulation they had just completed. The next class meeting followed exactly the same format, the only difference being this time the Beta culture was the topic of conversation. Jade held her own in these discussions.

*I am amazed at how everyone participating in the discussion was speaking in the voice of his or her simulated culture. Every time an Alpha opened their mouth, they*

---

[7]    In the reading assignment for that day Guiseppe Mantovani discusses the cultural encounter between Alvar Nunez and the Native Americans he encountered in the New World.

*reflected Alpha values, and every time a Beta spoke, it was with the best interests of Beta culture in mind. I did it too. This was fascinating to me, because we've absorbed the values of our respective cultures through our very skin, and during the somewhat heated discussion, we were each valiantly defending our own cultures.*

## Jade's Developmental Pathway: From School-Going Activity to Self-Discovery

Jade's class experience, as represented in these field note segments and our own documentation of events, placed issues of identity front and center because participation in the simulation actually required her to play the role of a specific kind of other with an easily recognized ethos/world view. As a result, the connections between goal formation and identity formation are even more tightly interwoven than they were in Jason's case. In an important sense, the forming of cultural identity is an excellent way to describe the process of culture formation, seen, so to speak, from the inside.

Jade chose the "COHI 130 Cross-Cultural Communication" class with the goal of fulfilling an upper division elective requirement. When she learned achieving this goal would require her not only to participate in the innovation of a simulated culture, but also to create and perform a role within that culture, she reported feeling unsettled and excited – precisely the response we hoped for in designing the course. Within this unsettled yet safe place inside the simulated culture, affiliation, play, and peer interaction gradually began to interact with her school-going activity as a means of resolving the multiple personally important issues of culture and identity she herself was experiencing.

This transformation was not instantaneous, nor does it imply that Jade gave up on the academic side of the course. From the beginning Jade performed her role as a university student perfectly. She came prepared to each class, turned in her assignments on time, and aced her quizzes. She also behaved in ways appropriate for a well-mannered Korean woman, both in the regular class discussions and in the simulation. While her written summaries of the readings were accurate, at first she did little to connect the theories they addressed with the class activities, and she struggled with the demands of the simulation. The first indication that Jade was beginning to form new goals with respect to her readings came only after Jade had begun to immerse herself in the trading game and a teammate found her participation to be inadequate – too meek to be competitive in the ways Betan culture demanded. In her field notes she defends her decision to behave more like a successful Betan and less like a nice Korean girl or even like a good student. In building her defense she invoked the authority of Giuseppe Mantovani (who we had read extensively in the class), quoting his admonition that "we are not cultural clones; we each have our own songlines to follow" (2000, p. 17).

Jade's final reflection described her own development in the class in terms of coming to a better understanding of the processes of culture and becoming a better communicator in cross-cultural environments. She credits these gains to being repeatedly put in situations where the goals, social rules, and cultural understandings she brought with her into class needed to be replaced by new ways of thinking about herself in relation to her identity as a Korean woman, with all of the values and dispositions that identity calls forth. Beta culture's progressive development into a highly aggressive and competitive society of traders held Jade in the precarious position of straddling the divide between the expectations of her Korean ethnic ideology and those of the Beta culture. As the quarter progressed, she drew more from the readings and class discussions to reconcile her actions in the class with these two conflicting ideologies.

## Conclusion

Our initial goal in this chapter was to document processes by which we have used CHAT principles to create educational activity in higher education. We think we have shown CHAT principles can in fact be used to create educational activity in a school. That is, we have created a form of activity in which goal formation that is in the service of major life tasks is a routine feature, providing sources of motivation that school going alone cannot provide. In each course, while working within a curriculum that could be taught by lecture and test-taking methods, the strategy of placing students in situations where they must innovate new practices to deal with the challenges they have been posed simultaneously reveals ways in which processes of identity formation are recruited as part of the problem-solving process. And, inversely, the ways uncertainties about identity encourage the recruitment of new problem-solving processes.

Both courses employed the strategies of destabilizing ordinary classroom practice, providing multiple sources of motivation by "mixing" leading activities, and ensuring reflective practices were a routine, instrumental aspect of the students' coursework. The resulting mixture of motives generated hybrid, unexpected (and unpredictable) problems for the students. Lacking a prepared script, they had to think for themselves. They had to form goals as part of a collective activity.

Routinely, the students confronted unexpected problems that arose out of seeking to create meaningful joint activity under conditions that, while half-baked at the start, had to be actively recreated as a part of the small group process of enculturation/cultural formation. "What should I do next?" now involved issues the students had never had to confront in their educational experience. The solution of those issues required a different mode of higher education, one that involved real educational activity motivated by central life concerns.

We illustrated the process of development with two cases studies, each drawing on the particular properties of the courses in which the two students were involved as well as their own personal positions.

So, in Jason's case: How do I show Manuel that, like him and his family, the people where I come from also live in crowded, communal conditions? How do I connect with him through the role of "outsiders together" so that I can promote his development?

In Jade's case: How do I deal with the double dishonesty of my group? Can I remain silent when injustice is done in my name? Can I be quiet when my own group conspires to cheat our fellow group members? How do I reconcile my desire to master the individualistic skills and dispositions of a Betan with my strong belief in group cohesion and mutual support?

While we started with a focus on goal formation and the creation of identity in more or less cognitive terms, we discovered along the way that our hybrid educational practices made very visible and available for analysis just how closely issues of identity are connected with the process of genuine educational activity, where goal formation and reflection are a routine part of the overall educational activity system the course represents. The multiethnic and multigenerational makeup of the students attending the class made such issues the source of genuine goal formation that clearly reflected back on their academic development. Jason and Jade, facing the different challenges inherent in the two learning environments, formed different sets of goals and worked on different aspects of identity formation. In the community-based practicum, Jason was motivated to reconsider his beliefs about Chinese and Mexican family life and values. When confronted with Manuel's difficult living circumstances he reached into his own past experience and brought forth pictures of the crowded living conditions in Hong Kong high rises as a means of maintaining his affiliation with Manuel as fellow outsiders to American language and culture. In the process of reconsiderations that were then aroused, the coursework led up to new career choices with their own consequences for commitment to family and being Chinese-American

In the class where culture-specific modes of life and identity were focal academic issues, Jade was specifically and almost obsessively focused on unpacking her own ethnic ideologies (plural to include Korean and American). What is gratifying is the way that she gradually came to embrace the academic readings as tools for her own self-explorations. Jason, on the other hand, could not so clearly articulate his confusions. He was still mulling things over when the class ended.

What impresses us especially about the field notes is the extent to which they do, in fact, illustrate the proclivity to systematically reconcile many different conflicting identities at once. Jade's notes are particularly impressive in this regard, almost as if she were describing herself using Erikson's own words.

In concluding, we note the limitations of the data we have offered in support of our ideas and the limits on their application. We have provided only two kinds of courses and one case study from each. However, the phenomena we report for the two students are ubiquitous in our corpus for each kind of class and we thought them most condensable for current purposes. However, we want to be clear that these are demonstration proofs regarding theoretical claims about the interrelationship of two psychological processes and cultural-environmental circumstances that make them particularly visible for analysis. Scaling up the application of the courses in the face of intense pressures on contemporary higher educational systems, where instructor to student ratios are often in the hundreds and climbing, would require more institutional commitment to this form of education than currently exists. In the meantime, the opportunity to combine teaching and research in the manner described here is sufficient good luck for a lifetime.

### References

Dewey, J. (1916). *Democracy and Education: An introduction to the philosophy of education*. New York: Macmillan.

Engeström, Yrjo. (1987). *Learning by Expanding*. Helsinki. Oriento-Konsultit Oy.

Erikson, E. H. (1968). *Identity: Youth and crisis*. New York: Norton.

Grotevant, H. D. (2001). The relationship code: Deciphering genetic and social influences on adolescent development (review). *Perspectives in Biology and Medicine*, **44** (1), 137–13.

Holland, D. and Lachicotte, W. Jr. (2007). Vygotsky, Mead, and the new sociocultural studies of identity. In H. Daniels, M. Cole, and J. V. Wertsch *The Cambridge Companion to Vygotsky*. New York. Cambridge University Press.

Kuhn, D. and Franklin, S. (2006). The second decade: What develops (and how)? In W. Damon, R. M. Lerner, D. Kuhn, and R. Siegler (Eds.), *Handbook of Child Psychology* (vol. 2, 6th ed., pp. 953–94). New York: John Wiley & Sons.

Lareau, A. (2002). Invisible inequality: Social class and childrearing in black families and white families. *American Sociological Review*, **67**: 747–76.

Leontiev, A. N. (1981). *Problems of the development of the mind*. (Trans. M. Kopylova) Moscow: Progress Publishers.

Lightfoot, C., Cole, M., and Cole, S. (2009). *The Development of Children*. Worth Publishers.

Marcia, James E. (2002). Identity and psychosocial development in adulthood. *Identity*, **2**(1): 7–28.

Mantovani, G. (2000). *Exploring Borders*. London: Routledge.

Mead, G. H. (1934). *Mind, Self and Society*. Chicago, IL: University of Chicago Press.

Penuel, W. and Wertsch, J. (1995). Vygotsky and identity formation: A sociocultural approach. *Educational Psychologist*, **30**: 83–92.

Shirts, G. (1977). *BaFa BaFa: A Cross-Cultural Simulation*. Simulation Training Systems, Del Mar.

Sullivan, S. and Duplaga, E. (1996). The BaFa BaFa Simulation: Faculty experiences and student reactions. *Journal of Management Education*, **21**(2): 265–72.

Vasquez, O. (2002). *La Clase Mágica: Imagining optimal possibilities in a bilingual community of learners*. Routledge.

Vygotsky, L. (1978). *Mind in Society: The development of higher psychological functions*. Cambridge, MA: Harvard University Press.

# 3

## Using a Cultural Historical Approach to Understand Educational Change in Introductory Physics Classrooms

### Chandra Turpen and Noah Finkelstein

### Introduction

Recent years have seen a shift in the goals of college (science) courses, from a model based on the dissemination of information, rote practice, and selection of students to a model that focuses on student engagement, conceptual foundations, and social interactions (Barr & Tagg, 1995; Bransford, Brown, & Cocking 2000). To achieve these goals in our classrooms, education researchers and curriculum developers have created a vast body of educational curricula and practices that place greater emphasis on peer interactions, problem solving, and students' conceptual development (Redish, 2003).[1] Despite the success of many of these efforts (Ruiz-Primo et al., 2011), we are sorely lacking in understanding how successful interventions take root and spread, and how variation in enactment leads to different outcomes (Finkelstein & Pollock, 2005; Henderson, Beach, & Finkelstein, 2011/2012). Cultural Historical Activity Theory (CHAT) (Cole, 1996; Engeström, 1993; Engeström, Miettinen, & Punamäki, 1999; Roth & Lee, 2007) provides us a model of learning-teaching-content-environment relationships that allows us to move beyond a focus on specific curricula, pedagogy, and content-based outcomes, while activity theory in particular (Engeström, 1993; Engeström, Miettinen, & Punamäki, 1999) focuses attention on a key unit of analysis, the activity system, which incorporates unpacking the complex interactions among curricula, students, faculty members, and institutional structures, and simultaneously calls our attention to the coordinated (or conflicting) goals of the activity systems. CHAT forefronts our understanding of the goals (outcomes)

---

[1] The National Academy of Science through the Board on Science Education is currently assessing the status, contributions, and future direction of discipline-based education research. See, for example, papers available at http://www7.nationalacademies.org/bose/DBER_Meeting2_commissioned_papers_page.html.

of our educational transformations rather than leaving these implicit. For example, classrooms can support radically different activity systems. One activity system may hold students accountable for bubbling in multiple choice exams and getting the right answers, where students' roles may be characterized as being students. Alternatively, we can construct classroom environments where students participate in making tentative judgments, engaging in argumentation, justification, and experiment, more like being a scientist. These less discussed goals of instruction reflect a long-standing and well-established contradiction in the goals of our higher education system – students as producers rather than consumers of (scientific) knowledge.

In the present chapter, we employ CHAT to study educational change in a physics department to demonstrate that while the new interactive approaches promoted in physics (and across many disciplines) can be used merely as more efficient tools to recapitulate traditional norms and goals, they can also be implemented to empower students as practitioners and producers of scientific practice within these educational environments. Indeed, we argue the same educational innovations may in fact lead to different goals and outcomes depending on implementation (the enacted activity system). From the CHAT perspective, learning (the appropriation and use of cultural tools, practices, and norms in collective practice) arises from participation in communities, using and observing the use of these tools in joint, goal-directed activity. Here we explore the idea that expertise is often distributed among participants, and more expert-like participants assume varying roles in supporting the engagement of individuals within a given cultural system. In this way, differences in the goals of these activity systems are of direct consequence for what participants learn. We study (1) how faculty enacting the same educational innovation can come to remarkably different outcomes and (2) how shifted course structures can support faculty development. We use CHAT in case studies of two of the most popular educational reforms in college physics, peer instruction and tutorials. In these studies, CHAT provides a mechanism for identifying which questions to ask, where contradictions exist, and how we might promote sustainable change in these systems.

## Adaptation Practices of Individual Faculty as a Driver of Instructional Change: The Case of Peer Instruction

Peer instruction (PI) is the most widely adopted pedagogical approach in introductory physics (Henderson & Dancy, 2009). According to its author, Mazur, peer instruction is a pedagogical approach in which the instructor stops lecture periodically to pose a question to the students (1997).

These questions or ConcepTests are primarily multiple choice, conceptual questions in which the possible answer options represent common student ideas. Mazur describes peer instruction as a seven-step process (1997; Crouch et al., 2007):

1) Question posed by instructor
2) Students given time to think
3) Students report individual answers
4) Neighboring students discuss their answers
5) Students report revised answers
6) Feedback to teacher
7) Explanation of the correct answer

Based on the information gathered, the class adapts to the level of student understanding. Even in this brief description of the pedagogical approach, we see that this tool has some transformative potential. As compared to a purely lecture-based course, PI reorganizes the roles and rules of the activity system by integrating feedback into an otherwise unidirectional communication structure. Similarly, PI emphasizes conceptual understanding (a new objective) and active student engagement (new roles).

Most educators will immediately recognize that this description is woefully underspecified. We illustrate how this pedagogical approach is enacted differently in two different classroom activity systems. Both classrooms are part of the introductory calculus-based physics sequence at the University of Colorado; however, they are taught by different instructors (Professor Red and Professor Green). These case studies demonstrate that the division of labor and rules of these two classroom activity systems vary dramatically and afford students with different opportunities to learn. We will see that in these two classrooms, the tension between students as consumers of physics knowledge and students as producers of physics knowledge is resolved in different ways.

Based on our observations, there are a variety of scientific practices (potential objectives) with which students can gain experience through the use of peer instruction, including:

i. To try out and apply new physical concepts
ii. To discuss physics content with their peers
iii. To justify their reasoning to their peers
iv. To debate physical reasoning with their peers
v. To formulate questions and ask questions
vi. To evaluate the correctness and completeness of problem solutions

vii.   To interact with physicists
viii.  To begin to identify themselves as sources of solutions, explanations, or answers
 ix.   To communicate in a public arena

While not traditionally assessed, many faculty value developing students' capacity with these sorts of practices. Our studies (Turpen & Finkelstein, 2009, 2010), drawing from audio data, observational notes, and records of student voting, demonstrate the potential for PI to support the development of these scientific practices; however, opportunities for development depend on the specifics of PI implementation. In all of the classrooms studied (Turpen & Finkelstein, 2009), students were found practicing the first four items in this list. However, there were large discrepancies in students' opportunities to engage in the remaining five practices. Case studies of Professors Red and Green illustrate these variations and the differing roles and rules for professor and student participation (the typicality of these cases is developed more thoroughly in Turpen & Finkelstein, 2009).

### Green PI Case Study: Calculus-Based Introductory Physics 2
Figure 3.1 shows the second PI question occurring midway through the class period. Prior to this question, the professor had briefly discussed the domain model of magnetism (magnets composed of smaller magnets) and described permanent magnets. The professor says, "It's time to go to the next chapter … electromagnetic induction." The professor continues, "I think that this is something that you can actually understand based on what we have done before. So I will start with asking a question on it before I have really started the chapter." The professor displays and describes the question: "So here I have a magnetic field going into the board and then a conducting ball, a metal ball, is moving through the magnetic field moving to the right. And if you remember now that a conductor has lots of valence electrons that can move around inside the conductor then you should be able to determine what will happen with this ball when it moves through this field. And there are options there, that it will be polarized in different directions or that it will not be affected at all" (see Figure 3.1). (For the unfamiliar reader, a moving electron in a magnetic field feels a force perpendicular to the direction of motion and the magnetic field.)

During the voting, the professor stands at the back left corner of the stage. He paces there for most of the voting time. Then the professor checks the incoming clicker votes. Meanwhile there seems to be a significant amount of discussion occurring among the students. The professor warns the students,

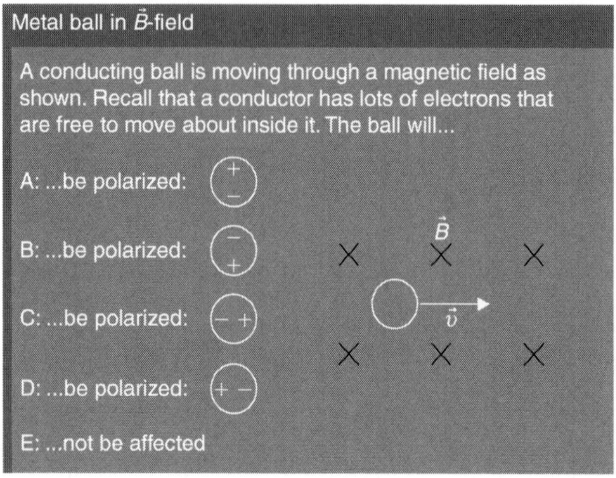

FIGURE 3.1. Screen shot of a PI question in Green's class (Correct answer: A). B represents the magnetic field; X's indicate the field is into the page.

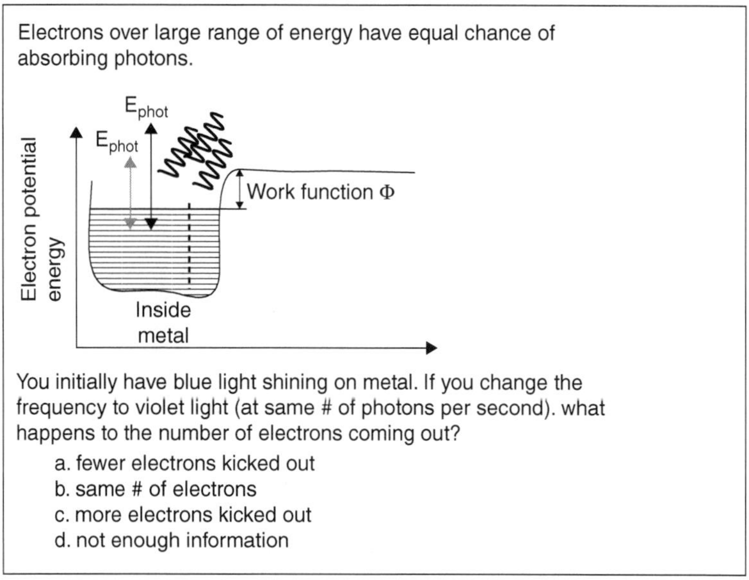

FIGURE 3.2. Screen shot of a PI question in Red's class (Correct answer: C).

"Okay, twenty more seconds." A little bit later the professor says, "Last few votes. Okay, I'll stop it there." The professor displays the voting results (A: 72% B: 17% C: 4% D: 2% E: 5%). The professor says, "Most people thought that it would be polarized for sure and … that it has a net positive charge on the top and a net negative on bottom. Can somebody explain how they determined that?" Pause. The professor calls on one student with his hand raised. The student explains, "Well, in the ball the positive charges are moving to the right and they are affected by a magnetic field that is going into the board so the force on the positive charges would be up, so they would move up. But for the negative charges in the ball their velocity would be negative so there the force would be pointing down on the negative charges … so those forces would force the positive charges to the top of the ball and the negative charges to the bottom of the ball." The professor responds, "Okay, Joe says the positive charges in the ball are moving to the right, so it's an effective current to the right. With a B-field into the board, the positive charges would be deflected by a force trying to push them up. And the negative charges are moving to the right, but it's an effective current for the negative charges to the left and B-field into the board, so the force on the negative charges would be pointing down to the bottom of the ball. Does this make sense? [pause]. Yeah, It does make sense." The students laugh at this comment.

The professor continues, "But is it completely true though? … Both of these things? Or is it just one of these things that is true?" The students respond in murmurs, "Only one, the second one." The professor continues, "Yeah, we usually think of the nuclei, the positive charges, in a conductor as fixed and it is electrons that move around, but it is perfectly fine to think of positive charges moving as well. We can't see positive charges are not moving around. But if we measure it, it will look like the positive charges have moved. Since usually … we will now consider current as well, which is like positive charges moving. So, it will be convenient to think of the positive charges moving as a result of force. Excellent. So I guess that I gave away that that was the correct response." The solution discussion period lasted approximately three minutes. The professor continues into a discussion of how this is an example of electromagnetic induction using examples from demonstration equipment.

### Red PI Case Study: Calculus-Based Introductory Physics 3

Figure 3.2 shows the second PI question of the class. The question is preceded by a discussion of what the work function is (the amount of energy required from an incoming photon to remove an electron from a metal). To represent the energy levels of the electrons in the metal, the professor has used an image of a well with balls stacked in it along levels and these balls are given kicks by photons. The professor has walked through an energy conservation argument for this exact physical situation when blue light interacts with the metal. The professor puts up a clicker question (see Figure 3.2). The professor says, "Enough of me yammering. Electrons can have a large range of energy and equal chances of absorbing a photon. Okay. So umm, If I come in with higher-energy light, initially you have blue light shining on a metal and if you change that frequency to violet light, at the same number of photons per second okay.... So I've increased the intensity, but I have the same number of photons coming in per second, but the energy in the violet photons is … bigger or smaller?" The students call out answers, mostly saying bigger. The professor continues, "Bigger, okay. What happens to the number of electrons coming out?" He says, "So get into your discussion groups and chit chat." The students begin to discuss with each other. The professor wanders around the front of the room talking to different students sitting in the front row. He later asks a different group of students across the room, "What do you guys think?" The professor continues to engage in a discussion with this group of students. Then the professor says, "Everybody in? Okay, Three, two, one. [Student Responses (A: 0%; B: 17%; C: 74%; D: 8%; E: 0%)] Okay, we might have an all-time high in attendance. Okay if we keep doing this do you know how many students we're going to have at the end of the semester? An infinite number. [The students laugh.] That's kinda cool. Students from all other universities are going to be piling into this class. So, I heard a bunch of great reasons. All of the reasoning was in essence correct that I heard; it's just that some of the reasoning was incomplete. So … someone want to give a quick stab at what's up?"

The professor points to one of the students. The student says, "I said that more electrons got kicked out because the photons have greater energy; they are going to knock out more electrons from deeper inside the metal than they would have before." The professor responds, "Okay does everybody agree that the purple or violet has greater energy than the blue? Okay, so then your argument is … if you got more energy, then you can scoop down into the metal deeper, because the length of that arrow is longer, right? Okay." The professor asks, "Does anybody want to retort?" The next student who speaks is inaudible on the recording, but the professor paraphrases the student's comment to the rest of the class, "Aaaha, so it could kick off. But wait a sec, there is enough from the blue to dig off from the top. Okay, so it could … " A student interrupts, "But don't all the electrons have an equal probability of getting hit?" The professor says, "Aaaha, But photons aren't very smart. They don't know what ones they're going to go for. So they all have equal probability. It's not like there's this hand guiding it." A student asks another question, "I thought there was always one photon kicking out one electron." The professor responds, "Yes, one photon always interacts with one electron, but we don't know which electron." A student asks, "Just those top electrons?" The professor responds, "No, it could be any of those electrons." Another few students speak. After the students seem to have made a good amount of progress on their own and have brought forward some of the key ideas, the professor displays his solution on a PowerPoint slide and walks through it fairly quickly.

In both Green and Red's classes, the role relationships between students are transformed as compared to a purely lecture-based course: students talk to each other in class, practice using physics concepts to solve problems, and justify their thinking to their peers. However, in Green's class, the role relationships between the instructor and the students are only changed minimally (still largely falling into an initiate, respond, evaluate (IRE) framework) (Cazden, 2001; Mehan, 1979; O'Connor & Michaels, 1993). In Green's case, only a single student explanation was elicited and this student's explanation was clear and correct. There is limited dialogue between professor and students throughout this activity. Following this correct student explanation, the professor communicated the correctness of this explanation and did not elicit additional student comments or questions even though more than 25 percent of the students had answered the question incorrectly. The outcomes in this activity system emphasize getting the correct answer. In Red's class, the role relationships between the instructor and the students are also significantly changed as compared to a purely lecture-based course. In Red's case, he wanders around engaging in dialogue with students. We see that multiple students contribute explanations (enacting different rules) where some "correct" and "incorrect" ideas are presented publicly. Professor Red fostered discussion and debate among his students. Red structured student-to-student dialogue during the solution discussion by positioning students to respond to or comment on other students' contributions. In Red's class, students are responsible for evaluating the correctness and completeness of the problem solutions proposed by their peers. In this way, the professor structured the students' interactions with each other to encourage debate, providing alternative explanations, arguing, defending, challenging, or clarifying each other's ideas (thereby demonstrating that different roles and rules can be enacted in similar classrooms). Students in these classrooms are given different opportunities to practice identifying themselves as sources and evaluators of solutions, explanations, or answers. The roles, rules, and outcomes in Red's class differ from those in Green's. Green and Red's classrooms represent two different resolutions of the same tension: the tension between giving students access to the canonical or scientifically accepted ideas (consumers of scientific knowledge) and giving students access to the practices/processes of doing science and constructing their own scientific knowledge (producers of scientific knowledge).

These differences in the enacted activity systems contribute to varying degrees of perceived emphasis on reasoning and sense making (in ways that are systematically recognizable to students) (Turpen & Finkelstein, 2010). For example, a multiple choice survey question asked students: "In class, how important is it for you to articulate your reasoning either to your peers or during whole class discussion?" Students in Red's course reported greater importance on articulating reasoning than Green's students (p<0.001 via Mann-Whitney U Test) (see Turpen and Finkelstein, 2010 for complete results). It appears that, although students do speak a significant amount in Green's class, the students that are contributing are usually contributing a clear and correct explanation to the question. Flawed student reasoning is not voiced equally in this class even on questions where there is a significant fraction of students incorrectly answering the question. Since incorrect ideas are not as likely to be shared, this reduces the emphasis on reasoning and sense making. It is the answer that is predominantly valued. Red's class demonstrates different outcomes from Green's class.

Now we turn to demonstrating how broader institutional structures can support redefining classroom activity systems and support faculty change in the process.

### Institutional Structures as a Driver of Faculty Change: The Case of Tutorials

The University of Colorado at Boulder (CU) physics department began using the University of Washington *Tutorials in Introductory Physics* (McDermott, Schaffer, & PEG, 2002) in 2003 (Finkelstein & Pollock, 2005). The adoption of this curriculum required a restructuring of the existing thirty-person activity system, the weekly section meetings associated with the large lecture: shifting content emphasis from computation to conceptual understanding; shifting student activity from watching, listening, and transcribing to actively discussing, reasoning, and problem solving; shifting student interactions from individual work to group work; and shifting the role of the educator from a source of answers to a source of guiding and focusing questions. These efforts were led by an experienced and highly knowledgeable physics education researcher, Professor Purple. This characterization of the roles, rules, and goals of the introductory physics course, as transformed through the use of tutorials, is supported by interview comments by Professor Purple (see Table 3.1). After replicating the student conceptual learning gains achieved at the University of Washington, the department began an effort to sustain the use of the tutorials (Pollock & Finkelstein, 2008).

TABLE 3.1. *Introductory Physics Activity System Based on Characterizations in Interviews*

| | "Orange Pre" Activity System | "Orange Post" Activity System | "Tut Purple" Activity System |
|---|---|---|---|
| Subject | | | |
| Tool (Key tool for learning) | Professor Orange End-of-the-chapter computationally focused problems from the textbook. | Professor Orange Tutorial activities tuned for the basic ideas and concepts without significant mathematics. | Professor Purple Conceptually based tasks within and outside the tutorials that build on common student ideas. |
| Division of Labor (Roles) | The role of the educator is to lecture and set high expectations of students to put in effort outside of class. The role of students is to take responsibility for their own learning by reading the textbook material and completing the extensive homework sets outside of class. | The role of the educators is to help keep students on task, but not to interfere with students' discussions with each other. The role of students is to focus on learning the physics through discussions with their peers. | Educators are expected to be a source of guiding and focusing questions (not sources of answers). Students are expected to actively discuss, reason, and problem solve with each other. |
| Community | 10% of students can follow and 90% of students cannot follow. | The student body has very diverse backgrounds. | All 600 students. |
| Rules | Students should do the problems by themselves, unless they are a "weak" student and need help. Students should take responsibility for their own learning. | Educators should remind students that they are here to learn and help student keep focused. Students should be talking about physics with each other in class. | Educators and students should focus on concepts and respect dialogue. |

*(continued)*

TABLE 3.1. (*continued*)

| | "Orange Pre" Activity System | "Orange Post" Activity System | "Tut Purple" Activity System |
|---|---|---|---|
| Object | Get through the material, and give students practice solving mathematical physics problems. | Engage students with the basic ideas or concepts without the added worry associated with the equations or formulas. | Motivate the students, get them thinking about physics, and get them to reflect on if the physics makes sense. |
| Outcome | Produce the brightest, top ten percent to populate the profession of physics. | Benefit the majority of students enrolled in the course. | Learn to monitor your own thinking and evaluate how you know what you know (which resembles the process of developing knowledge in science). |

*Note:* We note that the mediating relationships between nodes are suppressed, but important.

The department dedicated resources to support faculty members mentoring each other and engaging in reflective practice through co-teaching. Additional resources were made available to these faculty members, including a locally created instructors' manual, a lead graduate assistant to provide additional implementation support, a local expert in tutorial implementation, and undergraduate learning assistants (Otero et al., 2006) hired by the physics education research group to increase the teacher to student ratio in the sections. Most faculty development approaches tend to design interventions outside of classroom contexts to shift faculty members' conceptions. In our approach to sustaining the use of tutorials at CU, we posited that embedding faculty in new instructional situations (with additional resources) would support changing their teaching conceptions and practices. This approach aligns with CHAT's perspective on learning, where learning occurs through participation in activity systems. Here, learners engage with others employing the culturally valued tools and practices in joint, goal-directed activity. As such, the tools and practices employed become a critical part of learning. We question the assumption that faculty members must a priori be completely on board with the goals of the curriculum prior to teaching with it. Drawing on observations of classroom practice, analysis of course artifacts, and interviews with physics faculty, we describe the activity system of this introductory physics course based on the perspectives of two physics faculty members. One instructor, Professor Purple, is a physics education researcher and the originator of the tutorials reforms at CU, and the other, Professor Orange, had only very limited interaction with education research and volunteered to try out using the tutorials. Nonetheless, we see him shift over time. As even Professor Orange reflectively comments, "my general feeling about how to run this kind of class has also kind of evolved through the semester" (post-teaching).

We present evidence from interviews with Professor Orange spanning two different snapshots in time, one interview prior to teaching with the tutorials (labeled "Orange Pre") and one interview after a semester of teaching with the tutorials for the first time (labeled "Orange Post"). Orange illustrates his perceptions of the division of labor and rules of the introductory physics course prior to working with the tutorials: "I would prefer that they do their homework by themselves. I don't really encourage them to form student groups. I just don't like that kind of idea.... Of course, weaker students may want to form study groups" (pre-teaching). This sentiment stands in marked contrast to his comments made about the division of labor and rules after working with the tutorials: "If you don't give them somewhat close supervision they tend to drift away. You really need to ... not necessarily interfere with their discussions, but make it clear why we are here" (post-teaching). We see similar dramatic changes in how Professor Orange talks about the outcome or longer-term purpose of these activities. Prior to working with the tutorials, Professor Orange stated, "In physics education the focus is to produce the brightest. The focus is really more on the top ten percent of the students. The other ninety percent of the student mostly people say, okay you cannot follow" (pre-teaching). After working with the tutorials, Professor Orange reflects, "For the intro-level classes, seeing the students with such diverse backgrounds, maybe the way that we are doing it now is better.... We really focus on the average students not really the top one or five percent. I think that most of the students actually benefit from this type of practice" (post-teaching). Table 3.1 summarizes these activity systems in terms of the classic components of activities according to Engeström: subjects, mediating artifacts (tools), division of labor (roles), community, rules, and objects of focus, which leads to varying outcomes/objectives (Cole, 1996; Engeström, 1993; Engeström, Miettinen, & Punamäki, 1999). Three classroom activity systems are characterized by the perspectives of Professor Orange (pre and post instruction) and Professor Purple (post instruction) using language that paraphrases their interview descriptions of Physics 1 tutorial environment.

The observed shifts in Professor Orange's ways of talking about teaching likely depend on how Professor Orange participated with students and the curricular materials (which has not been the case with all faculty who have participated in teaching with the transformed curricula). Although the dynamics of this participation were not the subject of careful study, Professor Orange was observed to visit tutorial sections as they were running: sitting with students and listening to their discussions with each other. Professor Orange's participation in the implementation of the tutorials is likely critical to the change observed. We see Professor Orange's pre-descriptions are consistent with a delivery or consumer model of education, while post-descriptions move toward a participatory model.

## Conclusions

Faculty take part in little formal training in teaching and unsurprisingly often end up recapitulating their own histories of engagement in higher education (Lortie, 1975). Most efforts to transform the teaching of physics at the university level parallel the students' consumer-producer contradiction, often treating faculty as consumers of educational innovations. This view encourages an approach to educational change that targets individual physics faculty members to market to them and to convince them to use the innovation.

Other approaches to educational change focus on "structural constraints" or "institutional barriers," drawing attention to the historical patterns departments and universities have for accomplishing their work (Henderson & Dancy, 2007; Trigwell & Prosser, 1997). However, both of these models separate the individuals from their environments, which often leads to static descriptions of people and their environments. These approaches miss the potentially important interplay between individuals and their environments. CHAT provides a mechanism for understanding these critical interactions. By studying the distributed expertise within these systems (i.e., the faculty, the tutorial activities, learning assistants, weekly preparatory meetings, and role of other experts), we may understand the complex interplay in these cultural systems that allows for the development of both the systems and the members within them.

Using a framework that focuses on the activity system as the base unit of analysis, we have been able to document and understand the relations among key elements of our educational transformations. These analyses suggest progress (or resolution of existing contradictions) involves shifts in both individuals and environmental structures. We have shared two examples of change in higher education. In one example, the adaptation practices of an individual are the primary driver of change – faculty shaping environment. In the other, the shifted institutional structures are the primary driver of faculty change – environment shaping faculty. While both case studies occur within the context of physics, these accounts of change suggest that supporting meaningful transformation of educational practices in any discipline will require much more than engineering curricular solutions. We need to support the development of educational adaptive expertise in faculty (Borko & Livingston, 1989; Hatano & Inagaki, 1986; Hatano & Oura, 2003), so that these faculty members may negotiate complex settings and adapt educational innovations to local structures. In enacting change efforts in higher education, the use of CHAT allows us to attend to multiple, appropriate scales, as well as to note the key levers of change within an activity system.

We see that faculty and students (in coordination with the use of new tools) can co-construct new activity systems, modifying educational innovations (tools, roles, rules, and outcomes) in the process. In the case of PI, enactment of curricula was found to be of direct consequence for what students learned. In the case of the tutorials, faculty participation in newly arranged educational settings was of direct consequence for the instructor's learning. CHAT provides resources for understanding how faculty members can create spaces for students to participate in new ways and how institutions can create spaces for faculty members to participate in new ways – leading to different learning outcomes. If we are fundamentally interested in the development of students in these formal settings, the complex and dynamic interplay between individuals and the environment (settings, tools, and participants) will be integral to these accounts, and CHAT provides mechanisms for us to meaningfully include both in our discussions.

## References

Barr, R. and Tagg, J. (1995). From teaching to learning – A new paradigm for undergraduate education. *Change*, **27** (6), 12–26.

Borko, H. and Livingston, C. (1989). Cognition and improvisation: Differences in mathematics instruction by expert and novice teachers. *American Educational Research Journal*, **26** (4), 473–98.

Bransford, J. D., Brown, A. L., and Cocking, R. R. (2000). *How People Learn*. Washington, DC: National Academy Press. Available online at http://newton.nap.edu/html/howpeople1/.

Cazden, C. (2001). *Classroom Discourse: The language of teaching and learning*, 2nd ed. Portsmouth, NH: Heinemann.

Cole, M. (1996). *Cultural Psychology: A once and future discipline*. Cambridge, MA: Harvard University Press.

Crouch C. H., Watkins, J., Fagen, A. P., and Mazur, E. (2007). Peer Instruction: Engaging students one-on-one, all at once. *Reviews in Physics Education Research*, **1**(1).

Engeström, Y. (1993). Developmental studies of work as a testbench of activity theory: The case of primary care medical practice. In S. Chaiklin and J. Lave (Eds.). *Understanding Practice: Perspectives on activity and context*. New York, NY: Cambridge University Press.

Engeström, Y., Miettinen, R., and Punamäki, R. (Eds.). (1999). *Perspectives on Activity Theory*. New York, NY: Cambridge University Press.

Finkelstein, N. D. and Pollock, S. J. (2005). Replicating and understanding successful innovations: Implementing tutorials in introductory physics. *Physical Review Special Topics – Physics Education Research*, **1**, 010101.

Hatano, G. and Inagaki, K. (1986). Two courses of expertise. *Child Development and Education in Japan*, 262–72.

Hatano, G. and Oura, Y. (2003). Commentary: Reconceptualizing school learning using insight from expertise research. *Educational Researcher*, **32** (8), 26–29.

Henderson, C., Beach A., and Finkelstein, N. (2011/2012). Facilitating change in undergraduate STEM instructional practices: An analytic review of the literature (accepted). *Journal of Research on Science Teaching*.

Henderson, C. and Dancy, M. H. (2007). Barriers to the use of research-based instructional strategies: The influence of both individual and situational characteristics. *Physical Review Special Topics – Physics Education Research*, **3**, 020102.

(2009). Impact of physics education research on the teaching of introductory quantitative physics in the United States. *Phys. Rev. ST Physics Ed. Research*, **5**, 020107.

Lortie, D. (1975). *Schoolteacher: A Sociological Study*. Chicago, IL: University of Chicago Press.

Mazur, E. (1997). *Peer Instruction: A User's Manual.* Upper Saddle River, NJ: Prentice Hall.

McDermott, L. C., Shaffer, P. S., and PEG at the University of Washington. (2002). *Tutorials in Introductory Physics.* Upper Saddle River, NJ: Prentice Hall.

Mehan, H. (1979). *Learning Lessons.* Cambridge, MA: Harvard University Press.

O'Connor, M. C. and Michaels, S. (1993). Aligning academic task and participation status through revoicing: Analysis of a classroom discourse strategy. *Anthropology and Education Quarterly*, **24** (4), 318–35.

Otero, V., Finkelstein, N. D., McCray, R., and Pollock, S. (2006). Who is responsible for preparing science teachers? *Science*, **313** (5786), 445–46.

Pollock, S. J. and Finkelstein, N. D. (2008). Sustaining educational reforms in introductory physics. *Physical Review Special Topics – Physics Education Research*, **4**, 010110.

Redish, E. F. (2003). *Teaching Physics with Physics Suite.* Hoboken, NJ: John Wiley & Sons.

Roth, W. M. and Lee, Y. J. (2007). Vygotsky's neglected legacy: Cultural-historical activity theory. *Review of Educational Research*, **77** (2), 186–232.

Ruiz-Primo, M. A., Briggs, D., Iverson, H., Talbot, R., and Shepard, L. (2011). Impact of undergraduate science course innovations on learning. *Science*, **331**, 1269–70.

Trigwell, K. and Prosser, M. (1997). Towards an understanding of individual acts of teaching and learning. *Higher Education Research and Development*, **16** (2).

Turpen, C. and Finkelstein, N. D. (2009). Not all interactive engagement is the same: Variation in physics professors' implementation of peer instruction. *Physical Review Special Topics, Physics Education Research*, 5, 020101.

(2010). The construction of different classroom norms during peer instruction: Students perceive different. *Physical Review Special Topics, Physics Education Research*, **6**, 020123.

# 4

## Taking Responsibility for Learning: CHAT in a Large Undergraduate Class

### Gordon Wells

The past fifty years have brought major changes in the nature of higher education, both in the United States and in other technologically developed countries. Of these, the most important is the very substantial increase in the proportion of each age cohort that now enters some kind of tertiary institution. From the point of view of equality of opportunity, this is a significant achievement. Unfortunately, however, public funding of higher education has not kept up with the increasing numbers of students and this has led to a deterioration in the quality of that opportunity. This is seen most clearly in the increase in class size and the impact this has had on the nature of the learning experience. Now, instead of small tutorial groups, many classes contain over one hundred students, with introductory courses in popular subjects not infrequently reaching a thousand or more. This, taken together with the decreasing availability of funds to pay teaching assistants, has meant the opportunity for students to receive guidance and support from their teachers, either individually or in small tutorial groups, has become practically nonexistent. At the same time, with such large classes, there are few alternatives available to the teacher other than to present the course content through lectures supported by visual aids of various kinds. While a few students may be bold enough to ask questions, the class size makes genuine discussion between students and teacher impossible. Similar problems constrain the opportunity for students to express their understanding of and reactions to the course material in writing and to receive a personal response. With so many students, it is not possible for the teacher to read and respond to individually composed written papers; instead, educators tend to carry out assessment by means of short quizzes and multiple choice tests, with feedback taking the form of a score or a grade.

Unfortunately, these conditions only perpetuate the attitudes to learning developed during the K-12 years by so many young people, particularly those seen as "A" students. As they explain, to succeed in school requires one to excel at memorizing what the teacher or textbook presents as important and to deliver correct answers on the end-of-unit tests. It also involves learning to read the teacher's interactional style to give the responses he or she is hoping for. In other words, what comes to motivate these students' learning is success in pleasing the teacher and doing what is necessary to obtain good grades.

That students should have come to think of learning in these terms is not at all surprising, for it is implicit in the conception of school teaching that is all too frequently put forward at the level of university administration. Here is a short extract from an article I read some twenty years ago in the Ontario University Teachers' Association newsletter under the title "Great Teaching Means Mastery of Subject Matter and Transmission of Knowledge":

Knowledge needs to be transmitted in an effective and cogent manner for learning to take place.

At the elementary and secondary schools the emphasis in teaching is placed on transmitting facts. Children need this information as the basic elements in the development of knowledge.... During the pupil's first 12 or 13 years of schooling the major share of responsibility for knowledge acquisition rests with the teacher.... At the university level the student is expected to assume responsibility for knowledge acquisition.... It is at the university that the student is transformed into a self educator. (OCUFA, 1992, pp. 1–2)

This pronouncement contains several serious flaws, the most serious of which is the idea that learning occurs as the result of passive reception of the transmission of factual information. True learning – in the sense of coming to understand – is always an active process, since it involves questioning the connections between new information and what is already known and believed to be understood and then considering the implications of the new understanding. However, if the teacher alone decides what questions may be asked and what answers are acceptable, students are deprived of the opportunity to ask their own questions, test their own understanding, or offer alternative perspectives on the topic being studied. As a result, they do not learn to think critically about the material presented to them, but are encouraged instead to defer to authority and to evaluate their own ideas only against the criterion of acceptability to the teacher.

Equally flawed is the belief that students will readily assume responsibility for their own learning on entry to university. Having grown accustomed to depending on their teachers, they are reluctant to make decisions about how to engage with course material or to judge when they have succeeded.

And why should they give up the strategies that have proved successful in the past if the courses they take are taught in the same transmission mode?

### From School to College and Back Again

I have drawn attention to the connection between large university classes and the learning strategies students bring from school because my long-term goal is to change the orientation to learning and teaching that holds sway in a high proportion of schools. However, given the test frenzy that currently drives classroom instruction in countries around the world, it is clear this goal will not be easily achieved. With policy makers hell-bent on improving test scores and district administrators requiring teachers to spend substantial portions of each day on test preparation, it is not surprising that students come to believe test scores are the currency in which learning is measured and to develop strategies to succeed in this grade economy. Because policy makers pay little attention to the evidence accumulated on how people learn, it seems the only avenue for bringing about change is to use that evidence in the planning and enactment of teacher preparation and development.

One of my major responsibilities is to teach an introductory course in our university's teacher preparation program, and, over the last ten years, I have attempted to enact the principles I outline in this chapter in the way I organize the course. However, each year I meet with resistance from a proportion of the students, who are firmly wedded to the strategies that have worked for them in their education so far and who intend to teach their future students in the manner in which they were taught. Apparently, they have never experienced anything other than transmissionary teaching, even during their years of higher education – and some are graduates from my own university.

This is not the place to describe the ways in which I try – not always with success – to arrange experiences that will lead them to change their minds, as I have written about this elsewhere (Wells, 2011). However, the general approach I was developing proved very relevant when, some years ago, I was asked to teach an introductory course, entitled "Introduction to Theories of Education," in a program intended for undergraduates thinking about a career in education. When I learned that the course had been taught in the mode of three seventy-minute lectures a week to a class of 300 students, I was very reluctant to take it on, as the size and format of the class was in conflict with my beliefs about learning and teaching. However, I finally agreed on the condition that I could redesign the course in a different format, with the aim of coming as close as possible to realizing the principles I had been developing from my reading of Cultural Historical Activity Theory (CHAT), from working with K-12 teachers, and from reading and writing about my collaborative research with some of these teachers (Wells, 2001, 2009).

## Learning: From Experience to Understanding

The first and most important idea I wanted my students to understand was that any useful theory of education must be based on an understanding of how people *learn*, not only when taught in school, but, equally important, when there is no institutionally prescribed instruction. Here the research on learning in the years before school is particularly important. From this work it has become clear that, from birth, infants are self-motivated learners, making sense of their world through active engagement with their surroundings (Piaget, 1970). In addition, unlike other primates, human infants are born with a predisposition to treat other members of their species as intentional agents and to seek to understand their intentions; this makes it possible for them to learn through imitation of others' intentional behavior (Tomasello, 1999). By the second year, the human infant brings these general abilities to bear on learning the particular form of spoken language used by those around her. Once started, progress is rapid and within two or three years the child can initiate and participate in conversation about many aspects of daily life. Furthermore, as Halliday (1993) has pointed out, in learning to talk, the child is also appropriating the culture's ways of making sense of experience, since this is mediated by the grammar and vocabulary of the language.

This social, constructivist view of learning and development also brings to the fore the relationship of interdependence between society and its individual members. Since society preexists individual learners, it is from society that they appropriate the values, practices, and knowledgeable skills that shape who they become; at the same time, it is equally the case that society has been – and continues to be – maintained and transformed through the active participation of its individual members. Nevertheless, the relationship between individual and society is never direct; rather, it is necessarily mediated by situated, productive activities and interpersonal interactions with other members of the particular communities and activity systems in which individuals participate on particular occasions (Engeström, 1999; Wells, 2010).

The third key understanding about learning that has emerged in the last century is the importance of personal engagement. When the task we are working on or the problem we are trying to solve is of real personal interest, learning becomes engaging and the desire to achieve one's personal goals provides the motivation to sustain that engagement. Ensuring the learner's

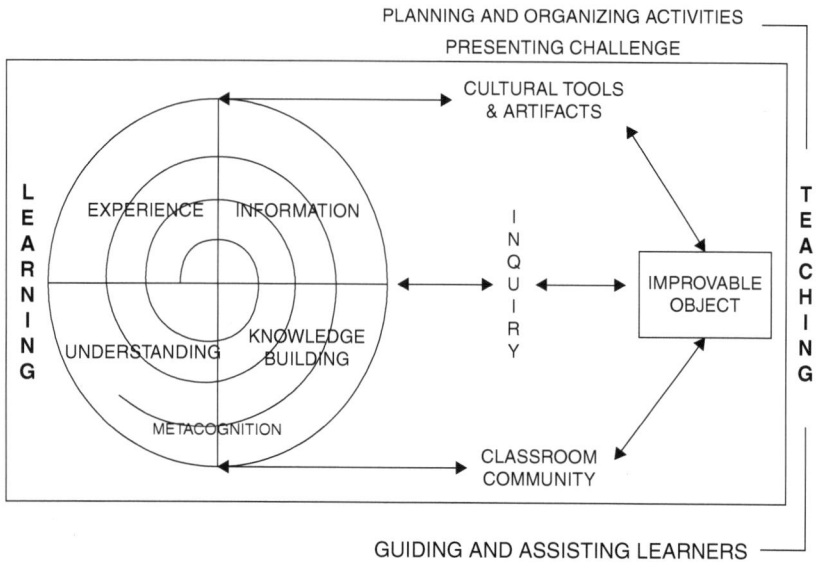

FIGURE 4.1. A model of the relationship between learning and teaching (adapted from Wells, 1999).

interest is thus of prime importance in the context of formal education. As Vygotsky wrote about teaching literacy, "teaching should be organized in such a way that reading and writing are necessary for something.... Writing should be incorporated into a task that is relevant and necessary for life" (1978, pp. 117–18).

With a similar end in view, Dewey (1938) argued education should be organized around inquiry, and in recent years this idea has been made more specific in the proposal that learning activities should start from significant or problematic features of students' experience and environment and have as their intended outcome a growth in students' understanding, where this is taken to mean, not simply factual knowledge, but knowledge growing out of and oriented to socially relevant and productive action (Cohen, McLaughlin, & Talbert, 1993).

Bringing these ideas together, I have attempted to represent some of the most important relationships among them in the form of a spiral of knowing, learning, and acting in the context of formal education (Figure 4.1).

Learning is at the heart of the diagram. As Lave and Wenger (1991) point out, learning can occur without deliberate teaching – as is the case in people's participation in the activities that make up family and community life and in many work situations. In most countries, however, it is also considered important to make provision in schools and colleges for the more systematic, guided learning necessary to master the various disciplines that underpin activities in technologically advanced societies. In such formal educational contexts, where learning is an intended outcome of activity, teaching has two major functions: the first is to select and manage the overall topic of inquiry, provide access to the necessary resources, and negotiate with the learners the challenges they will take on; the second is to monitor the progress of individuals and groups and to provide guidance and assistance as appropriate. This latter responsibility includes engaging individuals and the whole class in "metacognitively" reviewing the products and the processes of their learning so that they can take greater control over and responsibility for their efforts to achieve understanding (Olson & Bruner, 1996).

The cycle through the four quadrants of the diagram represents what is involved in carrying out a single challenging activity. On such an occasion, one starts with a personal resource of interpreted past *experience*, which provides the initial orientation for making sense of what is new in the current situation. The new is encountered as *information*, either through feedback from action into the world or from reading, viewing, or listening to representations of the experiences, explanations, and reflections of others. However, for this information to lead to an enhancement of *understanding* – which is the goal of all useful learning – it must be actively transformed and articulated with personal experience through *knowledge building* (Scardamalia & Bereiter, 2006).

Knowledge building can take a variety of forms, but all are essentially social and interactional in nature. Most typically, it takes place through face-to-face oral discourse (which may, of course, include reference to artifacts present in the situation, such as material tools, diagrams, graphs, and quotations from written texts of present or absent authors). The aim is to participate in a collective knowledge-building process to which all contribute, whether overtly or through responding internally to the contributions of others in the dialogue of inner speech. While knowledge building certainly occurs in problem-solving activities in everyday life, it is – or should be – a focal activity in formal educational contexts. Thus, one of teachers' most important tasks is to help students develop the skills required for participation in collaborative knowledge building and to use them in a sustained and focused manner.

So far, in explicating Figure 4.1, I have focused on a single opportunity for learning. But the diagram can also be seen as a representation of the cumulative nature of learning. For, while insights are frequently achieved on particular occasions of knowledge building in relation to a particular problem or issue, a change in the situation and/or the introduction of new information may expose the limits of what one thought one understood and thus call for further knowledge building. At a second level, therefore, the diagram can be seen as a continuing spiral of learning over time as new challenges set in motion new cycles of knowledge building and coming to understand.

It is at this level that the "improvable object" takes on its full significance as both goal and outcome of inquiry activity. In everyday life, major developments in understanding typically occur when participants face a challenge that requires the creation of a new artifact or practice or the improvement of an existing one. In educational contexts, such an object can take many forms, ranging from a functioning model or a symbolic representation (e.g., a map) to a work of art (e.g., a sculpture, poem, or a musical performance) and from a historical explanation to a geometric proof. Such an improvable object provides a clear focus for collaborative knowledge building, particularly if it is a representation of its creators' current understanding and a rationale has to be given for proposing a change. At this second level, then, Figure 4.1 represents a continuing progression through many cycles of "coming to understand."

Not represented in the diagram, but equally important, are the wider institutional and societal contexts within which all particular events occur. These create affordances for and constraints on what can be achieved. Thus, the events that constitute both individual cycles and progressions through the spiral need to be viewed from multiple perspectives, including those of the individuals involved, the classroom community, and the wider society of which that community is a part. However, these perspectives are not so much alternatives as different foci on the same overall activity; all have to be taken into account to understand the full complexity of any classroom event (Rogoff, 2003). In sum, in this model, learning is envisaged as a continuing "spiral of knowing," as learners continually traverse through the four quadrants of the cycle of knowing in particular places and times (Wells, 1999).

In taking on the undergraduate course on theories of education, I wanted not only to share this model with my students but also to enact it – as far as possible – in the organization of the course.

## Disrupting the "Delivery" of Curriculum

Whenever I read about "delivering the curriculum" in university documents I am reminded of how engrained the conception of education captured by this metaphor is at all levels of educational administration. I was therefore well aware of the difficulties I would encounter in trying to break out of the constraints of the standard model of first-year introductory classes. However, by putting forward my proposal for the course as an experiment and securing a small grant to evaluate it, I was allowed to go ahead with my plan.

From the point of view of scheduling, the main change was to retain the three class meetings each week but to change their function. Instead of three seventy-minute lectures, there was just one, of ninety minutes, on Mondays at 5 P.M. and a similar length section meeting later in the week. However, key to the new organization was that, within each of the ten sections of thirty students, the students would work in self-selected study groups of four to six students, meeting on their own each week for a period of one to one-and-a-half hours at any time convenient to the group members. This was the third class meeting; it was intended as a time for them to discuss the readings set for the week and to work on their group project. One of the main intentions for these study groups was that they would foster a more intimate peer network, a "safe space" in which, in the absence of authority figures, students would be more likely to engage in knowledge building and less likely to assume a passive role.

To familiarize the students with working as a group (since some had never had this experience), in the first section meeting they were asked to form groups at random and given a puzzle to solve. The puzzle was to arrange the numbers one to nine in a 3x3 matrix so that each row, column, and diagonal summed to the same number. They were asked to attempt the puzzle individually and then to work together to arrive at an agreed solution at their first group meeting. If they solved the puzzle quickly, they were asked to try to solve either the 4x4 or 5x5 puzzles, solutions to each of which share features with the first but differ in significant ways. Then, in the following section meeting, when each group reported on the strategies they used, some time was spent in metacognitive reflection on how they had proceeded individually and as a group and on formulating guiding principles for successful group work.

Having started with this small-scale "improvable object," the object for the next five weeks was for each section to tackle the global challenge of climate change by investigating ways of developing a more sustainable way of life. Section members individually proposed an aspect of this overall topic they would like to research and then formed groups of four to six on the basis of similar interests. Each group was to present the outcome of its work at a sustainability forum in its section meeting in the sixth week. Most of the groups' individual and collaborative research took place outside class, but, to the extent possible in the class time available, they were also assisted by the teaching assistant responsible for their section.

There were two main reasons for introducing this project. The theoretical rationale was to enable the students to experience in practice the theoretical model of learning through joint productive activity that was at the heart of the course. The second reason was to engage them in inquiry on a topic they personally chose under an umbrella theme of real social relevance and one that had the potential to change their own values and way of living as well as to prepare them to introduce this topic in their future work as teachers. While some students, despite my prior explanation, could not initially see the relevance of the group inquiry project in the context of a course on educational theory, most made the connection between theory and practice by the end of the course.

In the final four weeks, the second group project was more explicitly related to the ways of thinking about learning and teaching considered during the course. The challenge was to draw on their research on sustainability to design an appropriate curriculum unit on this topic for a grade level of their choice, using the theoretical principles they had appropriated from the course. Since many of the students planned to teach, this project was an exciting foretaste of their chosen careers, and even for those who had no specific plans it was a meaningful way of consolidating and applying the various components of the course.

In addition to the group projects, there were two kinds of individual assignments. The first was to keep a journal with at least one entry per week, responding to the topic of the week by reflecting on the readings and lecture and on the relationship of these to their own life experiences. Second, there were two essay assignments. The first, at mid-term, was on a self-chosen topic arising from the readings to date; students exchanged their first drafts with another member of their group, who was responsible for giving helpful feedback; the final draft was due a week later. The second essay assignment was to write a rationale for the curriculum unit their group had designed, justifying their decisions in the light of the ideas they had encountered during the course. Teaching assistants gave written responses to each essay and periodically to the journal entries. However, to dissuade students from second guessing how to get an "A," they were informed on the first day of class that they would not earn formal grades for individual assignments; instead, they would receive comments designed to help them improve the objects they had been working on. At the same time, they were told that the (institutionally required) final grade for the course would be based on the evidence of engagement shown in all their written work as well as in their section and group participation, week by week.

In contrast to the more student-centered orientation of the section and small group activities, the weekly lectures provided an introduction to each new topic and an overview of the ideas involved and of the principles that could be derived from them. At the same time, in keeping with CHAT theory, each lecture also incorporated more interactive episodes in which video clips, demonstrations, and open-ended questions were used to stimulate interaction among students, followed by more general discussion. These activities were intended to involve them more actively in collaborative knowledge building and thereby to sustain their interest and engagement. In later iterations of the course, I also invited students to send me questions arising from previous weeks so that I could revisit issues they found problematic.

However, within this organizational framework, the section meetings were the key component. They acted as a pivot, mediating between the lectures and readings on one hand, and the group and individual assignments on the other. The scheduled ninety minutes allowed for a variety of activities – reviewing the readings, hearing reports from the study groups, responding to students' individual assignments – and the relatively small size of the sections made genuine discussion more feasible. The teaching assistants were all very well prepared, in part because they were chosen from our doctoral and masters students, who had already encountered CHAT through coursework with me or another professor in the Education Department, and in part because we met in advance of the course, and regularly throughout, to plan activities and to discuss any modifications that seemed desirable in the light of feedback from the students. In addition, I made it my practice to visit each section several times during the course to meet with the study groups to hear how they were managing their time together and to offer any assistance that seemed appropriate. I also hoped in this way to overcome to some extent the impersonality of my role as lecturer and ultimate assessor of their performance.

### Evaluation and Feedback

At the end of the course each year, the students were asked to complete a questionnaire that sought their reactions to the different aspects of the course format as well as to its content; they were also invited to offer their ideas about how the course could better meet their needs. Many took up this latter opportunity and, year by year, their suggestions helped us to make several significant improvements.

Reviewing the responses received over the years, it is clear some undergraduates were disconcerted – at least initially – by our efforts to persuade them to take greater agency as inquiring learners. A major reason for the difficulty such students experienced was insightfully expressed by one of them as follows.

People seem to have such a hard time accepting Education 92B's philosophy and expectations and this is only because their previous school learning developed

certain modes of operation, habits, approaches to problem solving, ways of thinking that stand in stark contrast to the 92B approach. Undoubtedly it must prove
perturbing for students to find themselves in a context where they are unable to
use the habits and skills they have refined through their years in school.

However, from the outset, many students did understand and appreciate the
opportunity to develop their own understanding in collaboration with their
peers rather than simply accepting the teacher as the sole authority. There was
also evidence that the opportunities we created for students to reflect metacognitively on their experiences during the course enabled some to gain a
better understanding of themselves as learners. Furthermore, it was clear the
majority of students really enjoyed the opportunity to work in small groups
without an instructor – although some were initially skeptical about how the
work would be distributed among them and the value or feasibility of being
given responsibility for deciding how to use that time.

As mentioned earlier, we made several changes over the years in light of
the students' feedback, in particular by giving more explanation at the outset
for the format of the course and the reason for choosing sustainability as the
overall theme for the group projects. As a result, students increasingly came
to value their experiences during the course, some even reporting that, for
the first time during their undergraduate careers, they had learned to work
toward their own personal goals and, as a result, felt a new sense of empower-
ment around their education and their work. The positive tone of the following, fairly representative, quotation suggests these students were getting the
point and enjoying as well as benefiting from the experience.

It has been a real rewarding experience taking this course. I signed up for it at the
last minute to satisfy a GE [General Education] requirement, yet it has transpired
into so much more than that. I applaud and am inspired by the dedication, willingness, and desire people have shown (TAs included) to change our education
system for the better. I have learned a great deal about what needs to change not
only in the classroom, but in the public's eye as well, when it comes to assessment,
teaching, and understanding.

The culminating improvable objects in particular – the group designed curriculum units and the individual rationale for the design of the unit each
student wrote – proved very worthwhile for many of them. Not only was it
a meaningful way of putting their new understandings to practical use in a
"joint productive activity" (Dalton & Tharp, 2002), but it also prompted metacognitive reflection on their own learning, which made them more explicitly
aware of how the CHAT principles underlying the course could be a basis for
their future work as teachers.

Preparing a curriculum unit was difficult but it really hammered home everything we had done up to that point and all of the effective teaching methods we learned. I felt that by having to develop our own curriculum we were carried to a better understanding of specific theories. This class was amazing.

## Conclusion

While I have not changed my opinion about the undesirability of large classes, it does seem that attempting to apply CHAT principles in their design can make the student experience more educationally significant – at least for those open to the challenge of becoming more self-directed in their learning. Judging by students' comments, it also appears the opportunity to work in small study groups on related self-selected topics was a key factor. Collaborating in the creation or improvement of their chosen object not only channeled their motivation toward a common substantive goal but also created a social camaraderie that provided emotional satisfaction (Immordino-Yang & Damasio, 2007). The decision not to grade the groups' projects also seemed significant in reducing the problems that often arise when all members of the group are assigned the same grade despite perceived unequal contributions. Nevertheless, not all students appreciated the group assignments. For some, interpersonal incompatibilities made collaboration impossible; for others, the theme of sustainability was perceived as either irrelevant or too demanding. The choice of theme is thus clearly critical and the principles involved in selecting one that is both relevant to the course content and effective for the particular mix of students requires further research.

This course was planned with future educators in mind, but, in practice, it also attracted a sizable proportion of students who took it as part of the general education requirement, in some cases because it was the only general education course that would fit their schedule. The fact that some of these students found it a new and valuable learning experience suggests the CHAT principles underlying its design could, with adaptation, profitably be enacted in other disciplines.

## References

Cohen, D. K., McLaughlin, M. W., and Talbert, J. E. (Eds.). (1993). *Teaching for Understanding: Challenges for policy and practice.* San Francisco, CA: Jossey-Bass.

Dalton, S. S. and R. G., Tharp (2002). Standards for pedagogy: Research, theory and practice. In G., Wells and G., Claxton (Eds.), *Learning for Life in the 21st Century: Sociocultural perspectives on the future of education* (pp. 181–94). Oxford, Blackwell.

Dewey, J. (1938). *Experience and Education*. New York: Collier Macmillan.

Engeström, Y. (1999). Activity theory and individual and social transformation. In Y. Engeström, R. Miettinen, and R.-L. Punamaki (Eds.), *Perspectives on Activity Theory* (pp. 19–38). Cambridge: Cambridge University Press.

Halliday, M. A. K. (1993). Towards a language-based theory of learning. *Linguistics and Education*, 5, 93–116.

Immordino-Yang, M. H. and Damasio, A. (2007). We feel, therefore we learn: The relevance of affective and social neuroscience to education. *Mind, Brain, and Education*, 1(1), 3–10.

Lave, J. and Wenger, E. (1991). *Situated Learning: Legitimate peripheral participation*. New York: Cambridge University Press.

Olson, D. R. and Bruner, J. S. (1996). Folk psychology and folk pedagogy. In D. R. Olson and N. Torrance (Eds.), *The handbook of education and human development* (pp. 9–27). Cambridge, MA: Blackwell.

Ontario Confederation of University Faculty Associations (OCUFA) (1992). Great teaching means mastery of subject matter and transmission of knowledge. *Forum*, October, 1–2.

Piaget, J. (1970). Piaget's theory. In P. H. Mussen (Ed.), *Carmichael's Handbook of Child Development* (pp. 703–32). New York: John Wiley & Sons.

Rogoff, B. (2003). *The Cultural Nature of Human Development*. New York: Oxford University Press.

Scardamalia, M. and Bereiter, C. (2006). Knowledge building: Theory, pedagogy, and technology. In K. Sawyer (Ed.), *Cambridge Handbook of the Learning Sciences* (pp. 97–118). New York: Cambridge University Press.

Tomasello, M. (1999). *The Cultural Origins of Human Cognition*. Cambridge, MA: Harvard University Press.

Vygotsky, L. S. (1978). *Mind in Society: The development of higher psychological processes*. Cambridge, MA: Harvard University Press.

Wells, G. (1999). *Dialogic Inquiry: Towards a sociocultural practice and theory of education*. Cambridge: Cambridge University Press.

(Ed.). (2001). *Action, Talk, and Text: Learning and teaching through inquiry*. New York: Teachers College Press.

(2009). *The Meaning Makers: Learning to talk and talking to learn* (2nd ed.). Bristol, UK: Multilingual Matters.

(2010) Schooling: The contested bridge between individual and society. *Pedagogies: An International Journal*, 5: 37–48.

(2011). Motive and motivation in learning to teach. In D. M. Mcinerney, G. A. D. Liem, and R. Walker (Eds.), *Sociocultural Theories of Learning and Motivation: Looking back, looking forward*. Charlotte, NC: Information Age Publishing.

# 5

# CHAT and Student Writing

David R. Russell

Writing, often in conjunction with other media, is profoundly important to higher education, as it is to other modern institutions students will enter. Student writing mediates much of the activity of learning, and the most crucial parts, typically, such as assessment. Yet in higher education, writing often is devalued or even dismissed as a set of easily generalizable, elementary skills of transcribing speech or thought that students should have learned earlier in secondary or elementary school. This remedial model, and the tradition of complaint and cascading blame that goes with it, results not only in remedial courses but also, often, in the exclusion of student writing from the realm of serious inquiry and discussion in higher education.

Yet in many countries, higher education teachers, administrators, and policy makers have come to see writing as an important tool of learning and teaching. CHAT has provided concepts and research for using student writing as a means of meeting the pedagogic challenges this volume addresses (see Introduction). This chapter describes how CHAT-based research and interventions in several countries address specific issues of current higher education, and provides new answers, however partial. But first I briefly explain how writing, in CHAT terms, is more than a means for assessing students; it is a tool of university-level teaching, learning, and sociocognitive development.

For transmission models of communication, teaching/learning, and behavior, CHAT substitutes models of tool-mediated activity (see Figure 5.1). Writing (broadly seen as inscriptions on surfaces) is an extremely powerful and plastic cultural tool, as it is relatively permanent, often portable, and usually inexpensive to produce. It is therefore an efficient tool for (re)organizing and regulating thought and behavior. As such, it mediates not only thought, but also the social organization of literate cultures – think of laws, religious texts, maps (Bazerman, 2006; Goody, 1986).

Transmission Models                    Shared Tools Models

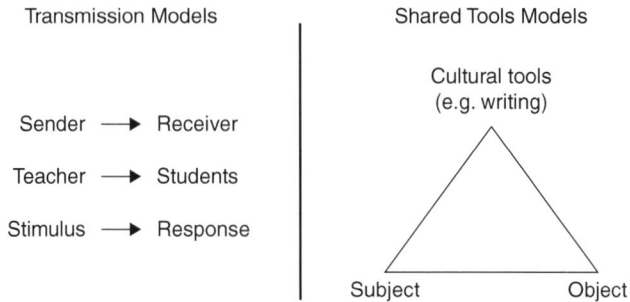

FIGURE 5.1. Transmission versus shared tool models of communication
(Russell, 2009).

For pedagogy, writing has broad potential as a tool of both learning and development, understood through the Vygotskian concepts of internalization and externalization. As the editors put it, "learning as not simply a matter of internalising what one is taught; rather, internalisation is complemented by a process of externalisation where learners take these ideas and work with them to shape what Vygotsky termed the social situations of their development." These concepts suggest writing is potentially much more than an autonomous transcription of speech or thought, a mere conduit of transmission. It is a tool for reorganizing and deepening thought. As E. M. Forster put it, "How can I know what I think until I see what I say?" (1971, p. 99). Or as another novelist, C. Day-Lewis, put it, we not only "write in order to be understood, we write in order to understand."

The central theoretical concept – from its Vygotskian origins in the work of James Britton and his colleagues (1975) – is that students not only learn to write but also write to learn. This concept provides a deeper understanding of writing than the sender-receiver model. Writing is a tool for *learning* instead of merely a tool for *assessing* learning. Writing is conceived as a means of engaging students with the problems and methods of a discipline as well as a means of sorting students.

James Britton's work (1975) inspired the language-across-the-curriculum (LAC) movement at the secondary level in the United Kingdom, which in turn inspired the writing-across-the-curriculum (WAC) or writing-in-the-disciplines (WID) movement in U.S. higher education, beginning in the 1970s (Russell, 2002). According to the most recent survey (Thaiss & Porter, 2010), more than half of the institutions of higher education in the United States and Canada who responded have some kind of program to improve student writing – and student learning through writing. Some 65 percent of PhD-granting universities reported such a program. WAC programs consist of such efforts as workshops for professors to learn techniques for improving students' learning through their writing, and often writing centers for students (Bazerman et al., 2005). And there are research and intervention efforts, though with different histories, in many countries, such as Australia, France, Colombia, Germany, New Zealand, Switzerland, and many others.

Recent large-scale survey research of more than twenty-three thousand students in eighty-two U.S. universities found that writing *with certain qualities* contributes significantly to student engagement and learning. The report concluded:

When institutions provided students with extensive, intellectually challenging writing activities, the students engaged in more deep learning activities such as analysis, synthesis, integration of ideas from various sources, and grappled more with course ideas both in and out of the classroom. In turn, students whose faculty assigned projects with these same characteristics reported greater personal, social, practical, and academic learning and development. (NSSE, 2008, pp. 20–21)

In a CHAT view, writing is important to student learning, but also to the intellectual activity of the disciplines. Researchers use writing to learn as well as to communicate. And they use highly differentiated forms (genres) of writing to do their work and "discuss" it in scholarly publications. Simply put, writing is specialized as well as transversal. Many aspects of writing are similar in all fields. All use the same basic grammar and spelling, and all pose problems, cite previous literature, give their methods and results, but they do so in very different ways, such that the writing in one field is often unintelligible to researchers in another. Writing is in fundamental ways different in each discipline, as it mediates the different activity of each.

In North American research on writing in higher education, the concept of genre-as-social-action, linked often to CHAT, has become important (Miller, 1984, 1994). A genre is not seen as a set of formal features, but as a typified response to a recurring need. Researchers write in certain ways because they think and communicate and manipulate certain objects in certain typical ways. Thus, students often find it difficult to move from the writing of one discipline to that of another, like "a stranger in strange lands," as the title of a seminal article on this put it (McCarthy, 1987).

Moreover, genres form systems or ecologies, which mediate systems or ecologies of activity (Bazerman, 1994; Spinuzzi, 2003). Those systems of activity and the genres that mediate them extend from researchers to professionals and publics beyond higher education. And they extend from researchers to students (Russell, 1997). The humble lab report in chemistry 101 is a reflection of – and potentially a step on a high scaffold toward – the work of scientists in professional laboratories. Thus writing is essential whether it is students creating new knowledge for themselves – what we call learning – or academics creating new knowledge for their fields – what we call research. Writing indexes the methods and epistemology of each discipline, the practices of each profession. But students are often not taught – but only expected to know or divine – the ways with words, that is to say, the genres of a discipline.

Research on writing in higher education often exposes and analyzes deep contradictions among the conflicting societal demands and interests in higher education, such as the rifts between "pure" and "applied" research (research for internal higher education interests and interests external to higher education). In relation to education, writing exposes the contradictions between the formation of students specifically (professionally) versus generally (for citizenship); for research (and reproduction) versus for professional practice (service); between the interests of teaching versus research. All are embodied in the tensions students and teachers experience in choosing and learning and writing the genres of higher education. And all reflect the great sea changes outlined in the introduction to this volume. I begin with the institutions that have the oldest and most numerous students – and those with the least status.

## Community Colleges and Adult/Further Education: Motivational Pathways of Texts

The first two of the three sea changes in higher education Wells and Edwards point to in their introduction – the broadening of higher education curricula to practical arts and sciences, and the expansions of higher education in both the number and types of students and the number and types of institutions – makes the cultural-historical contradictions of writing most dramatically evident. CHAT research has shown how the genres, audiences, and purposes for writing have also dramatically expanded, though often with little or no provision for, or even awareness of, the change on the part of teachers and administrators (Graves, Hyland, & Samuels, 2010). In a three-year longitudinal study in two UK further education colleges (similar to U.S. community colleges), Ivanic, Edwards, and Barton (2009) used activity theory, in combination with semiotic and discourse analysis, to describe the multiple and multimodal literacies (deliberately plural) of students and teachers in curriculums such as child care, catering, travel, and tourism.

Many of the students had worked or were currently working in the sector they were studying (common in these types of institutions), and all the students got extensive practical experiences as part of their curriculum (test kitchens, laboratory crèches, etc.). The researchers found that students had extensive and often very demanding literacy tasks in their everyday or work lives outside higher education. "Students engaged not only in vernacular literacy practices – that is, those which arise from their own interests and concerns – but also in a wide range of bureaucratic, more formal literacy practices which are demanded by the practicalities of their lives" (Ivanic, Edwards, & Barton, 2009, p. 180). Yet teachers and students rarely perceived these "outside" literacy practices as valuable.

What has become clear in our projects is that communication, which encompasses literacy practices, is an important part of the hidden curriculum in colleges. Yet all too often the communicative aspects of learning remain unacknowledged, literacies are treated as "belonging" in college or out of college, and students' everyday literacy practices remain untapped as resources for learning. As long as these tendencies continue, literacy in colleges and in other educational institutions will remain a constant "problem." (Ivanic, Edwards, & Barton, 2009, p. 190)

Ironically, students in vocational curricula were expected to produce a greater diversity of – and often linguistically more demanding – genres than students in academic courses, where they wrote only one (the academic essay). For example, students in child care wrote pamphlets for parents and students in catering developed menu prose and business plans, as well as academic essays. And vocational students experienced a contradiction in purposes and often great difficulty in writing, arising from this ambiguity in the curriculum.

The researchers concluded college staff needed to become aware of the literacies that mediate learning (Ivanic, Edwards, & Barton, 2009, p. 183). Based on the descriptive research, the teachers made changes in their practice to develop hybrid academic/workplace genres that engaged with students' everyday literacy practices. These "tended to increase their capacity for engagement and recall, and their confidence" (Ivanic, Edwards, & Barton, 2009, p. 186). For the researchers, "It is diversification and multiplication of literacy practices which is the issue and not the lack of them. If one seeks to impose a standardised view of literacy, then diversity and multiplicity will inevitably be problematic, but they could be a source of strength" (Ivanic, Edwards, & Barton, 2009, p. 181).

## Writing across the Curriculums: Contradictions in "General"/"Liberal" Education

CHAT has also been used to understand the differences among the discourses – and activities – of different disciplines, and therefore what is general or transversal about writing and what is not. As I mentioned earlier, writing indexes the epistemology and practices of each discipline, and it also maps in its genres the motivational and developmental trajectories expected of students. Russell and Yañez (2003; Yañez & Russell, 2009) studied a third-year Irish education history course in a large Midwestern public university (MWU), which students in fields other than history took to satisfy a university general education requirement (common in U.S. universities to broaden students' education). They wanted to understand obstacles to WAC (and the deeper attitudes, practices, and structures involved) in multiple contexts: the classroom, the broader university, and professional and civic contexts beyond it.

They found the assigned genres (book report, research paper) were defined very differently by the teacher and the students, which produced frustration in the students and tensions and disturbances in the classroom. By broadening the analysis to other activity systems (professional academic history, secondary school history teaching, and journalism), the researchers found the tensions were symptoms of deeper contradictions between the students and teachers' constructions of the object and motive of the course. The teacher perceived the assignments as genres of professional academic history useful for deepening students' critical thinking and making them more critically aware citizens, though the genres he assigned were those of professional academic historians rather than of civic discourse. The students perceived the genres as linked to the activity system of secondary school history or popular history for leisure reading, and even where the teacher's genres were understood, students did not perceive those genres of academic historians as relevant to their diverse professional pathways or future citizenship. Students expressed their sense of just doing it for a grade rather than for their future involvements, and they expressed alienation in their approach to the writing tasks.

From interviews with history faculty members and curricular/policy documents from the department and the university written over the last fifty years, the researchers traced the intertextual and intersubjective links between the classroom and the institution to identify deeper contradictions and a strategic ambiguity. When convenient, writing was conceived in terms of unproblematic transmission: a container or conduit for thought. "Content" is placed into written "form" and sent. Writing is a generalizable set of discrete skills necessary for critical thinking and democratic life. Students do not have to understand the relationship between the practices of academic history and their own pursuits. Citizenship is not a social practice into which one is enculturated but an accumulation of knowledge and skills taught to the masses – an ideology of mass education.

But when convenient, writing is alternatively conceived as a tool of enculturation in some specific social practice, such as the activity of doing professional academic history – an ideology of elite, meritocratic education. This strategic ambiguity allowed MWU to pursue contradictory motives in general education without confronting their consequences at the human level of teaching and learning. The strategic ambiguity made it possible for faculty members and administrators to alternatively invoke one and ignore the other of these two official motives when necessary or convenient in working out the division of labor. Graduate students, for example, taught the general education courses, freeing tenure-line faculty members for teaching majors and doing research. However, this strategic ambiguity over conceptions of general education and writing left the instructor, and his students from many disciplines, to wrestle with the consequences.

## STEM Education

Science, technology, engineering, and mathematics education (STEM) has been an important site of research on writing in higher education because of its prestige in the academic world and its links to powerful professional worlds. Moreover, STEM fields use not only alphabetic but also alphanumeric and graphical inscriptions.

Interventions using CHAT and genre as social action critically analyze some genre systems of formal schooling in light of research on literacy practices among professionals and students. Then the learning environment is re-mediated based on that research, often using Internet technology. The most demonstrably effective example is Labwrite, an online program used to teach students the processes of laboratory practice and lab report writing, common in natural sciences and engineering education (Carter, Ferzli, & Wiebe, 2004, 2007). The lab report is also common in workplaces for scientists, engineers, and technicians, but a genre whose classroom version often degenerates into a cookbook or worksheet formulaic genre. The researchers first did an analysis of university chemistry teaching and learning in laboratory contexts and the professional practices of scientists and engineers. Researchers drew on workplace studies of professionals researching and writing lab reports, classroom case studies of laboratory practices, and research on students' literacy practices in writing reports outside of the classroom/laboratory. The researchers then developed a web-based tool for leading students through the process of producing a lab report. In quasi-experimental, quantitatively analyzed studies, LabWrite was found to be significantly better than traditional instruction in improving students' 1) understanding of specific scientific concepts, 2) understanding of the scientific method, and 3) attitudes toward lab work (Carter, Ferzli, & Wiebe, 2004).

Rather than explicitly teaching the specific linguistic resources, LabWrite explicitly teaches the genre in the process of performing a rhetorical action in its target context of use, the activity of chemistry education in higher education. LabWrite leads students through the process of *doing* and *representing* (textually, mathematically, and graphically) a laboratory experiment. The instruction in "writing" a lab report begins before the students enter the laboratory, continues in the laboratory, and concludes after the students have left the laboratory. The goal of instruction is not to improve the students' writing per se, but to improve their learning: to teach scientific concepts and the scientific method using writing as a means. Because the students are writing to learn, they are assessed on their learning, not their writing. The genre is a tool for doing and learning science in the context of the course-specific laboratory, and the students learn the genre as a matter of course in doing the activity.

This approach shows particular promise. It is the only one that has proven effective (measured by quasi-experimental comparison methods) in teaching a genre to L1 adults. However, because the LabWrite study was confined to a very specific and regularized genre and activity system (the laboratory report in laboratory science instruction), the potential for transfer from formal schooling to professional spheres of activity beyond is not addressed, as Carter, Ferzli, and Wiebe point out (2004). Yet transfer is very often the goal of teaching genre, particularly in professional education. To address the problem of transfer, we must move beyond writing to learn toward writing to professionalize.

## Professional Education and Technologies of the Word

CHAT concepts of development and genre as social action have also informed research on the transition from writing in higher education to writing in professional work, fundamentally different activity systems nevertheless linked through systems of genres. This transition is crucial to understanding the contradictions of higher education, between traditional values of liberal education and new demands on higher education from employers, government employability agendas, and so on.

The most extensive study of the transition was conducted by a group of Canadian researchers (Dias et al., 1999; Freedman, Adam, & Smart, 1994). A central but uncomfortable finding is that there is little transfer between communication in the genres of professional education in higher education and communication in the genres of professional work. These researchers found that students attributed their learning to schooling (writing for the teacher, for a mark), even when teachers attempt to simulate the workplace by assigning workplace genres, having professionals in the field attend student presentations, and so forth. That is, students recognize and create texts as belonging to the activity (and genre) system of schooling, though the texts teachers assign for reading or writing may have been drawn from or intended for workplace systems of genres. The social motive of schooling (epistemic) is fundamentally different than that of work (pragmatic).

This fundamental contradiction in social motives generates other contradictions. Writing in schooling is primarily individual, is typically done for assessment, and leads to a mark. Incorporating other students' work is often considered cheating. Writing in professional environments is primarily collective, collaborative, and leads to a product or service. In schooling, then, there is little "document cycling" – feedback and revision loops common in professional workplaces (Paradis, Dobrin, & Miller, 1985).

An obvious intervention, then, is to immerse students in a target genre system *beyond* the classroom, in a workplace, as with internships or service learning, but this is expensive and difficult to control. Based on CHAT research on communication in professional organizations, researchers construct multimedia simulations of fictional organizations, represented by fictional Internet and intranet sites, to create an activity system that mediates between schooling and work (Fisher, 2006, 2007; Russell & Fisher, 2009) (see Figure 5.2). Students role play as they collaboratively engage in workplace-like activities in the fictional online learning environment, using the tools and genres typical in workplaces in a particular sector (databases, files of documents, meeting minutes, videotaped meetings, synchronous and asynchronous communication, etc.).

Students play the role of consultants (or interns) in a fictional organization. The "consultants" produce texts in a range of genres (written, oral, visual, and electronic) that arise in the fictional activity (and genre) system of the company. The texts are submitted to characters in the simulation, such as the CEO pictured here in a video (see Figure 5.2). And the characters reply to the students-as-consultants through a closed e-mail system (though it is actually – as the students are told – the teacher replying in character, using a special role-sensitive e-mail system). There is also a document server with a universe of documents from various departments of the organization. And in the interactions of fictional characters and students-as-consultants, that document universe is brought into circulation through the genre system, where students must act on deadlines, face ethical dilemmas seeded into the simulation, and deal with "emergencies," such as an anti-GMO demonstration outside the company headquarters. In other words, the elements of time and space, although fictional, are added to the fictional case to create

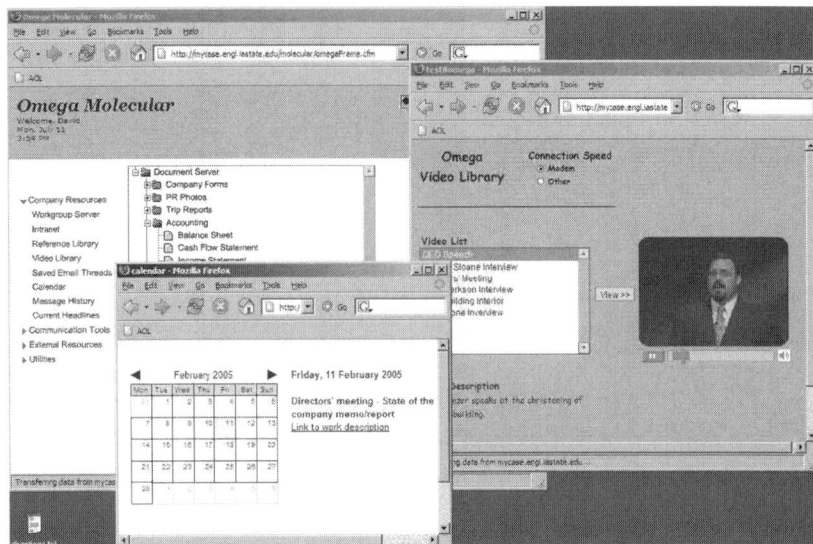

FIGURE 5.2. Online multimedia simulation of a fictional workplace.

a learning environment where students experience genre as social action in workplaces.

Research into students' learning in these environments suggests students are much more likely to attribute their learning in the online simulation environment to contexts of professional work than to contexts of schooling, as compared to their attributions of other parts of their courses that use more traditional learning environments (e.g., Blackboard™ and face-to-face instruction) (Fisher, 2006). These attributions seem to be shaped by the changes in classroom rules, division of labor, and community the simulation affords, and by the contradictions between the genre systems of schooling and workplace (mediated by the simulation as a teaching tool). For example, in engineering and business simulations, students draw freely from each other's work as it is posted to a shared file space and from the student work published in the simulation (students add to the simulation over time). This literacy practice is extremely atypical in classroom settings, where writing is primarily individual and done for assessment, and where incorporating other students' work is often considered cheating. But it is extremely typical in the workplace, where people often draw from a common pool of documents and where documents cycle through multiple readers in the division of labor. The goal of the online multimedia simulations is to exploit the contradictions between the two activity systems to produce reflective practice and reflective practitioners (Schön, 1983, 1987).

## Graduate Education and the Thesis/Dissertation: Lamination of Activity and Multi-Genre

The Master and PhD thesis (dissertation) has become a major issue with the exponential growth of this sector of higher education – and a major object of CHAT research for twenty-five years. From the first ethnographic studies of PhD students (Berkenkotter, Huckin, & Ackerman, 1988), research has found that students finally come to write the genre, but often at the price of profound conflicts of identity, long periods of inactivity, and other human and financial costs. Caught between the activity systems of the institution and its requirements, on one hand, and the discipline and its practices on the other, newcomers to the genre and activity of the thesis/dissertation bring their own sociocultural history and take an active role in learning to write it. Disciplinary enculturation is less a slow absorption or unconscious, passive assimilation and more a conscious, often chaotic battle, though often hidden from view.

Paul Prior's longitudinal studies (1998) have found that students at this level engage in a process of "gentrification," reclassifying texts, attributing similarities, as they learn – and sometimes reject – powerful disciplinary and institutional practices. Each student participates in multiple networks of activity simultaneously – university, department, discipline, committees, job market, family. And each must negotiate this "laminated" activity in writing this most important document of their career (See also Blakeslee, 1997; Casanave, 2002).

An ethnographic study of eleven students using activity theory (Lundell & Beach, 2003) isolated two central contradictions of graduate education revealed in their processes of thesis writing:

- Students must write in the format and style required by the rules of the department and university, but the formats and styles do not easily translate into presentation or publications for the job market.
- They must conform to the practices of the thesis director, who is often uninformed about the department/university rules, and who does not give them the rules.

Paré and Starke Meyerling's 2009 study of sixty PhD students and their thesis directors found that the thesis is not only a *double* genre – a last exercise at the university, a final test, but also, entirely or partially, the first significant contribution to the disciplinary conversations. The thesis is also a *multi*-genre, which responds to multiple exigencies, functions in multiple systems of activity, and is addressed to multiple readers. Not only does the thesis contain a number of distinct embedded genres, each difficult to master (literature review, essay, experimental report), but it also responds to different social actions in many contexts, including the dyad of the director and student, the thesis committee, the department, the university, the disciplinary community, hiring committees, and the broader social structures of research in the field. Thus, the thesis is perhaps the most complex genre written in the university (whether by students, teachers, or researchers) in its multiplicity of intellectual, rhetorical, and social demands.

## Conclusion

CHAT calls attention to the fundamental cultural tools of teaching and learning – and to their relation to the cognitive and social organization that extends beyond the teacher, the learner, and the classroom. Writing, like many cultural tools, tends to be invisible when people use it habitually, smoothly – or in A. N. Leont'ev's (1978) terms, when it is fully operationalized in some activity. Yet it disappears from conscious attention as one focuses on what one is writing, not on one's writing itself. In routine genres there seems to be no "writing," only "writing it up," the last and least interesting step. This invisibility is fine – useful – until it breaks down under the pressure of new challenges, and thus writing is bumped up into conscious attention with the attendant emotions. This is a normal part of learning to write a new genre in a new activity system (a scientist having to write a press release, for example (Smart, 2000)).

Yet for students, the genres of higher education – like the kinds of critical thinking those genres externalize and mediate – are for the most part new challenges for students, though the genres often go by the same names as those the students wrote in secondary school (essay, report), with the attendant confusion and unlearning necessary to sort out the differences in the kinds and disciplines of thinking/writing (Donahue, 2008; Graves, Hyland, & Samuels, 2010). So students must consciously wrestle with writing. They must struggle to acquire on their own the genre know-how that is for their professors so routinized, so operationalized in the activity and "content" of the field as to be invisible to them. Yet this is the very know-how on which not only students' grades but also their success beyond the university depends, in large part (as employer surveys so often point out (e.g., Bowers & Metcalf, 2008). This is the fundamental and unchanging challenge of teaching and learning with writing.

Yet in recent years, with the new challenges of higher education, what is true for individuals has become true for the higher education sector writ large. The old ways of teaching and learning (with) writing no longer work smoothly. Student writing development has thus become an object of conscious attention, a "problem" in higher education all around the world, because it reveals fundamental contradictions in contemporary higher education. Higher education sits between two contradictory pressures, what Burton Clark (1989) has called disciplinary excellence versus social equity. On one end, the intake end of social equity, far more students (and far more diverse students) come streaming into higher education – bringing in a far greater diversity of linguistic resources, not only international students but also students from different cultural and class backgrounds. Many of these new students do not know the ways of reading and writing that seem second nature to traditional students. Moreover, the patterns of participation have changed, with many students in higher education part time, balancing schedules and, more important, spending a large part of their time away from the academic environment and its traditional discourses.

On the other end, disciplinary excellence, higher education is also changing. Excellence used to mean reproducing an intellectual (and in many ways a social) elite, to carry on what was then the relatively stable work of the disciplines and professions. But changes in both knowledge and work mean postindustrial societies and economies need more "knowledge workers," and this knowledge work depends on written communication in and between specialisms. Higher education is essential to the employability agendas of modern societies, and this means higher education must use and teach more sophisticated and diverse genres of written communication. Students are leaving higher education to enter far more specialized and yet far more interdisciplinary workplaces. As the pace and complexity of global communication increases, the division of intellectual labor increases, and with it the importance of writing. Students will need greater linguistic and rhetorical flexibility to effectively enter and eventually transform professions and institutions.

Between these two contradictory pressures, a changing notion of social equity on one hand and a changing notion of disciplinary excellence on the other, sits student writing in higher education. Because it is no longer possible for higher education to simply skim the cream and pour the rest out, it is no longer possible to ignore issues of teaching and learning, and no longer possible to leave the problem of writing development solely in the hands of individual students, unaided by academic staff.

Attention to writing, given the CHAT take on pedagogy, is not a distraction from teaching content, but a means of teaching it more effectively, because content is seen not as a thing to be put into students' minds but as a resource for engaging with, communicating with, others and the world – most powerfully, usually, through writing. In this sense, writing is no longer a remedial subject, another course or courses to be taken outside a curriculum (the knee-jerk reaction of modern higher education to problems is to create another course). Writing is rather a shared responsibility, a means of teaching and learning and critical thinking for students and researchers. And as the tradition of CHAT research I have touched on here suggests, writing is also an interesting object of research and a tool of pedagogical experiment and reform in its own right.

## References

Bazerman, C. (1994). Systems of genres and the enactment of social intentions. *Genre and the New Rhetoric*, 79–101.

(2006). The writing of social organization and the literate situating of cognition: Extending Goody's social implications of writing. *Technology, Literacy and the Evolution of Society: Implications of the work of Jack Goody*. Mahwah, NJ: Lawrence Erlbaum Associates.

Bazerman, C., Joseph, L., Bethel, L., Chavkin, T., Fouquette, D., and Garufis, J. (2005). *Reference Guide to Writing across the Curriculum*. West Lafayette, IN: Parlor Press and The WAC Clearinghouse, http://wac.colostate.edu/books/bazerman_wac/. Retrieved from http://wac.colostate.edu/books/bazerman_wac/.

Berkenkotter, C., Huckin, T. N., and Ackerman, J. (1988). Conventions, conversations, and the writer: Case study of a student in a rhetoric Ph. D. program. *Research in the Teaching of English*, 9–44.

Blakeslee, A. M. (1997). Activity, context, interaction, and authority: Learning to write scientific papers in situ. *Journal of Business and Technical Communication*, 11, 125–69.

Bowers, M. Y. and Metcalf, M. A. (2008). What employers want and what students need: Integrating business communication into undergraduate and graduate business courses. *Proceedings of the 2008 Association for Business Communication Annual Convention*, 1–13.

Britton, J. N. (1975). *The Development of Writing Abilities (11–18)*. London: Macmillan Education.

Carter, M., Ferzli, M., and Wiebe, E. (2004). Teaching genre to English first-language adults: A study of the laboratory report. *Research in the Teaching of English*, 395–419.

Carter, M., Ferzli, M., and Wiebe, E. N. (2007). Writing to learn by learning to write in the disciplines. *Journal of Business and Technical Communication*, 21 (3), 278.

Casanave, C. P. (2002). *Writing Games: Multicultural Case Studies of Academic Literacy Practices in Higher Education*. Lawrence Erlbaum Associates.

Clark, B. R. (1989). The academic life. *Educational Researcher*, 18 (5), 4.

Dias, P., Freedman, A., Medway, P., and Paré, A. (1999). *Worlds Apart: Acting and writing in academic and workplace contexts*. Mahwah, NJ: Lawrence Erlbaum Associates.

Donahue, C. (2008). *Écrire à l'université: Analyse comparée en France et aux États-Unis*. Presses Univ. Septentrion.

Fisher, D. D. (2006). *Remediating the Professional Classroom: The new rhetoric of teaching and learning*. Iowa State University.

Fisher, D. (2007). CMS-based simulations in the writing classroom: Evoking genre through game play. *Computers and Composition* **24** (2): 179–97.

Forster, E. M. (1954). *Aspects of the Novel New York: Harcourt, Brace*.

Freedman, A., Adam, C., and Smart, G. (1994). Wearing suits to class: Simulating genres and simulations as genre. *Written Communication*, **11**, 193–226.

Goody, J. (1986). *The Logic of Writing and the Organization of Society*. Cambridge [Cambridgeshire]; New York: Cambridge University Press.

Graves, R., Hyland, T., and Samuels, B. M. (2010). Undergraduate writing assignments: An analysis of syllabi at one Canadian college. *Written Communication*, **27** (3), 293.

Ivanic, Roz, Richard Edwards, David Barton, Marilyn Martin-Jones, Zoe Fowler, Buddug Hughes, Greg Mannion, Kate, Miller, Candice Satchwell, June Smith, Dr. Richard Edwards, David Barton, Marilyn Martin-Jones, Zoe, Fowler, Buddug Hughes, Greg, Mannion, Kate, Miller, Candice, Satchwell, and June, Smith. *Improving Learning in College: Rethinking Literacies Across the Curriculum*. Routledge.

Leont'ev, A. N. (1978). *Activity, Consciousness, and Personality*. Englewood Cliffs, NJ: Prentice-Hall.

Lundell, D. B. and Beach, R. (2003). Dissertation writers' negotiations with competing activity systems. In Charles Bazerman and David R. Russell (Eds.), *Writing Selves, Writing Societies: Research from activity perspectives* (pp. 483–514). Fort Collins, CO: WAC Clearinghouse.

McCarthy, L. P. (1987). A stranger in strange lands: A college student writing across the curriculum. *Research in the Teaching of English*, 233–65.

Miller, C. R. (1994). Rhetorical community: The cultural basis of genre. In A. Freedman and P. Medway (Eds.), *Genre and the New Rhetoric* (pp. 67–78). London: Taylor & Francis.

National Survey of Student Engagement. (NSSE). (2008). *Promoting Engagement for All Students: The imperative to look within*. Bloomington, IN: National Survey of Student Engagement. http://nsse.iub.edu/NSSE_2008_Results.

Paradis, J., Dobrin, D., and Miller, R. (1985). Writing at Exxon ITD: Notes on the writing environment of an R&D organization. *Writing in Nonacademic Settings*, 281–307.

Paré, A., Starke-Meyerrin, D., and McAlpine, L. (2009). The dissertation as multi-genre: Many readers, many readings. *Genre in a Changing World, Perspectives on Writing* (pp. 179–95). West Lafayette, IN: Parlor Press and The WAC Clearinghouse http://wac.colostate.edu/books/bazerman_wac/.

Prior, P. A. (1998). *Writing/Disciplinarity: A sociohistoric account of literate activity in the academy*. NJ: Lawrence Erlbaum and Associates.

Russell, D. R. (1997). Rethinking genre in school and society. *Written Communication*, **14**(4), 504–54.

(2002). *Writing in the Academic Disciplines: A curricular history*. Southern Illinois University.

(2009). Texts in contexts: Theorizing learning by looking at genre and activity. *Rethinking Contexts for Learning and Teaching: Communities, activities and networks* (pp. 17–30). Taylor & Francis.

Russell, D. R. and Fisher, D. (2009). Online, multimedia case studies for professional education: Revisioning concepts of genre recognition. In J. Giltrow and D. Stein (Eds.), *Genres in the Internet: Issues in the theory of genre*, Pragmatics & beyond new series (pp. 163–91). Amsterdam; Philadelphia: John Benjamins Publishing Company.

Russell, D. R. and Yañez, A. (2003). "Big picture people rarely become historians": Genre systems and the contradictions of general education,. *Writing Selves/ Writing Societies: Research from activity perspectives.* Fort Collins, CO: The WAC Clearinghouse. Retrieved from http://wac.colostate.edu/books/selves_societies/.

Schön, D. A. (1983). *The Reflective Practitioner, How Professionals Think.* New York: Basic Books.

(1987). *Educating the Reflective Practitioner.* San Francisco, CA: Jossey-Bass.

Smart, G. (2000). Reinventing expertise: Experienced writers in the workplace encounter a new genre. *Transitions: Writing in academic and workplace settings,* 223–52.

Spinuzzi, C. (2003). *Tracing Genres through Organizations: A sociocultural approach to information design.* Cambridge, MA: MIT Press.

Thaiss, C. and Porter, T. (2010). The state of WAC/WID in 2010: Methods and results of the US survey of the International WAC/WID Mapping Project. *College Composition and Communication,* **61** (3), 37.

Yañez, A. and Russell, D. R. (2009). "The world is too messy": The challenge of writing in a general-education liberal arts course. *Composition(s) in the New Liberal Arts.* Cresskill, NJ: Hampton Press.

# 6

## Assessment in Higher Education:
## A CHAT Perspective

### Anton Havnes

### Introduction

Over the last couple of decades there has been a remarkable increase in research, policy initiatives, and developmental work in the area of assessment in higher education. Assessment has become an area of major concern. Knight framed it as the 'the Achilles' heel of quality' (2002, p. 107). It is of vital importance for the trust in higher education, but its validity and reliability are often challenged (Bloxham, 2009). There is an increasing demand from students and at the system level for feedback on students' achievements. The increase in the number of students and assessment events within programs has boosted the time teachers spend on assessment. The mix of purposes of assessment (e.g. certification, selection, directing learning, capturing students' time, diagnosing students' level of understanding, accountability, and funding) makes it hard to conceptualise.

In keeping with the focus of this collection on pedagogical practice, which puts students' learning in the centre, in this chapter I concern myself with the role of assessment in student learning, that is, assessment as an integral element of learning. My starting point is that assessment plays a significant role in defining and operationalising what students need to learn, as well as capturing students' effort and directing their learning practice. My intention is to outline key challenges in the assessment-learning relationship and ways forward in developing learning-oriented assessment, the formative dimension of assessment (Black & Wiliam, 1998; Bloom, 1969; Sadler, 1987; Scriven, 1967). I frame the discussion in the context of professional education and challenges raised in recent research, policy, and practice concerning assessment. This initial discussion leads up to the core question: How can Cultural Historical Activity Theory (CHAT) contribute to the understanding of the role of assessment in learning? How can we, based on CHAT, outline ways forward in developing learning-oriented assessment in higher education?

A particular approach to assessment has been developed under the CHAT paradigm: dynamic assessment (Feuerstein et al., 1980, 2003) and is often related to younger children and learning disabilities (Elliot, 2003, appendix). My intention is to frame the analysis in the context of the more extensive discussion in higher education on formative assessment and feedback (e.g. Birenbaum et al., 2006; Black and Wiliam, 1998; Gibbs & Dunbar-Goddet, 2009; Hattie & Timperley, 2007 Nicol, 2009, 2010; Sadler 1987, 2010; Shute 2008). The role of assessment in learning in higher education has stronger elements of independent learning and a learning-assessment-learning format than school-based learning among younger students and the test-teach-test format of dynamic assessment (Yeomans, 2008).

A core principle in CHAT is that two processes of human activity and development coincide. One takes place on the level of individual action, the other on the cultural, institutional, and professional levels. However, even at the individual level what we do is social in nature. The assessment I am involved in is largely attributed meaning by the institutional practice of assessment other assessors participate in. Likewise, students' learning is embedded in institutional practices and epistemic cultures (Nerland & Jensen, 2012), and the institutions and epistemic cultures, again, develop in the context of their interface with other educational and professional contexts and societal change. This implies that an analysis of the role of assessment in learning needs to expand the unit of analysis to include the institutional, cultural, and epistemic cultures and contexts in which assessment and learning are embedded – and their histories. It also implies a particular focus on assessment practices and students' learning in the perspective of what matters in professional practice beyond higher education. In the perspective of the CHAT principle that human action is fundamentally tool mediated (Vygotsky, 1978; Wertsch, 2003), students need to come to terms with both a set of material and conceptual tools and the domains of professional and cultural practices in which they are embedded and applied. In the context of learning, these conceptual and material tools are objects of learning that need to be transformed to tools that support professional and academic practices. These overall CHAT principles guide my exploration of higher education and assessment.

## Higher Education

Higher education has become increasingly complex. One characteristic of the expansion of higher education is the increase of undergraduate professional programs, for instance nursing, education, physiotherapy, journalism, accounting, and social work. Other professional programs – theology, law, and medicine, in particular – have long histories as university studies. For programs that have recently become part of higher education, the change has also been part of a professionalization process. For instance, moving nursing from hospitals to higher education institutions has made it more academic, emphasising scientific thinking, theory, and research-based knowledge. These newer higher education programs have, in other words, been subject to an academic drift (Kyvik, 2007, Kyvik & Lepori, 2010) that is still in progress.

Recognising the diversity of higher education and the strong position of the academic disciplines, in this chapter I focus on professional programs. I do not claim there is something that can be associated with a generic professional education. However, common issues arise across diverse professional programs like nursing, engineering, and journalism that have implications for what students learn, how they are taught, how they learn, and potentially for assessment. Firstly, they are 'hybrid, bridge institutions with one foot in the academy…and one in the world of practitioners' (Sullivan, 2005, p. 25). Professional practice implies applying scientific knowledge (Brante, 2011), which is general in nature, but in a professional context needs to be applied to specific tasks in particular settings, situations, and persons. The academic drift in many professional programs and the emphasis on theory and scientific knowledge potentially challenges their practice orientation (Bulterman-Bos, 2008). From extensive research on professional education at the Carnegie Foundation, Sullivan (2005) concludes medicine is the only professional education that has managed to bridge the gap between academia and the workplace. I will not explore that statement further here, only use it as an illustration of challenges in professional education. Secondly, the knowledge base that constitutes professional knowledge relies on a set of diverse disciplinary fields. Professional knowledge is theoretically heterogeneous. Social work programs are built around academic disciplines like law, psychology, sociology, and economics, in addition to the more practice-oriented 'social work'. Teaching includes school subjects (grounded on disciplines, e.g. literature studies, mathematics, history, and science), pedagogy, developmental psychology, and sociology. These sets of disciplines, subject areas, or fields of knowledge are weakly integrated (Grimen, 2008).

One of the key challenges of professional education is to bridge the theoretically fragmented knowledge base, as well as the academia-professional practice gap. Finally, when students enter the field of professional practice their main attention needs to be focused on the problem at hand and how to act (Dreyfus & Dreyfus, 1986). While theory and scientific knowledge is an object of study in the higher education context, it needs to be reframed as a tool for acting in concrete professional situations. In professional practice, theory is integrated in situated practice and embedded in professionals' approach to the flow of information and opportunities to act in the actual situation. This latter point could also be linked to the development of professional identities (Edwards, 2005, 2010; Holland et al., 1998) and a process of enculturation (Lave & Wenger, 1991; Wenger, 1998).

These integrative perspectives on professional knowledge frame the meaning and significance of the curricular components, but do not reduce the significance of any of the components in the building of professional knowledge. My position is that professional programs need to pay more attention to these challenges of integration, the theory-practice relationship in professional knowledge, and the boundary-crossing nature of professional education. In this context a crucial question is: How could assessment aid students' learning and the development of professionalism by supporting the learning of curricular components and also bridge modules, subject areas, contexts, theories, and practices?

## Assessment

There is a long and a short history of learning-oriented assessment. Gipps (1999) traces assessment in UK higher education back to mid 1800, when examinations were implemented at the very end of the program. The Humboltian University also had formal exams only at the end. However, 'students made presentations in seminars. Informal (formative) assessment was constantly taking place as students' papers were criticised by opponents and discussed by peers and the professor' (Dysthe & Webler, 2010, p. 253). There is a limitation in Gipps's analysis in that she only drew on formal examinations. In the formative meaning of assessment, assessment has probably been an element in the educational process since the emergence of formal education. Wilbrink (1997) describes extensive use of informal assessment, but not in the pretty version of the Humboltian University. In the earliest phases students had to present their ideas. The response students got from teachers took the form of punishment of students who did not meet the standards. Later, new regimes of rewards and then ranking of students developed. This was all part of the ongoing program.

As long as university education was for the higher classes and part of the self-recruiting of the next generation of scholars, there was no need of exams. Social status counted more than academic merits. Failing a candidate was extremely rare. The need of exams came along with the flourishing industrial capitalist economy and its call for trained professionals and managers. Certification became an educational issue as a means to regulate upward mobility in society (Gipps, 1999, p. 357). Since then the use of examinations and various forms of formal assessment have been at the core of higher education, serving certification and selection purposes.

Along with the modularisation of higher education has come the development of explicit learning outcomes at program, module, and assignment levels, all requiring formal assessment. Students' learning is now largely organised through assignments and formally assessed projects, which has led to assessment becoming both frequent and dominant. It has also led to questioning of the role of assessment in higher education. Alongside these changes, the shift from elite to mass education over recent decades has made learning a central issue. This takes us to the shorter history.

Over the past twenty years, there has been a process of change in the conceptions of assessment, away from the traditional view of assessment as a distinct practice at the end of the learning trajectory, separate from teaching and learning (Shepard, 2000). Now the constitutive nature of assessment is emphasised, in that it defines what students need to learn and drives educational practice (e.g. learning, teaching, and supervision) (Biggs, 1996; Havnes, 2004; Kvale, 1996; Sadler, 1987). In research, policy, and practice there is an increasing interest in assessment as a tool for directing, supporting, and correcting students' learning, as well as capturing their time and effort (Gibbs, 2006). Assessment is seen as an integral aspect of the learning process, in fact a prerequisite for learning. There is an expansion of focus from:

- outcomes to process;
- control of learning to support of learning;
- students being assessed to students also taking part in assessment; and
- assessment as a distinct practice to assessment as embedded in learning.

A series of review studies (Black & Wiliam, 1998; Hattie & Timperley, 2007; Shute, 2008) have documented that assessment and feedback are key factors in students' learning. The question, though, is: What changes are needed to realise the learning potential afforded by assessment?

Biggs (1996) and many others emphasise the need for aligning teaching, learning, and assessment. Birenbaum and colleagues (2006) called for a system change that would afford learning-integrated assessment. Resnick and Resnick also emphasised the significance of attending to assessment in curriculum development: you get what you assess, you do not get what you do not assess (1992, p. 59). Assessment should be built towards that which you want educators to teach. Finally, there has been focus on self-assessment and peer assessment, higher education, and employability (Knight & York, 2003), authentic assessment (Gulikers, Bastianens, & Kirschner, 2008), preparing students as lifelong (self) assessors (Boud, 2000), and assessment as an aspect of work (Kvale, 2008).

Research on learning-oriented assessment is often associated with constructivism and the notions of independent learning and learner self-regulation (Nicol, 2009; Sadler 1987, 2010; Wiliam, 2011). However, this emphasis on self-regulation, based on internal control of cognitive processes, is countered by an emphasis on student-teacher dialogue, peer assessment, and social interaction (e.g. Nicol, 2010). There is a mix of a self-regulated learning approach and a more sociocultural approach building on Vygotsky's theorising of the role of social interaction in learning.

Despite the wealth of research on assessment and learning in recent years, the conceptualisation of the role of assessment in learning is still in its early phase of development. While expectations of the effects on learning are high, there is a need for 'a frank and judicious dialogue' to move the theorising and practice forward (Bennet, 2011, p. 5). For instance, the actual effect feedback has on learning varies and is often even negative (Hattie & Timperley, 2007; Kluger & DeNisi, 1996). The main problem is to integrate assessment and feedback in teaching and learning, to attune assessment and feedback to students' level of understanding, and to apply assessment in further instruction. Students' reception and use of feedback is a key factor.

From this short narrative on developments in assessment a series of challenges in conceptualising and applying learning-oriented assessment emerges:

- the intermediate position of assessment in teaching and learning;
- the situatedness of assessment in assessment regimes, curriculum design, and professional development;
- notions of learning underlying learning-oriented assessment; and
- the relational agencies of teachers and students.

CHAT is a theoretical position that can serve as a springboard to come to terms with these complex issues and how they relate to professional education.

### A CHAT Perspective on Assessment

I took as a starting point the CHAT principle to expand the unit of analysis beyond the phenomenon under scrutiny (here, assessment). Here I focus on three core aspects of CHAT, all related to the expansion of the analysis beyond assessment as a specific activity: the developmental approach, the zone of proximal development (zpd), and levels of analysis.

*Developmental approach.* A key principle in CHAT is that everything must be understood in time in the perspective of its development. The 'historical' component in CHAT refers to the origin and inner dynamics of a phenomenon, not its appearance. 'To study something historically means to study it in the process of change' (Vygotsky, 1978, pp. 64–65). For instance, a student's achievement is explored in the process of his or her learning. Vygotsky was explicit about the role of assessment in learning in his elaborations of the zone of proximal development.

*ZPD – the social and the individual – the role of assessment.* A key idea in Vygotsky's theory of learning and development is that any function in the child's cultural development appears twice, or on two planes. First it appears in social interaction, then as an individual achievement. From this general law Vygotsky formulated the zone of proximal development (1978, p. 86). It implies that participation in problem solving under adult guidance or in collaboration with more capable peers is a forerunner of a child's development. Reframed to higher education, interpersonal problem solving is the forerunner of the student's professional or disciplinary development. It is 'this sequence [that] results in zones of proximal development' (Vygotsky, 1978, p. 90).

In a series of studies Vygotsky found that assessment (he used the term *psychological investigations*) could make an impact on children's progress. Instead of just stating their current level of development, assessment could inform future teaching and learning initiatives. Assessment information could be used to design problems that were 'harder than [the child] could manage on his own and provide some assistance: the first step in a solution, a leading question, or some other form of help'. With such support, some children could improve their achievements more than others. 'The discrepancy between a child's actual mental age and the level he reaches in solving problems with assistance indicates the zone of proximal development... This measure gives a more helpful clue than mental age does to the dynamics of intellectual progress' (Vygotsky, 1962, p. 103).

Vygotsky frames zpd as a 'tool in the process of education, a method [by which] we can take account of not only the cycles and maturation processes that have already been completed but also those processes that are currently in a state of formation, that are just beginning to mature and develop' (1978, p. 87). Thus, the zone of proximal development permits us to delineate the child's immediate future and his dynamic development state, allowing not only for what already has been achieved developmentally but also for what is in the course of maturing.

In line with these basic principles, Wertsch situates assessment at the centre of zpd: zpd deals with 'practical problems in educational psychology: the assessment of children's intellectual abilities and the evaluation of instructional practices' (1985, p. 67). Assessment serves to determine the actual developmental stage of the learner and to clarify the maturing processes and 'what is within her developmental level' (1985, p. 88). Wertsch (1985, p. 67) also cites a comment from Vygotsky's colleague and follower, Aleksei Leontiev, in Bronfenbrenner: 'American researchers are constantly seeking to discover how the child comes to be what he is; we in the USSR [in a CHAT perspective] are striving to discover not how the child came to be what he is, but how he can become what he not yet is' (Bronfenbrenner, 1977, p. 528).

These points also draw attention to the tool character of assessment, in this case assessment as a tool for learning, or a set of tools, since assessment takes diverse forms. Framing assessment as a tool for learning implies that content, timing, and modes of communication need to be altered, compared to assessment framed as a tool for certification or control of what has been learned. The tool character of assessment is also manifest in Vygotsky's account of the adult giving clues or hints to students. As such clues (e.g. hints, reminders of a concept or procedure, or the provision of a material tool) are attended to by the learner, they might take on the character of tools that support learning. In higher education concepts, models and diverse auxiliary tools are typically used in problem solving, analysis, and professional practice.

It is worth noting that Vygotsky relates zpd to the relationship between learning and development, and the aim is development (see Chaiklin, 2003 for an elaboration of this issue). It concerns 'the whole child [or student], as an integral person (p. 46), not a particular skill or the meeting of an assessment criterion or a specific predefined learning outcome'. Still, learning of specific skills is a prerequisite for development. Learning 'creates the zone of proximal development…learning is not development…learning is a necessary and universal aspect of the process of developing culturally organized, specifically human, psychological functions' (Vygotsky, 1978, p. 90).

Vygotsky's distinction between learning and development is essential in this analysis. Professional education leads to the formation of professional competence. It implies inclusion in a community of professional practice and the gaining of trust from society and the public to act independently as a professional. Becoming a professional involves achieving a position in society, dependent on who you are as a professional, not just the skills you possess. For instance, for the patient, undergoing surgery implies an act of trust; for the surgeon, it implies an act of responsibility. The learning of skills and problem-solving activities is a step towards development of the whole person.

ReframingChaiklin to the higher education context, zpd 'is not concerned with the development of skill of any particular task, but must be related to [students' professional] development', which brings the integrative aspect of professional education in focus (2003, p. 43).

*Levels of analysis.* However, the CHAT analysis 'is not limited to a developmental perspective'; it also 'includes…explanation of…external manifestations' (Vygotsky, 1978, p. 63). The local history of a disciplinary or professional context is part of a wider social and historical development. What teachers and students do with assessment in a local setting – and what they see as assessment – are aspects of the cultural or institutional practice of higher education. This implies that the meaning of assessment needs to be addressed at both these levels:

- assessment practices at the *action* level: how assessment is acted on by teachers and students and its influence on learning and development
- assessment practices at the *activity* level: how cultural, institutional, and collegial contexts constrain and afford assessment practices

Leontiev (1978, 1981) distinguished among different levels of human practice:

- *activity* – at the level of social systems
- *action* – at the level of individual action and interaction
- *operation* – at the level of the concrete operation, procedure, or behaviour.

The main level of analysis is the activity level. While the actions relate to the intentions of the actors, the activity is driven by a collective motive. To discover 'the true motive' of the participants in a social practice, we need to address the complex coordinated and joint activity of actors with different roles, tasks, and goals. These levels coincide in practice. What a person or group is doing in a particular situation can be explained at the levels of activity, of action, and of operations. When a teacher assesses a student paper, it can be seen as operation (e.g. following procedures – which, by the way, sometimes could be automated and done by a computer), action (e.g. intending to clarify points the student has not dealt with properly), or activity (taking the position as an assessor in higher education and representing the institutional system and the academic collegial culture).

As activity, the act of assessing students' work is 'a system in the system of social relations. It does not exist without these relations' (Leontiev, 1981, p. 47). 'Consequently, it is the activity of the others that provides an objective basis for the specific structure of individual activity' (Leontiev, 1978, p. 281). The wider context attributes the overall meaning of the series of diverse actions. Taking education as an example of an activity, the coordinated actions of many individuals constitute the activity: in particular the actions of a number of different students and subject teachers. These notions of levels of activity afford analyses of the embeddedness of human practice, as well as potential inner conflicts and dilemmas within this integrated system.

Engeström (1987) defined the main unit of analysis as the *activity system*, which includes both the active, participatory role of individuals, tools, the object, or motive the system is expected to accomplish, and the impact of the wider social system in which the agents operate. In what is often referred to as 'third generation activity theory', the argument goes even further: an activity system is also a system within a system of other activity systems. Institutional development and the interface with wider society and work life are at stake here (Engeström, 1996; Tuomi-Gröhn & Engeström, 2003). It means, for instance, that teacher education (which is both academic and preparation for work as a teacher) should be analysed in the perspective of how it interrelates with teachers' professional practice in schools and the activity of researching educational practice. The activity system model also affords conceptualising tensions within the system and between the system and other activity systems. To frame development of assessment in a CHAT perspective implies the exploration of these diverse levels, the potential conflicts between elements of the activity system, and the implications for assessment as intervention in learning. The starting point is to put development in the centre and to search for dynamics within the teaching-learning-assessment relationship and the educational system that make a difference.

Leontiev's point that it is the activity of others that provides the basis for how we act as individuals underscores the relational aspect of agency (Edwards, 2005, 2010). The role of assessment in learning depends on teachers and students working together. Assessment is an act of communication, an act that again needs to be acted on to support learning. In professional education, the heterogeneous knowledge base requires communication not only between a subject teacher and student, but also across modules, subject disciplines, and education-work boundaries. The role of assessment in learning is not a priori given, but continuously reconstituted in practice. CHAT provides an approach and concepts that afford exploring these processes across diverse levels of agency.

## Assessment in Professional Education – Conceptualisation and Ways Forward in a CHAT Perspective

In assessment research, policy, and practice, the role of assessment in student learning is regarded as essential. It has led to an increase in classroom assessment and to the extensive use of explicit learning outcome descriptions and assessment criteria at program, modular, and assignment levels. The demands on teachers to provide feedback to students are increasing – from institutions, students, and teachers themselves. However, the conceptualisation of the dynamics of the assessment-teaching-learning relationship is in its early phase of development (Bennet, 2011; Shepard, 2000). In the context of this discussion, it is essential to underscore that there is recognition of the need to embed the conceptualisation of the role of assessment in learning in a broader view of pedagogy, institutional development, and relationships to professional practice and society. CHAT can bring the discourse forward because it affords analyses of the complex integrative aspects of assessment practices, assessment systems, and theorising:

- the inner dynamics of the assessment-teaching-learning relationship
- the dynamics of the action and activity (system) level of assessment
- the dynamics of higher education and professional practice
- the interrelated nature and developments of these levels of assessment practices

The ground rule of CHAT that anything must be studied in the process of change puts assessment in the forefront of learning. Change cannot be perceived unless there is some form of assessment involved. Vygotsky was primarily interested in assessment as an intervention in the hands of teachers. More recent developments of CHAT (e.g. Edwards, 2010; Engeström, 1987) have emphasised the active involvement of the teacher, the learner, and peer students, which sets a theoretical framework for explaining the teaching-learning relationship as contingent upon the agencies of teachers and learners (Black & Wiliam, 2009; Sadler, 2010). Edwards's idea of relational agency can be taken to refer to the reciprocity and interdependence of the participation of diverse groups of participants in the educational process.

For instance, in the assessment literature, Sadler (2010) calls for exploring if – or how – students understand assessment feedback, which in turn influences how they use it in further learning. However, if we take a closer look at assessment at a structural or system level, and the sequencing of teaching, learning, and assessment, we often find that assessment is situated at the very end of the learning process, for instance, when an assignment is completed or at the end of a module (Gibbs & Dunbar-Goddet, 2009). The traditional use of assessment at the end of a (now shorter) learning trajectory is still intact. This timing of assessment runs contrary to the role of assessment as framed in Vygotsky's notion of the zone of proximal development.

In a study of postsecondary education, Torrance concluded assessment procedures and processes completely dominated the teaching and learning experience (2007, p. 291). The extensive use of explicit assessment criteria and follow-up in supervision and feedback might bring about an approach to teaching and learning where "'[c]riteria compliance" [comes] to replace learning' (Torrance, 2007, p. 282). There is a risk that the extensive use of assessment criteria might set the horizon of learning. Vygotsky's distinction between learning and development might be a springboard for coming to terms with the dangers of assessment being the ultimate aim of learning. In the modular structure of modern higher education, assessment is built around the subject elements of the program. Vygotsky, however, emphasises the course of development as 'much more unitary' than these instructional building blocks of a field of knowledge.

[T]he main psychic functions involved in studying various subjects are interdependent – their common bases are consciousness and deliberate mastery.... It follows from these findings that all the basic school subjects act as formal discipline, each facilitating the learning of the others; the psychological functions stimulated by them develop in one complex process. (1962, p. 102)

Professional development builds on the learning of modular components, but also involves a more unified professional development process (Grimen, 2008).

CHAT provides a conceptual framework that allows systematic analysis of the integration of diverse elements in the learning process, the knowledge base, and the various agents and agencies involved in higher education. Leontiev's three-level model frames the relationship between diverse levels of analysing assessment practices. In a CHAT perspective, the main level of analysis is the activity level. At this level, the activity of others provides the basis for what a given teacher does and what the students experience. It implies expanding the unit of analysis beyond a specific phenomenon (e.g. learning, teaching, assessment, teacher role, student role, institution, institutional guidelines and policies, and collegial cultures).

The CHAT unit of analysis includes the analysis of a phenomenon, an event, or the content of a curricular component and their inner dynamics. However, they need to be explored in the context of the wider configuration of diverse, interrelated practices, that is, at the level of educational activity of higher education. In professional education, the relationships of disciplinary knowledge and concrete, situated practice in school, health care institutions, social work, or engineering projects need to be included in the analyses. Teaching, learning, and assessment practices in higher education often tend to work contrary to such integrated analyses. For instance, in teacher education, a key problem is fragmentation of the knowledge base, theory, and practice and research-based and experience-based knowledge (Hammerness, 2006).

'The true object' of professional education can be framed as developing competence as a nurse, teacher, engineer, or other professional. I have emphasised the heterogeneous and integrating nature of knowledge. The object of professional education goes beyond each of these components. I have argued that such integration of a professional knowledge base cannot happen on the theoretical level; it has to take place in terms of practical syntheses. It is in the practice of teaching in a diversified classroom setting that, for example, mathematical knowledge, sociology, and development psychology integrate to professional teacher competence.

Knowledge represented by the component of the professional knowledge base is a set of tools in professional practice. These tools are integrated in the flow of perceiving, interpreting, and assessing the multilayered, ongoing activities in the classroom. However, in professional education, and frequently in professional practice, these tools need to be addressed as objects of learning. The use of mediating tools contributes to improving professional practice; we need to recognise and remind ourselves about when a tool is needed or relevant. Tools also need to be improved, revised, and modified. In the context of assessment, the individual components therefore require attention. However, the shift from being an object of learning to becoming a tool for attending to 'the true object' of professional practice also necessitates special attention, particularly in professional education.

### References

Bennet, R. E. (2011). Formative assessment: A critical review. *Assessment in Education: Principles, Policy and Practice*, **18** (1), 5–25.

Biggs, J. (1996). Enhancing teaching through constructive alignment. *Higher Education*, **32** (3), 347–64.

Birenbaum, M., Breuer, K., Cascallar, E., Dochy, F., Ridgeway, J., Wiesemes, R., and Nickmans, G. (2006). A learning integrated assessment system. *Educational Research Review*, **1** (1), 61–67.

Black, P. and Wiliam, D. (1998). Assessment and classroom learning. *Assessment in Education*, **5** (1), 7–75.

(2009). Developing the theory of formative assessment. *Educational Assessment, Evaluation and Accountability*, **21** (1), 5–31.

Bloom, B. S. (1969). Some theoretical issues relating to educational evaluation. In R. W. Tyler (Ed.), *Educational Evaluation: New roles, new means: the 68th yearbook of the National Society for the Study of Education (part II)*, Vol. 68(2), (pp. 26–50). Chicago, IL: University of Chicago Press.

Bloxham, S. (2009). Marking and moderation in the UK: False assumptions and wasted resources. *Assessment and Evaluation in Higher Education*, **34** (2), 209–20.

Boud, D. (2000). Sustainable assessment: Rethinking assessment for the learning society, *Studies in Continuing Education*, **22** (2), 151–67.

Brante, T. (2011). Professions as science-based occupations. *Professions and Professionalism*, **1** (1), 4–20.

Bronfenbrenner, U. (1977). Toward an experimental ecology of human development. *American Psychologist*, **32** (7), 513–31.

Bulterman-Bos, J. A. (2008): Relevance in educational research: Will a clinical approach make education research more relevant for practice? *Educational Researcher*, **37** (7), 412–20.

Chaiklin, S. (2003). The zone of proximal development in Vygotsky's analysis of learning and instruction. In A. Kozulin, B. Gindis, C. A. Ageyev, and S. M. Miller (Eds.), *Vygotsky's Educational Theory in Cultural Context* (pp. 39–64). Cambridge: Cambridge University Press.

Dreyfus, H. and Dreyfus, S. (1986). *Mind over Machine*. New York: Free Press.

Dysthe, O. and Webler, W.-D. (2010). Pedagogical issues from Humbolt to Bologna: The case of Norway and Germany. *Higher Education Policy*, **23** (2), 247–70.

Edwards, A. (2005). Relational agency: Learning to be a resourceful practitioner, *International Journal of Educational Research*, **43** (3), 168–82.

(2010). *Becoming an Expert Professional Practitioner: The relational turn in expertise*. Dortrecht: Springer.

Elliot, J. (2003). Dynamic assessment in educational settings: Realising potential. *Educational Review*, **55** (1), 15–31.

Engeström, Y. (1987). *Learning by Expanding*. Orienta-Konsultit: Helsinki.

(1996). Developmental work research as educational research, *Nordic Educational Research Journal*, **16** (3), 131–43.

Feuerstein, R., Falik, L., Rand, L., and Feuerstein, R. S. (2003). *Dynamic Assessment of Cognitive Modifiability*. Jerusalem: ICELP Press.

Feuerstein, R., Rand, Y., Hoffman, M. B., and Miller, R. (1980). *Instrumental Enrichment: An intervention program for cognitive modifiability*. Baltimore, MD: University Park Press.

Gibbs, G. (2006). Why assessment is changing. In B. Cordelia and K. Clegg (Eds.), *Innovative Assessment in Higher Education*, (pp. 11–22). NY: Routledge.

Gibbs, G. and Dunbar-Goddet, H. (2009). Characterising programme-level assessment environments that support learning. *Assessment and Evaluation in Higher Education*, **34** (4), 481–89.

Gipps, C. (1999). Socio-cultural aspects of assessment, *Review of Research in Education*, **24** (1), 355–92.

Grimen, H. (2008). Profesjon og kunnskap [Profession and knowledge]. In A. Molander and L. I. Terum, *Profesjonsstudier [Studies of Professions]* (pp. 71–86). Oslo: Universitetsforlaget.

Gulikers, J. T. M., Bastianens, T. J., and Kirschner, A. (2008). Defining authentic assessment: Five dimensions of authenticity. In A. Havnes and L. McDowell (Eds.) *Balancing Dilemmas in Assessment and Learning in Contemporary Education* (pp. 73–86). NY: Routledge.

Hammerness, K. (2006). From coherence in theory to coherence in practice. *Teacher College Record*, **108** (7), 1241–65.

Hattie, J. A. and Timperley, H. (2007). The power of feedback. *Review of Educational Research*, **77** (1), 81–112.

Havnes, A. (2004). Examination and learning. An activity-theoretical analysis of the relationship between assessment and educational practice, *Assessment and Evaluation in Higher Education*, **29** (2), 159–76.

Holland, D., Lachicotte, W., Skinner, D. and Cain, C. (1998). *Identity and Agency in Cultural Worlds*. Cambridge, MA: Harvard University Press.

Kluger, A. N. and DeNisi, A. (1996). The effects of feedback interventions on performance: A historical review, a meta-analysis, and a preliminary feedback intervention theory. *Psychological Bulletin*, **119** (2), 254–84.

Knight, P. T. M. (2002). The Achilles' heel of quality: The assessment of student learning, *Quality in Higher Education*, **8** (1), 107–15.

Knight, P. T. M. and Yorke, M. (2003). *Assessment, Learning and Employability*. London: Open University Press.

Kvale, S. (1996). Evaluation as knowledge construction. In Hayhoe, R. and J. Pan (Eds.), *East West Dialogue in Knowledge and Higher Education* (pp. 117–40). London: Sharpe.

(2008). A workplace perspective on school assessment. In A. Havnes and L. McDowell (Eds.) *Balancing Dilemmas in Assessment and Learning in Contemporary Education* (pp. 197–208). NY: Routledge.

Kyvik, S. (2007). Academic drift – A reinterpretation. In J. Eders and F. van Vught (Eds.), *Towards a Cartography of Higher Education Policy Change: A fesschrift in honour of Guy Neave* (pp. 333–38). Enschede: CHEPS.

Kyvik, S. and Lepori, B. (Eds.) (2010). *The Research Mission of Higher Education Institutions outside of the University Sector: Striving for differentiation*. Dortrecht: Springer.

Lave, L. and Wenger, E. (1991). *Situated Learning. Legitimate Peripheral Participation*. Cambridge: Cambridge University Press.

Leontiev, A. N. (1978). *Activity, Consciousness, and Personality*. Englewood Cliffs, NJ: Prentice Hall.

(1981). The problem of activity in psychology. In Wertsch, J. V. (ed.) *The Concept of Activity in Soviet Psychology*, (pp. 37–71). Armonk, NY: M. E. Sharpe.

Nerland, M. and Jensen, K, (2012). Epistemic practices and object relations in professional work. *Journal of Education and Work*, **25** (1).

Nicol, D. J. (2009). Assessment for learner self-regulation: Enhancing achievement in the first year using learning technologies. *Assessment & Evaluation in Higher Education*, **34** (3), 335–52.

(2010). From monologue to dialogue: Improving written feedback processes in mass higher education. *Assessment and Evaluation in Higher Education*, **35** (5), 501–17.

Nicol, D. J. and Macfarlane-Dick, D. (2007). Formative assessment and self-regulated learning: A model and seven principles of good feedback practice. *Studies in Higher Education*, **31** (2), 199–218.

Resnick, L. B. and Resnick, D. P. (1992). Assessing the thinking curriculum: New tools for educational reform. In B. Gifford and M. C. O'Connor (Eds.) *Changing*

*Assessments: Alternative views of aptitude, achievement and instruction.* (pp. 37–75) Boston, MA: Kluwer Academic Publishers.

Sadler, R. (1987). Specifying and promulgating achievement standards. *Oxford Review of Education,* **13** (2), 191–209.

(2010). Beyond feedback: Developing student capability in complex appraisal, *Assessment & Evaluation in Higher Education,* **35** (5), 535–50.

Scriven, M. (1967). The methodology of evaluation. In R. W. Tyler, R. M. Gagné, and M. Scriven (Eds.), *Perspectives of Curriculum Evaluation, Vol. 1,* (pp. 39–83). Chicago, IL: Rand McNally.

Shepard, L. A. (2000). The role of assessment in a learning culture. *Educational Researcher,* **29** (7), 4–14.

Shute, V. J. (2008). Focus on formative feedback. *Review of Educational Research,* **78** (1), 153–89.

Sullivan, W. M. (2005). *Work and Integrity.* San Francisco, CA: Jossey-Bass.

Torrance, H. 2007. Assessment as learning? How the use of explicit learning objectives, assessment criteria and feedback in post-secondary education and training can come to dominate learning, *Assessment in Education: Principles, Policy & Practice,* **14** (3), 281–94.

Tuomi-Gröhn, T. and Engeström, Y. (Eds.) (2003). *New Perspectives on Transfer and Boundary Crossing.* Amsterdam: Pergamon Press.

Vygotsky, L. S. (1962). *Thought and Language.* Cambridge, MA: MIT Press.

(1978). *Mind in Society: The development of higher psychological processes.* Cambridge: Cambridge University Press.

Wenger, E. (1998). *Communities of Practice: Learning, meaning and identity.* Cambridge: Cambridge University Press.

Wertsch, J. V. (1985). *Vygotsky and the Social Formation of Mind.* Cambridge, MA: Harvard University Press.

(2003). *Mind as Action.* Oxford: Oxford University Press.

Wilbrink, B. (1997). Assessment in historical perspective. *Studies in Educational Evaluation,* **23** (1), 31–48.

Wiliam, D. (2011). *Embedded Formative Assessment.* Bloomington, IN: Solution Tree Press.

Yeomans, J. (2008). Dynamic assessment practice: Some suggestions for ensuring follow up. *Educational Psychology in Practice,* **24** (2), 105–14.

# 7

## The Agency of the Learner in the Networked University: An Expansive Approach

### Russell Francis

*Information technology can be seen as a challenge and a change of the ways in which knowledge is transmitted in society. It is about changes on the societal level, in the ways organisations function but also about the individual. The exact consequences of these processes are difficult to talk about when you are in the middle of them, the dynamic is however visible on many levels.* (Säljö, 2004, p. 225)

### Introduction

Recent years have witnessed 'smart mobs' (Rheingold, 2002) mobilising in Iran, Tunisia, Egypt, and Libya to resist oppression and bring about social change. In the wake of these grassroots uprisings, news agencies started to celebrate the transformative potential of social media (Empire, 2011). The hyperbole surrounding the revolutionary potential of social media has been disputed (Bennett, 2008; Morozov, 2011). Nevertheless, the so-called Arab Spring alerted the wider public to the emerging possibilities for disempowered grassroots communities to use social media to connect, mobilise, and share information. Significantly, the uprisings in Iran (2008) and later North Africa (2010/11) were heavily supported by a global diaspora of human rights campaigners who enthusiastically micro-blogged digitised acts of oppression – captured on cell phones – across the Twitter sphere. Indeed, as the authorities cracked down, emblematic images of oppression spread rapidly through globally interconnected networks via Facebook wall posts and YouTube podcasts.

In educational contexts, a comparable process of disruption has become more visible. Originally, struggles over control and access to knowledge were confined to the margins. For example, debates about the emergence of fan fiction remix cultures (Black, 2005) and game modding cultures (Postigo, 2007) tended to be regarded as fringe skirmishes between zealous 'creatives' and profit-motivated media franchises (Jenkins, 2006). Indeed, libertarian calls to 'free culture' (Lessig, 2005) raged on the blogosphere for months, sometimes years, before the emergence of ethically motivated initiatives like the Open Education Movement (Iiyoshi & Vijay Kunar, 2008), the Wikimedia foundation, or the Creative Commons licensing scheme. However, the spirit of openness – which finds its origins in the culture of free and open software development (Kelty, 2008) – has since become a formidable force for change in higher education. In turn, researchers and educational professionals are beginning to recognise the need for fundamentally new models and conceptual tools for understanding the networked university cultures. This chapter suggests some of the ways Cultural Historical Activity Theory (CHAT) might be deployed to tackle this research challenge.

## A Dialectic of Disruption

Sociotechnical change invariably leads theorists to question dominant metaphors for thinking about knowledge work. In several articles, Säljö (2002, 2004, 2010) adopts a broad cultural-historical perspective to explore the interrelationships between learning, cognition, and sociotechnical change. This work powerfully suggests how changes at a discursive level are inextricably bound up with sociotechnical reconfigurations. In recent times, this has resulted in the dominance of 'performativity' metaphors, like Clark's (2003) 'mindware upgrades' that emphasise the hybrid (i.e. technology enhanced) nature of knowing and learning (Säljö, 2010). However, from a cultural-historical perspective, disruption at the discursive level has always been inextricably bound up with sociotechnical change.

In this section, I identify some of the more notable ways technological innovations have stimulated disruption in contemporary debates about the implications of media change for learning and literacy. The aim is to identify underlying contradictions and contextualise disruption – at a discursive level – as part of a dialectical process of sociotechnical change. The analysis covers a period of approximately two decades.

The mid 1990s witnessed a great deal of speculation about the emergence of a tech-savvy 'digital generation' (Green & Bigum, 1993; Prensky, 2001; Tapscott, 1998). In the years that followed, humanistic scholars engaged in heated debates about what it meant to be literate in an emerging media environment (Durrent & Beavis, 2004; Gee, 2003; Kress, 2003; Lankshear & Knobel, 2003; Snyder, 2002). At the same time, ethnographic studies of digital cultures revealed young people creating, sharing, and learning through play and self-discovery (Facer et al., 2003; Jenkins, 2006b; Sefton-Green, 1998). James Paul Gee (2003) published an influential book entitled *What Video Games Have to Teach Us about Learning and Literacy* and Sefton-Green (2003) posed the question: 'End of School' or just 'Out of School?' sensitising educationalists to a widening gap between learning in and beyond formal educational contexts. Overall, scholarly works of this kind draw attention to the ways digital (sub)cultures offer young people alternative arenas to create, share, publish, and be recognised for their creative and intellectual endeavours.

Throughout this period, schools and universities spent millions on developing information and communication technology infrastructures to support student learning in higher education. Moreover, funding agencies provided generous support for a variety of progressive technology-enhanced learning projects. Nevertheless, even the most progressive learning design initiatives (Dalziel, 2003; Masterman, Lee, & Francis, 2005) took insufficient account of the need to respect self-directed or interest-driven practices. In short, there is little evidence to suggest the 'digital dissonance' identified by Clark and colleagues (2009) has been harmonised. Arguably, many 'progressive' initiatives remained stuck in what Lankshear and Knobel (2003) describe as an 'outsider mindset'.

What did become visible was the 'lack' of impact of many centrally implemented ICT initiatives (Somekh, 2004). For example, Crook and Light (2002, p. 171) noted that 'electronic seminar spaces were unused by over 90% of course tutors'. Similarly, Muukkonen (2005, p. 535) and colleagues discuss the 'interrelated difficulties' that arise when tutors attempt to integrate online discussion forums into structured courses of study. More cynical treatments constructed the rise of course management software as a neoliberal strategy designed to increase accountability through surveillance (Knox, 2010) or to reduce administrative costs by foisting more clerical duties onto academic staff (Ferreira, 2010).

Gee's (2000, 2004) work on online 'affinity spaces' provides a good example of a conceptual innovation designed to shift the way we think about how, why, and where learning occurs. The concept draws attention to the ways social media allow people with similar interests to connect and share their interests and passions, irrespective of their age, class, geographic location, or institutional affiliation:

Young people today are confronted with and enter more and more affinity spaces. They see a different and arguably powerful vision of learning, affiliation, and identity when they do so. Learning becomes both a personal and a unique trajectory through a complex space of opportunities (i.e. a person's own unique movement through various affinity spaces over time) and a social journey as one shares aspects of that trajectory with others. (Gee, 2004, p. 89)

Significantly, conceived as a conceptual tool, the notion of an online affinity space does not simply describe an emerging form of communicative practice. From a cultural-historical perspective, it is also important to consider how conceptual tools might shape the ways both learners and learning designers understand media change. In this respect, conceptual breakthroughs must be regard as part of an dialectical process of sociotechnical reconfiguration.

Today, the social web supports myriad new opportunities for self-directed learning (Ito et al., 2008, James et al., 2008; Selwyn & Grant, 2009). My doctoral work explored what I described as the *shifting locus of agency for regulating and managing learning* (Francis, 2008). It focussed attention to the diverse ways advanced learners creatively appropriate digital tools and online resources in everyday life. The study suggested that tactical innovations, observable through micro-genetic observations of students' everyday use of digital tools, had started to drive a process of systemic change in the culture of higher education from the bottom up.

Change, it seems, is upon us. Nevertheless, it is far from clear that universities, in their current form, provide the most viable context to support students' personalised 'trajectories of participation' (Ludvigsen et al., 2011) in this brave new world. Indeed, this cultural shift has been associated with anxieties about the capacity of academics to stay in control (Nijhuis & Collis, 2005). For example, in a provocative article entitled 'Screw Blackboard, let's do it on *Facebook*', Selwyn (2007) reports on students' rejection of institutional virtual learning environments in favour of social networking platforms they manage for themselves. Moreover, given widespread government cutbacks and substantial rises in student fees (UK context), it appears students have already started to question whether a university education is worth it (Woolcock, 2009).

In the United Kingdom, the Joint Information Systems Committee (JISC) and Higher Education Academy (HEA) did sponsor nontechnical 'learner voice' studies that attempt to understand students' experiences of change and ground recommendations for policy and practice (CLEX, 2009; Conole & Creanor, 2007; Hemmi, Bayne, & Land, 2009; Masterman, 2009; Sharpe et al., 2006). However, these studies tend to be produced for and remain preoccupied with the implications for centralised information services. At a discursive level, there is a tendency to assume the future of university learning can be controlled and managed from the centre. In this respect, these studies didn't fully embrace the possibility that systemic change in the culture of higher education is driven from the bottom up by the changing practices of the students themselves.

To a degree, the recommendations that emerge are preframed in a model that assumes the university remains the central site of learning in young adults' personalised learning trajectories. Nevertheless, researchers are starting to recognise this problem. For example, Hanke has argued: 'In a strange sense, all faculties have become adjuncts to their university-based media system, which is both open and closed to the media environment outside the university; a cultural shift in which the "network university" implies a "polydimensional pluriversity"' (2010, p. 3). For these reasons, it seems critical that we start to frame insights emerging from empirical work in this area within a broader cultural-historical framework; a framework that can help us understand the intersections between change at a microgenetic, ontogenetic, and cultural-historical level of analysis.

### CHAT, Higher Education, and Expansive Transformations

Cultural Historical Activity Theory (CHAT) offers a methodological and conceptual toolkit that can help us address this research challenge. CHAT provides a framework that allows researchers to understand transformative processes at multiple levels of analysis. The editors of this volume provide a better introduction to the central tenets of CHAT than is possible within the scope of this chapter. However, it is worth pausing to consider how CHAT develops one of Vygotsky's critical insights. Vygotsky's work draws attention to the ways human beings regulate their own actions, intentions and mental processes – from the outside – with the aid of a designed environment:

But Man subjects to himself the power of things over behaviour, makes them serve his own purposes and controls that power as he wants. He changes his environment with the external activity and in this way affects his own behaviour, subjecting it to his own authority. (Vygotsky, 1997, p. 212, cited in Engeström, 2005, p. 312)

For CHAT researchers, insights of this kind provide the key to understanding the riddle of human agency. Indeed, the notion of *imposing control from the outside* has become a core concept in contemporary 'expansive' research (Sannino, Daniels, & Gutiérrez, 2009).

Engeström's work (1987, 1996, 2005, 2006, 2009) continually emphasises the capacity of individuals and collectives to take control over their own learning and development. These studies often use vignettes to illustrate how individuals and/or collectives are *breaking away* from institutionalised practices with the aid of new mediational means. For example, Engeström's (2006) work on

Italian school students vividly illustrates how learners use designed cognitive tools (i.e. cheating slips) to escape double binds (i.e. to pass impossible rote memorization tests). He notes:

Almost without exception, they conclude that daring to prepare their elaborate cheating tools, or the second stimuli was a personal breakthrough into self-confidence and pride through the realization that what they did was not wrong – what was wrong was the system of education strangled by exams and assessment. This was all the more interesting as many students mentioned in passing that they actually did not need to use their cheating slips in the exam situation – it was sufficient that they had prepared them, both in terms of careful selection and presentation of knowledge and in terms of at least equally careful construction of the physical artefacts typically with the assistance of mothers, fathers and other relatives. (Engeström, 2006, p. 22)

In this passage the act of breaking away is associated with a heightened state of awareness. In short, students recognise their own feelings of inadequacy are manifestations of underlying contradictions, as opposed to their own personal deficiencies. The process of designing the cheating slips leads to a renewed sense of 'self-confidence' as they begin to recognise that an outdated system is in need of radical reform. In this respect, the act of breaking away empowers the students to develop a renewed self-confidence in their own potential as learners.

In general, expansive ways of thinking draw attention to the capacity of individuals (and collectives) to connect with others and take a proactive role in transforming the context of their own learning and development (Sannino, Danniels, & Guttierez, 2009). From this perspective, expansive transformations are conceived as critical junctures in dialectical developmental processes in which existing tensions and contradictions are periodically transcended. Indeed Engeström often frames his work in distinctively Hegelian-Marxist terms:

Recent work based on dialectics and the cultural-historical theory of activity points towards three major challenges to the development of both Vygotsky and Piaget: (1) instead of just benign achievement of mastery, development may be viewed as partially destructive rejection of the old; (2) instead of just individual transformation, development may be viewed as collective transformation; (3) instead of just vertical movement across levels, development may be viewed as horizontal movement across borders. (1996, p. 1)

This is quite unlike models that conceptualise development in terms of organic growth, or apprenticeship models that explore how individuals are progressively enculturated into existing communities of practice (Lave & Wenger, 1991; Rogoff, 1990, Wenger, 1998). Indeed, expansive ways of thinking offer a powerful resource for thinking about the ways students are rejecting traditional modes of instruction, using the Internet to connect with others who share similar interests, and cultivating globally distributed personal networks that transcend institutional and geographical boundaries.

Insights of this kind have functioned as germ cells in my own thinking about the implications of media change for higher education. This chapter suggests how CHAT can help us understand the predicament of university students caught up in a process of transition. I focus on the ways students are negotiating contradictions and using new media to transform the quasi-virtual contexts of their own learning and development.

## Breaking Away from the Traditional University

This section suggest how the changing practices of students is driving a process of bottom-up transformation in contemporary networked universities. It draws on empirical work I completed as a doctoral student. The study focussed on graduate students' informal use of new media in everyday life (Francis, 2008; Francis & Furlong, 2008). All informants were graduate students who had long histories of Internet use. All lived in a collegiate environment and enjoyed access to the Internet through a fast, always on Ethernet connection. Further, all might be regarded as highly resourceful practitioners (Edwards, 2005, 2010).

In the original study, data collection and analysis became progressively focussed on the *digitally mediated practice* of sixteen graduate students. Multiple qualitative methods were used to develop an holistic understanding of goal-directed practices. Interview data was also used to contextualise specific practices within individuals' personal-historic live trajectories. Emblematic vignettes, that combined rich description and screenshots, were then used to reconstruct and represent emblematic practices. These vignettes also served to ground the work of conceptual development.

The study found that students routinely used web-based technologies in combination with institutionally managed information resources for both course-related study and self-education. Emergent practices (i.e. crowd sourcing information of Stumble Upon, uploading PowerPoints on Slide Share, or watching 'keynotes' as well as pop videos on YouTube) were typically pioneered by a small group of early adopters. However, these practices soon caught on and started to spread. This was not a planned, uniform, or centrally orchestrated process. Innovative practices sprang up and broke out as individuals discovered new tools, tinkered with their affordances, pioneered new study tactics, and told their friends.

Selected students experienced breakthroughs – which they often discussed with pride – when they discovered how to use web-based resources to escape double binds. For example, Anastasia, a student of evidence-based social work, despaired at the seemingly impossible task of learning multivariate regression analysis, with the aid of paper-based hand-outs, in a traditional seminar room:

> It wasn't very helpful for me, not only for me but for several of us on the course. We had never done statistics and found it difficult … because this system with hand-outs, learning statistics on handouts, it wasn't very good for me – the Professor would come with handouts that would have ANOVA and under ANOVA he'd have the SPSS table but I did not see how he did it or what all these figures meant. And he'd say 'you can see from this ANOVA test that this number is significant.' I would think why is this significant? What does this mean? This is all completely useless to me! (Anastasia cited in Francis, 2008, p. 182)

Nevertheless, with access to the Internet, Anastasia designed a sophisticated ecology of digital tools and resources that empowered her to teach herself multivariate analysis. A section of a vignette reconstructed from observation data suggests this strategy in action:

> During observation, she switched back and forth between resources exploiting the affordances specific to each: a clear explanation, a particular helpful diagram or a particular helpful screen shot sequence demonstrating how to conduct specific ANOVA tests using SPSS. In one procedure she switched between three or four online resources and a book, *SPSS for Social Scientists*, whilst simultaneously attempting to apply the test on her own data set on the SPSS program installed on her computer. Web-based instruction appeared to inform practices but problems encountered whilst attempting to apply the test also inspired her to seek further explanation from both online and offline resources. (Anastasia cited in Francis, 2008, p. 184)

The case illustrates how a student who found herself in a double bind started to seek out second stimuli (i.e. statistical websites) and set about designing a virtual learning environment that empowered her to pursue an independent self-directed learning agenda.

Significantly, Anastasia's determination and resourcefulness appeared related to a deep-seated commitment to becoming a social scientist capable of putting social work on a more scientific footing. Many of her coursemates simply opted to do assignments that did not involve advanced statistical analysis. In this respect, Anastasia's internalised commitment to becoming a certain 'kind of person' (Hacking, 1994; Gee, 2004) shaped the way she appropriated and made use of statistical websites. The designed digital ecology allowed her to proceed relatively independently in a self-generated and digitally mediated zone of proximal development. In turn, this quasi-virtual context mediated (and motivated) a developmental process directed towards the actualisation of her 'projective identity' (Gee, 2003, 2004). In short, Anastasia's internalised commitment to a strong projective identity had started to function as the object-motive (Leont'ev, 1978) of her lifelong learning agenda.

Dozens of observations revealed students exploiting access to new media to expand opportunities and to pursue self-directed learning agendas. For example, Ardash, a medical anthropologist, described how he started using the Amazon.com book recommendation system, as opposed to the university library system, to conduct exploratory literature searches. The library system seemed slow and inefficient by comparison. Further, he found the user-generated reviews and recommendations on Amazon.com extremely helpful when attempting to judge the relevance of a particular book for his specific research purposes. Moreover, he argued the system had helped him develop an insight into the various 'webs of influence' between authors. Later I discovered a student of politics, philosophy, and economics teaching himself Spanish by 'ripping' entire episodes of *Mimi Vice* from Bit Torrent and watching them first in English with Spanish subtitles and then in Spanish with English subtitles. Similarly, Marcia, a student of anthropology, described how she taught herself about the history of breakdance and its relationship to hip-hop music through the comparative analysis of breakdance videos uploaded to YouTube. All of the students seemed actively engaged in the process of creatively appropriating digital tools and resources to position themselves in zones of proximal development.

In general, insights of this kind suggest the importance of allowing students time and space to explore self-directed learning agendas that are closely coupled to their emerging identities. Nevertheless, this vision of learning seems increasingly out of step with a higher education system characterised by rising student fees, increasing student-to-staff ratios, and the progressive encroachment of externally imposed performativity targets (Rensfeldt, 2010). In short, the idea of a university that allows students to pursue an intellectual odyssey through diverse and esoteric domains of knowledge might not fit neatly into a neoliberal performativity culture that puts a premium on 'measurable outputs' (Roberts, 2007) rather than the need to cultivate a supportive community of academic practice that nurtures aspiring intellectuals as they quest to fulfil their critical and creative potentials.

With the emergence of the social web, students started to appropriate social media to create peer learning networks that transcend institutional boundaries. Moll, Tapia, and Whitmore (1997) use the term 'funds of living knowledge' to suggest how an extended family operates as a living system of shared knowledge and expertise (see also, González, Moll & Amanti, 2005).

The concept originated from a cognitive anthropology of Mexican working-class families. It draws attention to ways family members exchange knowledge and expertise essential for a family's collective functioning. This process is mediated through the 'household': a metaphor the authors use to suggest an amalgam of ritualistic practices (e.g. coming together for family meals and special occasions) that help to nurture an ethic of mutual responsibility among family members. In time, this notion became a germ cell that helped me understand how social software accounts (e.g. MSN Messenger, Friendster, and Facebook) can function in the capacity of a virtual household and allow individuals to stay closely connected to friends and family members as they make horizontal developments across boundaries. In multiple cases, I found students turned to particular individuals – often old friends and family members – for help and support rather than coursemates and tutors. For example, Miss Lullaby used MSN Messenger to create a sense of shared endeavour with current coursemates as she worked on assignments alone in her study room. She commented: 'it helps us have friendships', 'it helps the normal feel of a friendship', and 'it increases the solidarity we feel for each other'. Indeed, she routinely used social media to nurture relationships with friends and colleagues within her department. However, at critical moments, when, for example, she faced an important deadline and her supervisor was away on fieldwork, she turned to a close friend who lived 'back home in California' to provide detailed critical feedback on her dissertation.

Despite the fact that her friend 'hated' looking at her work, an ethic of mutual reciprocation existed between the two, a commitment developed through their undergraduate years at UCLA where they shared a dorm, went to college parties, prepared for exams, and graduated together. The pair sometimes argued like sisters. However, they'd been operating as a system of living knowledge for many years. Seemingly trivial practices (e.g. the posting of away messages, tagging of photographs, and the sending of electronic gifts) seemed to nurture the bond of trust and obligation that existed between the two. The fact that they now lived thousands of miles apart didn't interrupt their collaborative working relationship. Far from it, Miss Lullaby explained how she felt more inclined to rely on the feedback provided by an old friend – however critical it might be – rather than expose her weaknesses to coursemates and tutors.

In a world in which social software technologies have become integrated into the fabric of everyday university life for millions of students across the globe, it seems highly likely that globally distributed funds of living knowledge have already become a significant resource that helps individuals learn across institutional and geographical boundaries. For this reason it seems vital that we conduct further empirical research to explore how students are leveraging the distributed expertise accessible through their social software accounts.

### Using CHAT to Peer into the Future of (Self) Education

Contemporary developments in CHAT can also help us conceive how emergent practices – afforded by a social web – might continue to disrupt and subvert institutionalised practices. For Engeström (2006), distributed file-sharing communities (Uricchio, 2004) and the open source development movement (Di Bona et al., 1999, cited in Engeström, 2006) are used to illustrate how 'wild fire' activities spring up out of 'mycorrhizae' and break out without a centralised locus of control:

Mycorrhizae formation is simultaneously a living, expanding process (or bundle of developing connections) *and* a relatively durable, stabilized structure; both mental landscape or 'mindscape' (Zerubavel, 1997) and a material infrastructure. (Engeström, 2006b, p. 14)

The term *mycorrhizae* is borrowed from studies of fungus (Allen, 1991, cited in Engeström, 2006). It is used to suggest invisible criss-crossing networks that grow beneath institutional structures. Despite their relative invisibility, Engeström stresses that 'mycorrhizae' can grow to enormous sizes.

The visible mushrooms are reproductive structures. Even these structures are sometimes quite large, but the invisible body of the fungus, mycorrhizae, can be truly amazing. When molecular techniques were used, one Michigan fungus (Amillaria bulbosa) which grew in tree roots and soil and had a body constructed of tubular filaments was found to extend over an area of 37 acres and have the weight of 110 tons, equivalent to a blue whale. (Engeström, 2006, p. 12)

In many respects, the notion of 'breaking away into mycorrhizae' (Engeström, 2006) can help us understand emergent processes at a more abstract level of analysis. Indeed, students' capacity to break away into globally distributed criss-crossing social networks that grow, like mycorrhizae, invisibly beneath the surface of institutional structures, might prove critical for their capacity to survive and flourish in an increasingly competitive high-tech knowledge economy.

In the age of the laptop university (McVay, Snyder, & Graetz, 2005), students can take their personal networks and digitised libraries with them as they migrate across contexts and institutional boundaries. Furthermore, user-generated virtual worlds (Bayne, 2008), massively multiplayer online role-playing games (Linderoth & Bennerstedt, 2007; Nardi & Harris, 2006; Steinkuehler, 2006), and a burgeoning variety of 'video republics' (Buckingham & Willett, 2009; Hannon, Bradwell, & Tims, 2008) provide new opportunities for lifelong learning relatively independently of the traditional university. The re-emergence of folk learning models documented by Ponti's (2011) research on Massively Open Online Courses (MOOCs) is potentially even more significant. In short, students have choices and some, it seems, are choosing to break away into web-based mycorrhizae that support radically personalised self-directed learning agendas. As a result, students do not depend on the structures and hierarchies of the traditional university to the same degree.

The sudden rise of Academia.edu, a social networking tool designed for academics, might be regarded as the latest mycorrhizae-like activity system to break out. The platform allows students, faculty members, and independent researchers to share, collaborate, and coconstruct knowledge under the radar of the traditional university. What started as a seemingly trivial innovation – the latest fad, not to be taken too seriously – suddenly sprang up, broke out, and started to spread. Academia.edu now provides research students and staff members with an alternative quasi-virtual context for the exchange of academic knowledge and expertise. This web-mediated social space is not institutionally sanctioned. Nevertheless, not unlike the tree roots that support the growth of mycorrhizae studied by fungologists, it provides structures that allow students and junior staff members to work on their academic identities as they seek out opportunities, share work, and make connections across the globe with others who share their research interests. In combination with the rapid emergence of wildfire activities (e.g. micro-blogging vodcasts of academic lectures from TED.com), practices supported by Academia.edu have become inextricably interwoven into the real-virtuality of everyday university life. Therefore, understanding how students are appropriating these tools to learn, collaborate, and share may be a central challenge for those interested in peering into the future of higher education.

Interestingly, students in the UK have also started to appropriate social media to protest against the progressive privatisation of higher education in the post-debt crisis. In one notably grassroots campaign act, students use digital video to record each another 'milking' themselves in random public spaces (Kingsley, 2012). The recordings of these symbolic acts of resistance are then remixed and tactically spread through subterranean networks via social media (i.e. Facebook wall posts) in an attempt to mobilise others, raise awareness, and build solidarity. This grass roots campaign is typical of the ways disempowered groups are taking a stand with social media. However, in this case it seems designed to resist the progressive transformation of universities into profit-motivated corporations. The transformative impact of symbolic acts of resistance remains questionable. However, in a world in which some students are beginning ask fundamental questions about the 'worth' of institutionalised forms of higher education, it seems likely that alternative sites of learning – not governed by the neoliberal logic of cost cutting, efficiency gains, and measurable outputs – may continue to thrive. If so, we shall need new models and new metaphors to conceptualise learning beyond the boundaries of the traditional university.

## Conclusion

This chapter has attempted to illustrate how CHAT offers a powerful resource that can help us lift research focused on students' informal use of new media above a descriptive level and understand the implications of media change for higher education at multiple intersecting levels of analysis. It suggests some of the ways universities have become sites of struggle; struggles which are becoming 'visible on many levels' (Saljö, 2004) and have widespread implications for how students learn, how knowledge circulates, and how universities function as cultural institutions in contemporary society. The exact consequences remain hard to predict. However, this chapter foregrounds what I describe as the shifting locus of agency for regulating and managing learning. More specifically, it illustrates some of the ways students are breaking away from depending on centralised services and learning 'under the radar' in traditional universities in globally interconnected subterranean networks. This trend seems set to continue. Nevertheless, it seems likely further tensions and contradictions will continue to emerge.

This chapter also suggest metaphors that encourage us to think about education as a process of preparing students to pass exams and get high-paying jobs are now being displaced by metaphors that encourage us to conceive of education as an identity project (Gee, Hull and Lankshear, 1996; Emirbayer, & Mische 1998; Holland *et al*, 1998; Wenger, 1998; Gee, 2000, 2004; Poleman, 2006; Francis, 2010; Erstad *et al.* 2009; Erstad & Sefton-Green, 2013; Wells, 2007). This approach opens the door to thinking about some of the ways young adults learn, grow, and develop through participating in diverse activities, dialogues, and networks both on and offline. In time, new models may help educational professionals develop an expanded understanding of more practical questions. For example, how much freedom and time should students be given to participate in clubs and societies, take placements, or volunteer for good causes during the course of their studies? The conceptual toolkit

offered by CHAT provides a powerful resource that can help us reconceptualise and reevaluate these activities as we attempt to understand developmental
processes at multiple intersecting levels of analysis. In this respect, it provides
a solid foundation that may allow us to rethink the real implications of media
change for the future of (self) education.

## References

Allen, M. F. (1991). *The Ecology of Mycorrhizae.* Cambridge: Cambridge Uni
versity Press.

Bayne, S. (2008). Uncanny spaces for higher education: Teaching and learning in virtual
worlds. *Association for Learning Technology Journal,* **16**(3): 197–205.

Bennett, L. (ed.). (2008). *Civic Life Online: Learning how digital media can engage youth.*
Cambridge, MA: MIT Press.

Black, R. W. (2005). Online fan fiction: What technology and popular culture can
teach us about writing and literacy instruction. *New Horizons for Learning Online
Journal,* **11**(2).

Buckingham, D. and Willett, R. (2009). *Video Cultures: Media technology and everyday
creativity.* Basingstoke and New York: Palgrave Macmillan.

Clark, A. (2003). *Natural-Born Cyborgs: Why minds and technologies are made to merge.*
New York: Oxford University Press.

Clark, W., Logan, K., Luckin, R., and Oliver, M. (2009). Beyond Web 2.0: Mapping the
technological landscape of young learners. *Journal of Computer Assisted Learning,*
**25**, 56–69.

CLEX. (2009). *Higher Education in a Web 2.0 World: Report of an independent committee
of inquiry into the impact on higher education of students' widespread use of Web2.0
tools.* Bristol: CLEX. Available from: http://www.jisc.ac.uk/publications/general-
publications/2009/heweb2.aspx#downloads.

Collins, A. and Halversont, R. (2010). The second educational revolution: Rethinking
education in the age of technology. *Journal of Computer Assisted Learning,*
**26**, 18–27.

Conole, G. and Creanor, L. (2007). *In Their Own Words: Exploring the learner's perspective on e-learning.* London: JISC. Retrieved from: http://www.jisc.ac.uk/media/
documents/programmes/elearningpedagogy/iowfinal.pdf.

Crook, C. and Light, P. (2002). The Virtualization of Learning and the Cultural Practice
of Study. In S. Woolgar (Ed.), *Virtual society?: technology, cyberbole, reality* (pp. 153–
175). Oxford: Oxford University Press.

Dalziel, J. (2003). *Implementing Learning Design: The Learning Activity Management
System.* Paper presented at the ASCILITE 2003, Adelade, Australia. Retrieved from
http://www.lamsinternational.com/documents/ASCILITE2003.Dalziel.Final.pdf.

Durrent, C. and Beavis, C. (eds.). (2004). *P(ICT)ures of English: Teachers, learners and
technology*: AATE.

Edwards, A. (2005). Relational agency: Learning to be a resourceful practitioner.
*International Journal of Educational Research,* **43**, 168–82.

(2010). *Being an Expert Practitioner: The relational turn in expertise.* Dordecht:
Springer.

Empire. (2011, 20th March). Social networks, social revolution: YouTube, Facebook and Twitter have become new weapons of mass mobilisation. Aljazeera.net. Available from: http://english.aljazeera.net/programmes/empire/2011/02/20112161453211698 6.html.

Engeström, Y. (1987). *Learning by Expanding: An activity theoretical approach to developmental research.* Helsinki. Available from http://lchc.ucsd.edu/mca/Paper/Engestrom/expanding/toc.htm.

(1996). Development as breaking away and opening up: A challenge to Vygotsky and Piaget. Available from: http://lchc.ucsd.edu/mca/Paper/Engestrom/Engestrom. html.

(2001). Expansive learning at work: Toward an activity-theoretical reconceptualization. *Journal of Education and Work,* **14**(1), 133–56.

(2005). Networking to create collaborative intentionality capital in fluid organisational fields. *Advances in Interdisciplinary Studies of Work Teams,* **11**, 307–36.

(2006). Development, movement and agency: Breaking away into mycorrhizae activities. Osaka: Centre for Human Activity, Kansia University. Retrieved from http:// www.chat.kansai-u.ac.jp/publications/tr/v1_1.pdf.

(2009). The Future of Activity Theory: A rough draft. In A. Sannino, H. Daniels & K. D. Gutiérrez (Eds.), *Learning and expanding with activity theory* (pp. 303–27). Cambridge: Cambridge University Press.

Emirbayer, M. and Mische, A. (1998). What is agency? *The American Journal of Sociology,* **103**(4), 962–1023.

Erstad, O., Gilje, Ø., Sefton-Green, J., and Vasbø, K. (2009). Exploring 'Learning Lives': Community, identity, literacy and meaning. *Literacy,* **43**(2), 100–06. doi: 10.1111/j.1741–4369.2009.00518.x

Erstad, O. and Sefton-Green, J. (Eds.). (2013). *Identity, Community and Learning in the Digital Age.* Cambridge & New York: Cambridge University Press.

Facer, K., Furlong, J., Sutherland, R., and Furlong, R. (2003). *ScreenPlay: Children and computing in the home.* London: RoutledgeFalmer.

Ferreira, J. M. (2010). The university of the 21st century: The will to technology or the will to knowledge. *Canadian Journal of Media Studies,* **7**. Available from: http:// cjms.fims.uwo.ca/issues/07-01/Ferreira.pdf.

Francis, R. J. (2008). *The Predicament of the Learner in the Mew Media Age: An investigation into the implications of media change for learning.* DPhil. University of Oxford. Available from: http://ora.ox.ac.uk/objects/uuid:ocbd0185-c7ed-4306-b34e-993acd125e96.

(2010). *The Decentring of the Traditional University: The future of (self) education in virtually figured worlds.* New York and London: Routledge.

Francis, R. J. and Furlong, J. (2008). *Web 2.0 in University Life: A sociocultural approach.* Paper presented at the American Educational Research Association Conference.

Gee, J. P., Hull, G., A. and Lankshear, C. (1996). *The New Work Order: Behind the language of the new capitalism.* St. Leonards, N.S.W.: Allen & Unwin.

Gee, J. P. (2000). Identity as an analytic lens for research in education. *Review of Research in Education,* **25**, 99–125.

(2003). *What Video Games Have to Teach Us about Learning and Literacy.* New York; Basingstoke: Palgrave Macmillan.

(2004). *Situated Language and Learning: A critique of traditional schooling.* New York and London: Routledge.

Green, B. and Bigum, C. (1993). Aliens in the classroom. *Australian Journal of Education,* **37**(2), 119–41.

González, N., Moll, L. C., and Amanti, C. (Eds.). (2005). *Funds of knowledge: theorizing practices in households, communities, and classrooms.* Mahwah, N.J.: Lawrence Erlbaum Associates.

Hacking I. (1994). The looping effects of human kinds. In D. Sperber, D. Premack, and A. J. Permack (Eds.), *Causal Cognition: A multidisciplinary approach.* (pp. 351–83). Oxford: Clarendon Press.

Hanke, B. (2010). Introducing media, knowledge and the networked university. *Canadian Journal of Media Studies,* 7. Available from: http://cjms.fims.uwo.ca/issues/07-01/Introduction%20to%20CJMS2.pdf.

Hannon, C., Bradwell, P., and Tims, C. (2008, 10th June). *Video Republic.* London: Demos. Retrieved from http://www.demos.co.uk/publications/videorepublic.

Hemmi, A., Bayne, S., and Land, R. (2009). The appropriation and repurposing of social technologies in higher education. *Journal of Computer Assisted Learning,* **25**(1), 19–30.

Holland, D. C., Skinner, D., Lachicotte, W. J., and Cain C. (1998). *Identity and agency in cultural worlds.* Cambridge, Mass.: Harvard University Press.

Iiyoshi, T. and Vijay Kunar, M. S. (eds.). (2008). *Opening up Education: The collective advancement of education through open technology, open content and open knowledge.* Cambridge, MA: MIT Press.

Ito, M., Horst, H., Bittanti, M., Boyd, D., Herr-Stephenson, B., Lange, P. G., and Robinson, L. (2008). *Living and Learning with New Media: Summary of findings from the Digital Youth Project:* The MacArthur Foundation. Retrieved from http://digitalyouth.ischool.berkeley.edu/files/report/digitalyouth-WhitePaper.pdf.

James, C., Davies, K., Flores, A., Francis, J. M., Pettingill, L., Rundel, M., and Gardner, H. (2008, 22nd Feb). *Young People, Ethics and the New Digital Media: A synthesis from the Good Play project.* Cambridge, MA: Harvard Graduate School of Education. Retrieved from http://pzweb.harvard.edu/ebookstore/pdfs/goodwork54.pdf.

Jenkins, H. (2006). *Convergence Culture: Where old and new media collide.* New York: New York University Press.

Kelty, C. M. (2008). *Two Bits: The cultural significance of free software.* Durham, NC and London: Duke University Press.

Kingsley, P. (2012, 26th November). Milking: An udderly bizarre student trend, *The Guardian.* Retrieved from: http://www.guardian.co.uk/education/shortcuts/2012/nov/26/milking-udderly-bizarre-student-trend.

Knox, D. (2010). A good horse runs at the shadow of the whip: Surveillance and organizational trust in online learning environments. *Canadian Journal of Media Studies.*

Kress, G. (2003). *Literacy in the New Media Age.* London: Routledge.

Lankshear, C. and Knobel, M. (2003). *New Literacies: Changing knowledge and classroom learning.* Buckingham: Open University Press.

Lave, J. and Wenger, E. (1991). *Situated Learning: Legitimate peripheral participation.* Cambridge: Cambridge University Press.

Leont'ev, A. N. (1978). *Activity, Consciousness and Personality.* Englewood Cliffs, NJ: Prentice Hall.

Lessig, L. (2005). *Free Culture: The nature and future of creativity*. New York: Penguin Books.

Linderoth, J. and Bennerstedt, U. (2007). *Living in World of Warcraft: The thoughts and experiences of ten young people*. The Swedish Media Council. Retrieved from http://www.medieradet.se/upload/Rapporter_pdf/World_of_Warcraft_eng.pdf.

Ludvigsen, S., Rasmussen, I., Krange, I., Moen, A., and Middleton, D. (2011). Intersecting trajectories of participation: temporality and learning. In S. R. Ludvigsen, A. Lund, I. Rasmussen, and R. Säljö (Eds.), *Learning across Sites: New tools, infrastructures and practices* (pp. 105–21). Oxford and New York: Routledge.

Masterman, L. (2009). *Thema: Exploring the experience of masters' students in the digital age*. Oxford: JISC. Retrieved from https://mw.brookes.ac.uk/download/attachments/918039/Thema+Technology+Report.pdf?version=1.

Masterman, L. and Lee, S., with Francis, R. (2005). *Evaluation of the Practitioner Trial of LAMS: Final report*. Oxford: The Joint Information Systems Committee (JISC). Retrieved from: http://www.jisc.ac.uk/uploaded_documents/LAMS%20Final%20Report.pdf.

McVay, G. J., Snyder, K. D., and Graetz, K. A. (2005). Evolution of a laptop university: A case study. *British Journal of Educational Technology*, **36**(3), 513–24.

Moll, L., C., Tapia, J., and Whitmore, K. F. (1997). Living knowledge: The social distribution of cultural resources for thinking. In G. Salomon (ed.), *Distributed Cognitions: Psychological and educational considerations* (pp. 139–64). Cambridge: Cambridge University Press.

Morozov, E. (2011). *The Net Delusion: How not to liberate the world*. London and New York: Penguin Books.

Muukkonen, H., Lakkala, M., and Hakkarainen, K. (2005). Technology-Mediation and Tutoring: How Do They Shape Progressive Inquiry Discourse? *Journal of the Learning Sciences*, **4**(4), 527–66.

Nardi, B. and Harris, J. (2006). Strangers and Friends: Collaborative Play in World of Warcraft. Proceedings Conference on Computer-supported Cooperative Work. New York: ACM Press. Pp. 149-158.

Nijhuis, G. G. and Collis, B. (2005). How can academics stay in control? *British Journal of Educational Technology*, **36**(6), 1035–49.

Poleman, J. L. (2006). Mastery and appropriation as a means to understand the interplay of history learning and identity trajectories. *Journal of the Learning Sciences*, **15**(2), 221–59.

Ponti, M. (2011). Sociotechnical relations in the creation of an interest-driven open course. *E-learning and Digital Media*, **8**(4), 408–22.

Postigo, H. (2007). Of mods and modders. *Games and Culture*, **2**(4), 300–13.

Prensky, M. (2001). Digital natives, digital immigrants. *On the Horizon*, **9**(5).

Rensfeldt, A. B. (2010). *Opening up Education*, PhD. University of Gothenburg, Gothenburg.

Rheingold, H. (2002). *Smart Mobs: The next social revolution*. Cambridge, MA: Perseus.

Roberts, P. (2007). Neoliberalism, performativity and research. *International Review of Education*, **53**(4),349–65.

Rogoff, B. (1990). *Apprenticeship in Thinking: Cognitive development in social contexts*. Oxford: Oxford University Press.

Säljö, R. (2002). My brain's running slowly today – the preferences for 'things ontologies' in research and everyday discourse on human thinking. *Studies in the Philosophy of Education*, **21**, 389–405.

(2004). Educational conversations and information technological revolutions in human history. *Folkbildning.net: An anthology about 'folkbildning' and flexible learning* (2nd rev. ed., pp. 211–27). Stockholm: The Swedish National Council of Adult Education.

(2010). Digital tools and the challenges to institutional traditions of learning: Technologies, social memory and the performative nature of learning. *Journal of Computer Assisted Learning*, **26**, 53–64.

Sannino, A., Daniels, H., and Guttierez, K. D. (2009). *Learning and Expanding with Activity Theory*. Cambridge: Cambridge University Press.

Selwyn, N. (2007). *'Screw Blackboard... do it on Facebook!': An investigation of students' educational use of Facebook*. Paper presented at the Poke 1.0 – Facebook social research symposium. Available from http://www.lse.ac.uk/collections/informationSystems/newsAndEvents/2008events/selwynpaper.pdf.

Selwyn, N. and Grant, L. (2009). Researching the realities of social software use – An introduction. *Learning, Media and Technology*, **34**(2), 79–86.

Sharpe, R., Benfield, G., Roberts, G., and Francis, R. (2006). *The Undergraduate Experience of Blended E-learning: A review of UK literature and practice*. The Higher Educational Academy. Available from http://www.heacademy.ac.uk/research/.

Snyder, I. (ed.). (2002). *Silicon Literacies: Communication, Innovation and Education in the Electronic Age*. New York: Routledge.

Somekh, B. (2004). Taking the sociological imagination to school: An analysis of the (lack of) impact of information and communication technologies on education systems. *Technology Pedagogy and Education*, **13**(2), 163–81.

Steinkuehler, C. A. (2006). Massively multiplayer online videogaming as participation in discourse. *Mind, Culture and Activity*, **13**(1), 38–52.

Tapscott, D. (1998). *Growing up Digital: The Rise of the Net Generation*. New York ; London: McGraw-Hill.

Uricchio, W. (2004). Beyond the great divide: collaborative networks and the challenge to dominant conceptions of the creative industries. *International Journal of Cultural Studies*, **7**(1), 79–90.

Vygotsky, L. S. (1997). *The Collected Works of L. S. Vygotsky. Vol 4. The History of the Development of Higher Mental Functions* (R. W. Reiber and M. T. Hall, trans.). New York, Boston, London, Dordrecht, and Moscow: Plenum Press.

Wenger, E. (1998). *Communities of Practice: Learning, meaning, and identity*. Cambridge: Cambridge University Press.

Wells, G. (2007). Who we become depends upon the company that we keep. *The International Journal of Education Research*, **46**, 100–103.

Woolcock, N. (2009, 10th June). Rising fees and loans make students ask whether higher education is worth it. *The Sunday Times*. Retrieved from http://www.timesonline.co.uk/tol/news/uk/education/article6143763.ece.

# 8

# Supporting Access to Science and Engineering through Scientific Argumentation

Tamara Ball and Lisa Hunter

## Introduction

Over the past several decades, numerous educators, policy makers, and educational researchers have advocated providing research experiences to promote the retention and advancement of all students in science, technology,
engineering, and mathematics (STEM) and broadening participation in
STEM to include more students from nondominant backgrounds in particular (Dunbar, 1995; Hofstein & Lunetta, 1982, 2004). Studies of undergraduate
research experiences typically analyze educational outcomes using self-report
interviews or survey data to report on the perceived value of the experience
as evidenced in students' increased self-efficacy or changing attitudes toward
STEM. However, less is known about how students interact with a mentor as
they engage in research, or how different characteristics of the learning environment might render that interaction effective, productive, and inclusive.
Mentors are largely responsible for defining the parameters and objectives for
a student's project, and then facilitating the completion of the project while
ensuring the student is productively participating in the valued practices and
processes of the disciplinary field. Mentored research projects typically take
place over a semester or a summer, and include a variety of different kinds
of student-mentor interactions. Undergraduate research experiences can be
stand-alone events or part of a program that integrates additional activities
through workshops, seminars, or courses. This chapter presents a summary of
our findings from a study that followed six students through a program that
integrated coursework with a research position. We observed and recorded
their engagement in scientific argumentation – a practice highly valued by
professional researchers. Scientific argumentation is central to productive
participation in STEM as a way of generating new understandings, of articulating those understandings to others, and of persuading others of the merit

of new findings (Berland & Reiser, 2009; Duschl & Obsborne, 2002). It is also inextricably embedded within the norms and practices of STEM culture, which can differ significantly from students' everyday lives – for some students more than others. Supporting participation in this valued practice is rarely an explicit goal of student research experiences but may be an overlooked avenue for broadening participation in STEM.

Using Cultural Historical Activity Theory (CHAT) to develop our methodology and analyze our results, our study illuminates local conditions that support and constrain students' explaining practices during a mentored research experience. The findings reported here focus on the tools (semiotic and material), participant structures, power dynamics, action goals, and discourse structures that organized interactions in the research environments we observed. We provide evidence that some conditions promoted opportunities for student interns to engage in scientific argumentation more frequently than others. These findings extend prior research on the efficacy of research apprenticeships at the undergraduate level and on STEM learning – particularly around the role of inscriptions. We show the effectiveness of an inscription for engaging interns in scientific practice and reasoning depends in part on the historicity of that inscription relative to the intern. We conclude by summarizing the practical implications of these findings and provide examples of how they can inform the design and mentoring of student research, laboratory courses, and programs. Our findings suggest that, by supporting the practice of scientific argumentation, these programs could more effectively support the productive participation of students from diverse backgrounds and thus broaden access to STEM.

## Cultural Historical Activity Theory

CHAT maintains that learning, understanding, skill development, and changes in human practice are all outcomes of social processes, including not only interaction with other people but also engagement with human artifacts and built environments (Cole, 1996). These outcomes are produced, yet also constrained, by several interrelated sociocultural elements or "features" that can together be described as an "activity system" (Cole & Engeström, 1997; Engeström, 1999). Different activity systems form around and are organized by the shared purposes or "goals" that bring people together. In turn, these organizing goals result from particular historical events leading up to that occasion. Participants in joint activity do not all perform the same action at once, rather they take on *positional roles* defined by different contributions: specialized yet coordinated tasks that, additively, form a unit of activity organized by the group's mutual pursuit of an emerging purpose or *action goal*. Different positional roles are defined in part by what an actor is actually doing in the moment (e.g., trying something for the first time versus facilitating someone else's attempt) and in part by an inherent division of labor (e.g., someone has to be the player in order for another to take on the role of coach). The shared purposes that motivate and organize activity depend on the ability of participants to coordinate their actions, which in turn depends on their ability to communicate and establish a joint focus of attention (Rommetveit, 1992, 2003; Tomasello, 1999; 2005). Collective action, therefore, also depends on the available symbolic and material resources that mediate the ways various operations are accomplished, including communicative operations that use symbolic gestures and language to coordinate the exchange of information and focus attention. These *mediational means* include everything from the lead in a pencil used to write down a number, to the symbolic representation of a number, to the concept of numeracy itself. While these resources are constantly involved in the production of new ideas and new technology, they are themselves the "artifacts" of prior human activity. They embody and carry forward the past experiences of individual participants as well as the collective meanings and uses established through social processes. Finally, CHAT theorists recognize that, while the actions of individuals are not determined by the social systems in which they participate, their *agency* exists only insofar as it is part of the continuing and evolving system of dialectic and interactional relationships that connect them to other people and to their social and material environments (Stetsenko & Arievitch, 2003).

Consistent with the emphasis in CHAT on artifact-mediated action, previous research in science education has demonstrated the importance of "inscriptions" for developing and communicating scientific concepts (Latour & Woolgar, 1979; Roth, Bowen, & Masciotra, 2002; Roth & McGinn, 1998). Following these authors, we use the term *inscription* to distinguish between what is represented in a person's mind and "materially embodied representations." In contrast to "mental representations," inscriptions (including graphs, tables, diagrams, photographs, drawings, etc.) are directly available for public viewing and can be used to share meaning. Previous research on inscriptions has demonstrated their value in summarizing large amounts of data in economical ways, coordinating face-to-face interactions, translating initially divergent understandings into mutual concepts, supporting verbal arguments, and stabilizing otherwise malleable meanings as they are communicated across communities of practice (Bowen & Roth, 2002; Lemke, 2001). Inscriptions have proven especially valuable to students in instructional settings. For instance, Roth and McGinn (1998) show how students used drawings to understand the relative contributions of each of three layers of soil in a total sample, after the soil had settled. In their study, Roth and McGinn found the students' drawings were important in enabling teams of students to compare individual understandings with what their peers understood, as well as with more authoritative understandings represented in published inscriptions.

## Context and Background to the Study

This chapter is part of a larger study of an undergraduate research apprenticeship program developed and implemented for seven years by the Center for Adaptive Optics (CfAO), one of five research organizations in the original cohort of Science and Technology Centers approved for funding by the National Science Foundation's Office for Integrative Activities in 2000. CfAO staff members planned an apprenticeship program that would engage students in research early in their college education. They recruited students from community colleges and transfer students to increase participation from groups underrepresented in science and engineering. Knowing that the students recruited to the program were likely to have had less exposure, fewer role models, and a more limited range of educational experiences than students from dominant groups, the CfAO designed a program to supplement the research experience by including a one-week preparatory course, a communication curriculum integrated into the entire eight-week program, and public speaking events. The preparatory course includes a series of intensive lab activities collaboratively designed and taught by graduate students and postdoctoral researchers simultaneously participating in a CfAO professional program designed to scaffold inquiry-based pedagogy. The principal data for this study were collected in 2006 and 2007 while interns moved through the eight-week program. These data include results from (a) in-depth interviews with interns, mentors, and program coordinators, (b) ethnographic field notes, and (c) video and audio recordings of six interns – three in 2006 and three in 2007. These six interns were part of two larger cohorts of students selected for the program (the program had twenty-one total participants in 2006 and 2007).

## Methodology

Our analysis uses CHAT to characterize the local conditions in the interactive settings that held potential for CfAO interns to participate in scientific argumentation. We used StudioCode digital editing software to code the video and audio recordings of the six undergraduate students collected over the eight-week period. Recordings of interns working in isolation and scenes that involved primarily recreational "social talk" (e.g., talk about plans for the weekend) or logistics (e.g., a meeting location) were excluded from our database. The remaining recordings show interns working and interacting with the CfAO instructional team during the first-week preparatory course and weekly three-hour communication course meetings thereafter, with research mentors at their respective host research sites, and during weekly meetings that served as the backbone of the communication course.[1] We subdivided daily recordings into smaller analytic units called "episodes." The criteria for segmenting interaction into episodes were drawn directly from CHAT; we identified key changes in one or more of the organizing features of the evolving activity systems we observed and used these to define the boundaries of a new episode. For example, a new episode was identified when the introduction of a particular resource/artifact, such as a sketch on a whiteboard, shifted the focus of attention (i.e., from the practical mechanics of some technology to the conceptual physics underlying its operation), even though the basic action goal (understanding how to use the equipment), participant structure, and roles remained unchanged. We also developed a coding system to characterize key "conditions" affording or constraining scientific argumentation in each designated episode. Further details regarding this coding system are reported elsewhere (Ball, 2009).

A coding scheme to identify and distinguish among different verbal and nonverbal discursive contributions – or "moves" – presented by interns in our sample was also developed. This coding process involved: (a) distinguishing intern-initiating moves from responses; and (b) deciding whether the function of an intern move that offered information was explanatory or merely informative. Some initiating moves functioned only to demand information and did not include explanatory or informative clauses (e.g., "What should I call this graph?"). However, other initiating moves included at least one informative or explanatory clause (e.g., "the problem was that here you have to include an 'L' to complete the function"). When this occurred, the move was double coded as both initiating and as either explaining or informing. Other intern moves that did not involve the exchange of substantive information (e.g., "I don't know") or that simply acknowledged new information (e.g., "oh" or "I get it") were not counted.

---

[1] For additional information about how this sample relates to the full set of recordings, and what proportion of the interns' total summer experience this data corpus represents, see Section III.

We used a nonparametric two-sample signed rank test, otherwise known as the Wilcoxon Rank Sum Test, to test hypotheses about whether contrasting conditions defining different kinds of episodes would coincide with significantly more or fewer instances of intern explaining moves. These hypotheses were tested by matching pairs of contrasting *episode sets* and comparing the frequencies of intern explaining move rates counted in each set. Hypotheses about which combinations of episode descriptors would (a) form a meaningful episode set and (b) yield significant results were based on relevant literature, field observations, results of a previous analysis (see Ball, 2009), and an initial review of raw intern explaining move frequencies. Comparisons between matched pairs relevant to this analysis and that yielded significant results[2] are presented in Table 8.1.

## Findings

The results of our analysis of contrasting episode sets show that the specific composition of a learning environment does impact and influence an intern's participation in scientific practice. We provide summaries of our quantitative results organized into four thematic categories, which correspond to four of the seven key features of the CHAT activity system described by Wells (1999, 2007) as follows:

Feature 1 • Mediating Artifacts: *Intern-Generated Inscriptions*
Feature 2 • Action Goal: *Treatment of the Problem as Unresolved*
Feature 3 • Participant Structure: *Agency and "Hands-On" Manipulation*
Feature 4 • Intertextuality: *Responsive Discourse Patterns*

To be clear, our results do not suggest any single feature of an activity, occurring on its own, is more influential than another. Rather, our findings show the importance of understanding how the dynamic *interplay* over time and between different theorized features of an activity system shaped the quality of these interns' participation in scientific practice. To make this clear, we present a narrative example, or vignette, which allows the reader to understand in greater detail, one of the four CHAT features applied to organize our quantitative findings.

### *Mediating Artifacts:* Intern-Generated Inscriptions
Comparisons of matched episode sets 1 and 2 and sets 3 and 4 (see Table 8.1) tested a hypothesis about the importance and influence of the tools and artifacts

---

[2]  The results shown here represent only a subset of the total comparisons completed. Additional (including nonsignificant) results are reported in Ball (2009).

TABLE 8.1. *Comparison of Explaining Rates in Hypothesis-Driven Episode Sets*

| Comparison of Explaining Rates in Hypothesis-driven Episode Sets | | |
|---|---|---|
| **Hypothesis 1: Activities involving inscriptions promote more opportunities for interns to participate in scientific argumentation.** | | |
| | **Episode Selection Criteria** | **Wilcoxon Results** |
| Set 1 | All inscriptions | No significant difference |
| Set 2 | Non-verbal gestures, Language, Written Text | $Z = 1.9$, $p=.55$ |
| Set 3 | Intern generated inscriptions | Higher explaining rate in Set 3 |
| Set 4 | Inscriptions created by others | $Z = 1.8$, $p = .01$ |
| **Hypothesis 2: Problem solving activities treated as open-ended or unresolved promote more opportunities to participate in scientific argumentation.** | | |
| | **Episode Selection Criteria** | **Wilcoxon Results** |
| Set 5 | Interns working as engineers or investigating scientific phenomenon<br>Interns manipulating material world<br>Problem solving treated as having pre-determined solutions | Higher explaining rate in Set 6 |
| Set 6 | Interns working as engineers or investigating scientific phenomenon<br>Interns manipulating material world<br>Problem solving treated as having open-ended or undetermined solutions | $Z=2.2$, $p=.03$ |
| **Hypothesis 3: Interns manipulating the physical world, and showing intiative and agency, gain more opportunities to participate in scientific argumentation.** | | |
| | **Episode Selection Criteria** | **Wilcoxon Results** |
| Set 7 | Intern manipulating material world<br>Intern takes initiative<br>Intern directs activity or focus of attention | Higher explaining rate in Set 7 |
| Set 8 | Intern manipulating material world<br>Others take initiative<br>Others direct activity or focus of attention | $Z=2.2$, $p=.03$ |
| Set 9 | Intern manipulating material world<br>Intern shows initiative<br>Intern directs activity or focus of attention | Higher explaining rate in Set 9 |
| Set 10 | Others manipulating material world<br>Others lead initiative<br>Others direct activity or focus of attention | $Z=2.9$, $p=.01$ |
| **Hypothesis 4: Discourse structured in dialogic (responsive) pattern will promote more opportunities for explaining than monologic (authoritative, declarative) patterns.** | | |
| | **Episode Selection Criteria** | **Wilcoxon Results** |
| Set 11 | Interns working as engineers or discussants<br>Data interpretation or assessment goals organize activity<br>Dialogic discourse structure | Higher explaining rate in Set 11 |
| Set 12 | Interns positioned as engineers or discussants<br>Data interpretation or assessment goals organize activity<br>Monologic discourse structure | $Z = 2.6$, $p = .01$ |

these interns used to accomplish reasoning tasks. We predicted interns would make more explaining moves in episodes that involved inscriptions than in those that did not.[3] Surprisingly, we found this comparison alone did not yield a significant difference. Holding the interns' participant roles constant, we found the mean explaining move rate for episodes that involved inscriptions (set 1), was not significantly different from the mean rate associated with episodes that involved only oral language or other representational means (set 2). However, we did find that the mean explaining move rate associated with episodes that involved only *intern-generated inscriptions*[4] (set 3) was significantly higher than the mean explaining move rate associated with episodes that involved any other type of representational means, including other inscriptions created by someone other than the interns themselves (set 4).

### *Action Goal:* Treatment of the Problem as Unresolved

Comparisons of different types of episodes included in sets 5 and 6 tested a hypothesis about the importance of the action goal(s) organizing different activity systems. Our results show that interns who were working side-by-side with collaborators as engineers or scientific investigators and who were able to manipulate research tools made explaining moves more frequently when the problem they were working on was treated as undetermined (set 6) than when treated as if there was already an expected solution (set 5). It should be emphasized that, in making this distinction, the focus was on how the problem or question *was treated by the participants during the interaction*, rather than on whether a solution to the problem exists ontologically. The significance of these results seems even greater given that comparisons of two sets of problem-solving episodes organized around other kinds of action goals (e.g., information gathering, formative assessment, data interpretation) did not yield significant differences. This is consistent with CHAT insofar as the action-goal(s) that organize activity are presumed to exist only as emerging constructs generated by participants (Lemke, 1995).

### *Participant Structure:* Agency and Hands-On Manipulation

Comparisons of episode sets 7 and 8 and 9 and 10 tested a hypothesis about the agency or initiative demonstrated by an intern with respect to the material

---

[3] This prediction is based on previous research in science education, which has focused on the role of inscriptions in science reasoning and learning activities.

[4] Intern-generated inscriptions include graphs, charts, drawings, tables, sketches, and so forth that interns were either personally responsible for creating on their own, or those the interns substantially modified.

world and/or as expressed through dialogue. We predicted that interns would participate in scientific argumentation more readily when they were in direct control of the material tools or equipment mediating the interaction as compared to when someone else was directing their actions or controlling the material environment. While we did not find significant differences for mean explaining move rates in this comparison we did find significant differences *when multiple indicators of an intern's agency were in play*. Even when interns had the opportunity to manipulate the material world, they still made significantly fewer explaining moves when someone else was controlling the focus of attention or micromanaging the intern's actions (sets 7 and 8). This shows that simply ensuring interns have a hands-on experience was not enough; interns needed to be situated "in the driver's seat" to gain opportunities to participate in scientific argumentation. Of even greater significance was the finding that, when interns were *not only* manipulating tools or equipment *but also* initiating the topic of conversation, leading the action, or directing the focus of attention (set 9), they made significantly more explaining moves than when someone else was controlling the focus of attention or directing their actions (set 10).

### *Intertextuality:* Responsive Discourse Patterns

A fourth set of comparisons was motivated by a long history of research on discourse patterns in classroom interaction, which has established the difference between authoritative (or "monologic") and responsive (or "dialogic") exchanges between students and teachers (Lotman, 1988; Wells, 2002). For the purposes of this analysis we compared intern explaining rates associated with episodes that involved either problem solving or interpretive work *and* were structured by responsive (dialogic) discourse patterns (set 11) with episodes characterized by those same conditions but structured by authoritative (monologic) discourse patterns (set 12). Not surprising, we found that on average intern explaining move rates were significantly higher in episodes that involved responsive as compared to authoritative discourse patterns.

### Narrative Vignette: The Role of Inscriptions

To demonstrate how the combination and interdependence of different theorized features of an activity system shape learning, we focus on one set of findings – those related to the *role of inscriptions* – and provide more detail. We focus on the role of inscriptions in particular because we believe our findings directly inform ongoing research into the importance of inscriptions for STEM learning and STEM practice. Our quantitative results suggest that when interns in this study were personally responsible for creating or modifying the inscriptions they later used to evaluate, understand, and explain scientific data or engineering designs they were much more likely to participate in scientific argumentation than when using "established" inscriptions created by others. Evidence for the influential role of inscriptions (as mediating artifacts) on scientific practice and understanding is already well established (Kozma, 2003). Our findings, however, complicate and build on earlier research to show that it is not only the presence or absence of an inscription that makes the greatest difference to those just beginning to engage in STEM, but rather the relationship between the authorship of an inscription and how learners use it. Moreover, our results demonstrate that the power of an inscription to mediate practice is realized through, and interdependent with, the dynamic tensions that link this *"tool-in-use"* (Wells, 1999; Wertsch, 1998) to the way other features/aspects of an activity system play out.

The vignette outlined in this section illustrates the changing dynamic between Holly and her mentor, Jordan, as they worked with a set of inscriptions (a series of spectral "maps") they were using to characterize photometric data emitted by galaxies more than halfway across the universe and captured by telescopes. The vignette contrasts two different episodes of interaction at a point in Holly's internship when Jordan was training her to apply a coding scheme previously developed by the research group sponsoring her project. This scheme, known by the research group as "Z-spec," used descriptive codes designed to standardize, catalogue, and quantify interpretations of spectral information representing these distant galaxies. The contrasted episodes show differences between interactions organized around *established inscriptions* (i.e., those previously generated by someone else) and those organized around inscriptions that were the outcome of Holly's self-initiated efforts.

In the first episode, Holly and Jordan focused on a data set previously formatted and catalogued by other researchers. From the start, Jordan, seated next to Holly, monitored Holly's actions closely and controlled or "directed" the interaction, despite the fact that Holly was the one actually using the keyboard and computer terminal. In this episode, Jordan made all but one of the initiating moves, made declarative statements about coding, issued detailed directions (e.g., telling Holly exactly what to type), made several evaluative comments (e.g., "That's good"), and generally controlled the interpretive/decision-making process.

Under these conditions Holly's verbal responses were highly compliant, and her contributions were limited to a few tentative observations (e.g.,

"Ahhh – O2?") while her other moves were limited to requests for confirmation ("Umm, but that's good, yeah?"), acknowledgments of Jordan's dominant perspective ("Oh yeah, that's right. Sorry, I was actually thinking…"), or appeals for approval. Thus, while the inscriptions they viewed in this episode did appear to help coordinate their joint focus of attention and enabled Holly to follow Jordan's reasoning more closely, they opened up relatively few opportunities for Holly to make original contributions, and were not instrumental in promoting exchanges that involved Holly in scientific argumentation.

The conditions changed, however, when Jordan was called out of the room to assist a colleague. Upon his return, about twenty minutes later, Jordan found that Holly had ventured to enter codes on her own, which Jordan promptly suggested they review together. We observed that, while the overarching purpose of their work remained the same (i.e., training Holly to use the Z-spec coding system), there were important shifts in several defining features of the activity system (including their positional roles and the dominant discourse structure), and thus the organizing dynamic between the intern and her mentor. A most noticeable difference was that displays that they were jointly focusing on were now the products of Holly's own efforts.

As they reviewed these files, Holly became more proactive and concomitantly engaged more readily in the practice of scientific argumentation. Holly made three out of four initiating moves in the episode following Jordan's return, as compared to one of six in the earlier episode. Holly was more assertive in calling attention to defining aspects of the spectral displays/maps, at one point even interrupting Jordan mid-sentence to make her own point heard ("Well, there's two [galaxies] in this one, so…"). Holly not only offered unsolicited interpretations (e.g., "It actually has some nice H-beta…"), but she acted on those interpretations promptly (entering Z-spec codes), without waiting for Jordan's approval. As Holly became more expressive, Jordan had more opportunities to learn about and acknowledge her interpretations of the data (e.g., "That's a good assumption on the redshift"), ask follow-up questions, and build on Holly's observations with other kinds of responsive moves (e.g., "It's also bad extraction – which you can see because the O-2 lines…").

A defining moment in this episode occurred when Holly attempted to persuade Jordan of her own conclusion – that she had discovered what the research team referred to as an "off-ser."[5] To convince Jordan, Holly used a

---

[5] "Off-sers" = serendipitously discovered galaxy "offset" in the display from the coordinates of a target galaxy.

calculator to demonstrate how she determined the object's redshift[6] using the available information.

> HOLLY: And so this is the one where I found the "off-ser" ((opens the next file)).
> JORDAN: ((studies the monitor display))
> HOLLY: And so I calculated – you know…
> JORDAN: The red shift?
> HOLLY: Where the – yeah where the red shift would be and it matched up with H-beta ((indicates a point in the display marked as H-beta)).
> [*Holly uses calculator to retrieve some of her earlier calculations…*].
> HOLLY: And, so let's see – [*talks herself through several steps in the calculation*]. So it would have been at seven – zero – one – seven and so… ((moves cursor to locate coordinates on screen)).
> HOLLY: Right there [*whispers for emphasis*].
> JORDAN: Oh, H-beta?
> HOLLY: Yeah.
> JORDAN: Okay. Yeah, that's, that's it. Good job, *good job*, gooooood JOB.

This vignette shows that Holly was more proactive and made a greater proportion of initiating moves when using inscriptions that she was, at least in part, responsible for generating. More to the point, in her attempt to persuade Jordan of her discovery of the off-ser and in demonstrating how she arrived at this conclusion, Holly was participating in the practice of scientific argumentation, which can be viewed as integrating three operational goals: sense making, articulating, and persuading (Berland & Reiser, 2009). Holly not only used her demonstration as a means of *articulating* the relationship she was interpreting (i.e., *sense making*) between the H-beta emission line and redshift value, but she also used it as a way of *persuading* Jordan of the validity of her interpretation.

Obviously Holly could not have been expected to make as many explaining moves at the outset of her training, before she was introduced to the tools of the trade and before she had a chance to actually work with the data. However, our observations of how this situation shifted to allow Holly to make more explaining moves should not be taken for granted or considered inevitable. We observed plenty of instances when mentors continued to dominate an interaction with their intern long after an intern had become familiar with the

---

6  *Redshift* is a term used by astronomers to characterize an increase in the wavelength of radiation emitted by a celestial body as a consequence of either the Doppler effect (corresponding to objects within the Milky Way) or the expansion of the universe (corresponding to objects in deep space).

tools or procedures central to the research, even when the main task involved reviewing data entries, interpreting results, and so forth. We also remind our readers that this vignette illustrates what proved a significant pattern in our quantitative data – namely, that interns regularly made more explaining moves during episodes in which the focus of attention was organized around inscriptions the interns had been in some way responsible for producing.

## Discussion

Previous research has established the power of inscriptions to mediate scientific thinking and practice and to support scientific communication. Furthermore, research on technology in science learning and teaching has demonstrated how using inscriptions can make abstract concepts accessible, inspectable, and arguable, and how visual modeling activities are "mutually constitutive" in the translation of quantified and/or databased records of observations of natural phenomena into usable ideas (Latour, 1993; Roth & Tobin, 1997; Bowen & Roth, 2002). Our findings qualify the implications of this existing body of research because they suggest educators also need to consider the historicity of an inscription in relation to the user. In our study, the potential for inscriptions to promote changes in an intern's ability to participate in scientific argumentation was related to the work the intern had invested in producing or modifying that inscription. This finding is generally commensurate with research in the CHAT tradition on how learners appropriate new knowledge or practice. Learners are much less successful in knowledge building when they only (passively) view demonstrations or receive transmitted information/instruction as compared with when they can use presented information, directions, or demonstrations to produce or accomplish something new (Moschkovich, 2004; Wells, this volume; Wertsch, 1979; Wertsch & Stone, 1999).

While the vignette illustrating interaction between Holly and Jordan was selected to foreground the role of inscriptions, it also illuminates the interdependence of the key features of the activity system in play. The potential for these inscriptions to transform the nature of their interaction depended on the co-occurrence of changes in other features of the activity system, including the discourse patterns, the organizing action goals, and the positional roles adopted by Holly and Jordan. For example, the fact that Holly was physically in command of the research tools (keyboard, cursor, calculator, and so forth) might have influenced Holly's willingness to continue coding by herself after Jordan stepped away. In our study, we noted multiple examples of shifts in an intern's show of initiative that corresponded to instances when a supervising mentor relinquished physical control of material tools or equipment if they also simultaneously relinquished their authority or position in the "driver's seat." Additionally, on this occasion the problem they were solving (e.g., whether or not there was sufficient evidence of an off-ser) was treated as one that could be resolved in any one of a number of possible ways (i.e., assertions depended on what evidence of unidentified galaxies was established as valid) rather than as having a predetermined solution (e.g., an off-ser was presumed to exist and the task was to identify verifying evidence). Our quantitative analysis also revealed multiple episodes when an intern's participation in scientific argumentation coincided with a focus on problems treated as open-ended rather than predetermined.

## Implications for Practice

Involving students in research, whether in an authentic research project or in a laboratory course that mimics research, has the potential to productively engage students from a broad range of backgrounds in STEM. The presumption, however, that merely providing access guarantees newcomers the chance to participate in authentic research practices, such as engaging in scientific argumentation, is not always fulfilled in practice. It was for this reason that we conducted this study. Our intention was to learn whether there are localized conditions in a research experience that noticeably promote or constrain scientific argumentation in actual practice. We relied on our understanding of CHAT to organize our findings according to four features, which we believe can also guide the design of learning environments and mentoring practices within them so that novice researchers are enabled to participate in STEM authentically. From this perspective, we conclude with some succinct suggestions for applying the results of this study to inform educational practice.

*Learner-generated inscriptions.* Mentors can prioritize what types of inscriptions are used and when. They can adopt strategies that encourage learners to generate and then employ their own inscriptions. Mentors can be intentional in using and building on learners' inscriptions and, as appropriate, avoid temptations to rely only on expert or canonical inscriptions.

*Treatment of a problem as unresolved.* When planning a student project, mentors can consider how to organize necessary steps or sub-tasks. Rather than presenting them as routine, the mentor can relate tasks and outcomes to a question or problem and emphasize the need to identify and consider alternative solutions or explanations. Mentors can design an entry point into the project that opens and encourages different pathways to a solution. On a day-to-day basis, mentors can transform errors into skill-building opportunities;

rather than jumping in with the quick fix, mentors can refocus attention on what remains unresolved or problematic and why.

*Agency in hands-on manipulation.* Mentors can be intentional in their decisions as to which instruments, equipment, or techniques newcomers need to understand at a deep level versus those they don't. When a deeper understanding is the goal, the mentor can stand back to let newcomers fumble and find their own way.

*Responsive discourse patterns.* Rather than routinely offering their own explanations or resolutions, mentors can watch for opportunities to use responsive discourse moves that encourage students to "make observable" their new and emerging understandings.

These are but a few suggestions for how our results can inform efforts to mentor students involved in research, whether in the field or during a laboratory or capstone project course. The quality of the interaction between student researchers and their mentors is critical to the success of the apprenticeship model and for ensuring research training works as a transformative experience that advances unlikely candidates into STEM, rather than turning them away. Our findings provide evidence that research apprenticeships do not always involve students in scientific practices as expected. However, they also show how different conditions of a learning environment can be intentionally adapted to promote more opportunities for students to engage in scientific argumentation. We are convinced further applications of CHAT for analyzing and interpreting observations of mentoring in practice will be critical to practical efforts focused on changing the demographics in STEM.

## Acknowledgments

This material is based on work supported by: the National Science Foundation (NSF) Science and Technology Center program through the Center for Adaptive Optics, managed by the University of California, Santa Cruz (UCSC) under cooperative agreement AST#9876783; UCSC Institute for Scientist & Engineer Educators; and UCSC Graduate Division.

## References

Ball, Tamara B. *Explaining as Participation: A multi-level analysis of learning environments designed to support scientific argumentation.* Thesis (Ph.D.), University of California, Santa Cruz. Retrieved from Digital Dissertations Databases.(Accession Order No. 613216695).

Barab, S. and Plucker, J. (2002). Smart people or smart contexts? Cognition, ability and talent development in an age of situated approaches to knowing and learning. *Educational Psychologist,* **37**(3), 165–82.

Berland, L. and Reiser, B. (2009). Making sense of argumentation and explanation. *Science Education*, **93**(1).

Bowen, G. and Roth, W. (2002). Why students may not learn to interpret scientific inscriptions. *Research in Science Education*, **32**(3), 303–27.

Cole, M. (1996). *Cultural Psychology: A once and future discipline*. Cambridge MA: Harvard University Press.

Cole, M. and Engeström, Y. (1997). A cultural-historical approach to distributed cognition. In G. Salomon (Ed.), *Distributed Cognitions: Psychological and educational considerations*, (pp. 1–46). Cambridge: Cambridge University Press.

Dunbar, K. (1995). How scientists really reason: Scientific reasoning in real-world laboratories. In R. J. Sternberg and J. Davidson (Eds.), *Mechanisms of Insight*. (pp. 365–95). Cambridge, MA: MIT Press.

Duschl, R. and Osborne, J. (2002). Supporting and promoting argumentation discourse in science education. *Studies in Science Education*, **38**(1), 39–72.

Engeström, Y. (1999). Activity theory and individual and social transformation. In Yrjö Engeström, Reijo Miettinen, and Raija-Leena Punamäki, (Ed.), *Perspectives on Activity Theory*, (pp. 19–38). Cambridge: Cambridge University Press.

Hofstein, A. and Lunetta, V. (1982). The role of the laboratory in science teaching: Neglected aspects of research. *Review of Educational Research*, **52**(2), 201.

(2004). The laboratory in science education: Foundations for the twenty-first century. *Science Education*, **88**(1), 28–54.

Kozma, R. (2003). The material features of multiple representations and their cognitive and social affordances for science understanding. *Learning & Instruction*, **13**(2), 205–26.

Latour, B. and Woolgar, S. (1986). *Laboratory Life: The construction of scientific facts*. Princeton University Press.

Latour, B. (1993) *We Have Never Been Modern* (Catherine Porter, trans.). Cambridge, MA: Harvard University Press.

Lemke, J. L. (1995). *Emergent Agendas in Collaborative Activity*. Paper presented at the Annual Meeting of the American Educational Research Association, San Francisco.

(2000). Across the scales of time: Artifacts, activities, and meanings in ecosociological systems. *Mind, Culture and Activity*, **7**(4), 271–90.

(2001). Articulating communities: Sociocultural perspectives on science education. *Journal of Research in Science Teaching*, **38**(3), 296–316.

Lotman, Y. (1988). The semiotics of culture and the concept of a text. *Soviet Psychology*, **26**(3), 52–58.

Moschkovich, J. (2004). Appropriating mathematical practices: A case study of learning to use and explore functions through interactions with a tutor. *Educational Studies in Mathematics*, (55), 49–80.

Rommetveit, R. (1992). Outlines of a dialogically based social cognitive approach to human cognition and communication. In A. H. Wold (Ed.), *The Dialogical Alternative: Towards a theory of language and mind*. Oxford: Oxford University Press.

(2003). On the role of "a psychology of a second person" in studies of meaning, language and mind. *Mind, Culture and Activity*, **10**(3), 205–18.

Roth, W., Bowen, G., and Masciotra, D. (2002). From thing to sign and "natural object": Toward a genetic phenomenology of graph interpretation. *Science, Technology & Human Values*, **27**(3), 327.

Roth, W., Bowen, G., and McGinn, M. (1999). Differences in graph-related practices between high school biology textbooks and scientific ecology journals. *Journal of Research in Science Teaching*, **36**(9), 977–1019.

Roth, W.-M. and McGinn, M. K. (1998). Inscriptions: Toward a theory of representing as social practice. *Review of Educational Research*, **68**(1), 35–59.

Roth, W. M. and Tobin, K. (1997). Cascades of inscriptions and the representation of nature: How numbers, tables, graphs, and money come to re-present a rolling ball. *International Journal of Science Education*, **19**, 1075–91.

Sandoval, W. A. and Millwood, K. A. (2005). The quality of students' use of evidence in written scientific explanations. *Cognition and Instruction*, **23**(1), 23–55.

Stetsenko, A. and Arievitch, I. (2003). The self in cultural-historical activity theory: Reclaiming the unity of social and individual dimensions of human development. *Theory & Psychology*, **14**, 475–50.

Stetsenko, A. (2005). Activity as object-related: Resolving the dichotomy of individual and collective planes of activity. *Mind, Culture, and Activity*, **12**(1), 70–88.

Tomasello, M. (1999). *The Cultural Origins of Human Cognition*. Cambridge, MA: Harvard University Press.

Tomasello, M., Carpenter, M., Call, J., Behne, T., and Moll, H. (2005). Understanding and sharing intentions: The origins of cultural cognition. *Behavioral and Brain Sciences*, **28**, 675–735.

Vygotsky, L. S. (1987). The development of scientific concepts in childhood (N. Minnik, trans.). In *The Collected Works of L. S. Vygotsky* (Vol. 1, *Problems of General Psychology*, pp. 146–209). New York, NY: Plenum.

Wells, G. (1999). *Dialogic Inquiry*. Cambridge: Cambridge University Press.
  (2002). Dialogue in activity theory. *Mind, Culture and Activity*, **9**(1), 43–66.
  (2007). Semiotic mediation, dialogue and the construction of knowledge. *Human Development*, **50**(5), 244–74.

Wertsch, J. V. (1979). The concept of activity in soviet psychology: An introduction. In J.V. Wertsch (ed. and trans.), *The Concept of Activity in Soviet Psychology*, M. E. Sharpe, Armonk, NY, 144–88.

Wertsch, J. *Mind as Action*. New York: Oxford, 1998.
  (1999). Alterity in human communication. *Communication: An arena of development*, 17–30.

Wertsch, J. and Stone, C. (1999). The concept of internalization in Vygotsky's account of the genesis of higher mental functions. *Lev Vygotsky: Critical Assessments*, **1**, 363–80.

# 9

# Using CHAT to Understand Systems to Support Disabled Students In Higher Education

## Jan Georgeson

### Introduction

This chapter explores how CHAT helps us to understand how students with a disability operate within the systems designed to support them through their undergraduate degrees. The discussion draws on a national study that followed a cohort of disabled students through their undergraduate courses at different UK universities between 2005 and 2008 (Fuller et al., 2009). Recent changes in legislation meant universities were required to make reasonable adjustments so disabled students would not be disadvantaged by their impairments in comparison with their peers and to fulfill a Disability Equality Duty leveled on all public bodies to avoid discrimination.

As part of the national study, I examined the disability services and academic departments in one university in the north of England, seeing them as separate but interdependent activity systems (Georgeson, 2009). The object of activity for each was the support of students who met the criteria as "disabled" and the general object motive was that students should not be disadvantaged by their impairment. I adopted a Cultural Historical Activity Theory (CHAT) framework for this analysis because, as I spoke to staff members, it became apparent their response to the need to support disabled students was complicated, shaped by local practice, central regulation, institutional values, and subject-specific discourses. Also the data set was diffuse; recruitment of participants had been uneven and anticipated differences along arts/science old/new university divides had not emerged. An activity theory analysis allowed an exploration of how disability support played out differently in different departments with different histories and different stakeholders. Staff members and students alike operated within support systems in different ways, and for some the experiences of discerning the best way to participate in the systems was shaped by and continued to shape how they responded to disability.

There were no simple stories; what individual staff members did was influenced by what they brought from other parts of their lives and their past experiences of disability support, with variation in how staff members in different parts of the systems used their experiences to work with disabled students. Students' participation in systems for disability support also varied according to their previous experience of support and their response to their own impairment. It became apparent that learning how to operate within university support systems contributed to students' understanding of their own disability and the extent to which they accepted, accommodated, or rejected the label of disabled student. Students were not passive recipients of support, but neither did they have a strong voice in organizing how support was structured and administered. Analysis therefore needed to reflect how staff members and students operated within the constraints of the system, and the extent to which they identified with the positions offered to them within the system. I also wanted to document their understandings of what the system afforded, how much room they had to maneuver and act with agency and invention.

I turned to the work of Holland, Lachicotte, Lave, and colleagues on the theory of social practice (Holland et al., 1998; Holland & Lave, 2009). Social practice theory, like CHAT, takes activity as its central focus, but foregrounds subjects as actors in activities developing self-understandings in cultural contexts. The approach seeks to "move us away (but not completely) from cultural determinism and situational totalitarianism to make (some) way for the importance of improvisation and innovation (agency)" and has been usefully employed to "focus on different social contexts of education and how the worlds formed in these contexts helped shape how people came to make sense of themselves in these worlds and in society" (Urrieta, 2007, pp. 107–108).

This approach captured both the sense of restriction and creativity in working toward solutions, and the effects this had on students' and occasionally staff members' self-understandings, including their "abilities to form and be formed in collectively realized 'figured worlds,'" like universities, which "supply the contexts of meaning for actions, cultural productions, performances, disputes, for the understandings that people come to make of themselves and for the capabilities that people develop to direct their own behaviour in these worlds" (Holland et al., 1998, pp. 49, 60).

In the next section, I briefly show how activity theory helped to explore the ways disability support was operating as a network of systems, before using concepts from social practice theory to go beyond the abstraction of division of labor (Holland et al., 1998, p. 41) and focus on understanding individual students as inhabitants of the cultural world of the university.

## Disability Support as a System

The disability support systems offered tools, such as physical aids and adjustments to assessment procedures, whose use was constrained by regulation and shaped by subject discipline and the institution's own values and priorities. Analysis revealed contradictions within and between central and departmental structures, some of which stemmed from familiar tensions between standards and inclusion agendas (Georgeson, 2009).

This analysis prompted a closer examination of the object of activity within different departments, from the perspective of academic and administrative staff members. The university had long-standing links with industry and a tradition of widening participation. Staff members were concerned that students should develop work-appropriate personal qualities, such as toughness and resilience, alongside their degrees. For some staff members, this ran counter to the need to make reasonable adjustments for disabled students, such as allowing extra time in exams or engaging sign language translators. As one lecturer (who also worked in industry) commented:

When I'm interviewing in an industry context and if somebody had a degree, what I've got to be very careful of is it's not a devalued degree. Meaning? If everything has been done for them, – as a batsman in a cricket team, if they've had a runner for them as well – if they had a whole host of backing to get that qualification.

The twin priorities of developing subject knowledge and professional readiness led to conceptual tools that accommodated difference. These varied across departments and produced localized variation in staff members' response to disability. For example, staff in an engineering department enthusiastically reported "tinkering" with the support systems for a student with ADHD until they arrived at a combination that worked, while a performing arts lecturer pointed to her discipline's emphasis on exploring everyone's frailties and weaknesses to reveal inner strengths, which she judged supported a truly inclusive ethos.

There was also variation within departments in individual staff members' motivation to support disabled students; some took it as a moral imperative but for others it was a performative compliance, and this affected the extent to which they were prepared to bend the rules and offer students flexibility. Some staff members were openly suspicious of students' motivations:

Students have a strong incentive to put "dyslexia" if they get more time in exams; they should not get more time even if they have a disability of that nature; it undermines our credibility.

Several people discussed their personal experience of disability, either their own or that of family members, and explained how this shaped their approach to support for disabled students. Their positions in departments also influenced what they could do. Examining systems for support for disabled students from staff members' points of view revealed complexity and contradictions, as well as creativity in how they worked within the rules, using the conceptual and procedural tools at their disposal.

Differences in what staff members thought they were doing and how and why they did it meant disabled students' experiences of support varied across the institution. But students' motivations, use, and interpretations of the system also varied. It became apparent they sought to act with agency within the system, making choices about which conceptual and physical tools they would use so they could reconcile the reality of receiving disability support with their sense of identity (Fuller et al., 2009, pp. 96–113).

## Introducing the Five Case Studies

To illustrate how students with different needs operated within the system of disability support, responding to its constraints and making use of its affordances, I discuss five students. These case studies show how, over time, the students developed understandings of their own needs and how they might be met within the system. The students were self-selecting: one student had mobility impairment and was on a faculty of arts course with strong technological elements; four declared dyslexia; of these, two were studying arts subjects and two were on technology courses. Two of the five (one dyslexic and one mobility impaired) were mature students who had always lived in the region; the other three came from other parts of the country to study, one straight from school, one following a gap year, and the third was starting again having left another university after a term. The students were interviewed once or twice a year during the three years of their course. Four individuals in the group gave permission for researchers to interview their lecturers, and one student was also observed during a teaching session.

## On the Boundaries of Disability

For different reasons, all five students positioned themselves on the boundaries of disability. Dyslexia is specifically covered in disability legislation under the broad category of a disability that affects "memory, or ability to concentrate, learn or understand," but might not conform to most people's "social image" (Holland & Lave, 2009, p. 9) of a disability. The legal definition of disability – a physical or mental impairment that has a substantial and long-term adverse effect on your ability to carry out normal day-to-day activities – is much wider than many people might expect. For many "it is only about wheelchair users or people with sight and hearing impairments" (Peter Fox, disability training manager; quoted in Redford, 2007), a view perhaps perpetuated by the presence of a wheelchair user in the universal logo for disability.

Although there are recurring debates in the media demonstrating suspicion about the status of dyslexia as a disability (see, for example, David Mills's article for the *Daily Telegraph*, January 15, 2007), dyslexia is now by far the largest single category of disability reported in university statistics and has shown a marked increase in recent years (15 percent of disabled first degree undergraduates in 1994/5; over 50 percent in 2009/10; HESA, 2011). This has been accompanied by a corresponding decrease in the number of students declaring an unseen disability (from 52 percent in 1994/5 down to 13 percent in 2009/10). While many other factors could contribute to this effect, it is tempting to suggest students who might previously have declared an unseen disability are switching to declaring dyslexia.

One might assume, therefore, that there is something about the category "dyslexic" that students are comfortable with, at least at the point at which they declare their disability. However, it is a category about which teaching staff members felt ambivalent or even suspicious. The students who had declared dyslexia also expressed uncertainty about its status as a disability during interviews. Nonetheless, it emerged that using the label "dyslexic" offered different benefits to the students in the study.

All four dyslexic students found themselves involved in a system for disability support for the first time. While they had been at school, they had received help via systems to meet special educational needs. Provision for special educational needs applies only to pupils of school age; therefore, if they required additional support after leaving school they had to declare a disability. This involved independent assessment and subsequent allocation of funding (Disabled Students' Allowance; DSA) to pay for extra support. To receive the support from which they had benefited at school, they were obliged to place themselves in a new category – that of disabled student – which positioned them differently, and often at a disadvantage, in relation to their fellow undergraduates. When asked what they understood by the term *disability*, the students responded with a student in a wheelchair, revealing what was for them the prototypical disabled student inhabiting the figured world of the university – somebody quite different from the way they saw themselves.

The fifth student's mobility impairment qualified him as disabled. He too was ambivalent about being categorized as disabled, as it was important to him to operate as normally as possible. The support available to him as a disabled student, however, helped him cope with other difficulties that would not have been categorized as disabilities. I now discuss each student in turn.

## Ben: A "Very, Very Borderline Dyslexic"

Ben started his course in computer gaming after leaving school. He had struggled to get his problems with reading and spelling recognized at school, but was eventually assessed as dyslexic and received a statement of special educational needs entitling him to extra support. He had a clear idea of his difficulties: poor spelling, handwriting, and eye-hand coordination; memory problems, and slow reading speed. He had chosen a course in computer programming, which he found easy – "it's just something I can do" – and achieved a 2:1 upper second class degree with a lot of hard work and a very active social life.

He appreciated the unproblematic way that, as a dyslexic student, he had been able to enter the university's system of disability support, in comparison with the struggle he had had to gain this status and access help in school. However, when I looked carefully at what he actually got out of the university systems for support, it was very little: dyslexia-alert stickers for the small amount of written work he did not produce on a computer – "It's nice to put the little sticker on the top, to say, 'don't mark me on my spelling, punctuation or grammar.'" – and extra time in examinations. He didn't apply for DSA (although entitled) to buy extra equipment or to pay for printing. However, his unproblematic assumption of the position of dyslexic student in the support system gave him recognition from peers and staff that he had certain difficulties and the acceptance that these were just who he was. His fellow students teased him about his spelling, but this only seemed to cement his place in the group without positioning him less favorably:

I get a lot of gyp from friends about it, because of my spelling. But I just laugh at them.

We're very close, there's like twenty of us in our group, and banter gets passed round. So it's something that I have, that I am, so it's something that gets mentioned. But equally then, other people get stick for different things, so it's nothing that I find offensive or inappropriate. And if I ever ask for any help off anyone they would give it to me.

While he comfortably identified as dyslexic, he did not consider himself disabled. This was possibly because his particular context (a computing course with access to strategies to make assessment easier for dyslexic students) did not, in fact, disable him:

I've managed to do something to almost get around it. [the label of disability] is something that I've taken on, because it benefits me. I've had to push to get myself recognised as dyslexic, because I'm very, very borderline; my spelling is bad, and my handwriting is terrible, so it's something that I need, but it's not something that people have been willing to offer before. I wouldn't say [the label of dyslexic] is positive, I wouldn't say it was negative, it's just something that I am. It comes with its drawbacks, but then, people will try and help you so you get advantages from it as well. So it's not positive or negative, it's something that almost balances itself out.

Ben also noticed that, with the incremental structure of the course, staff members used the same conceptual tools in "building" students that programmers used to develop characters in a game; the tutors were *"just building us up so that we can do everything."* For Ben, therefore, the tools and strategies provided by the disability support system (extra time in exams and assessment stickers) worked successfully with the strategies and tools provided by his chosen discipline (spellcheckers and incremental learning). But there was also a consonance in values between the two systems; the disability support system involved making specified reasonable adjustments for particular categories of students, in the same way the programmers made little additions to build particular characters. Ben could add "+disability support" to his own character without changing who he was, a very, very borderline dyslexic.

## Bella: Contradictions over Disclosing Dyslexia

Bella was a dyslexic student taking a degree in acting. She knew she had weaknesses with spelling, reading, and memory; she had struggled in these areas through school, but had only been officially diagnosed as dyslexic after starting at university. Bella did not, however, see herself as disabled and was uncomfortable about disclosing dyslexia, even though the position of "dyslexic actor" in the acting world was presented as advantageous. Staff told her dyslexic actors are valued because of their creativity, but Bella was reluctant to declare dyslexia to visiting tutors and directors. Her tutor commented:

In my understanding there is a clear relationship between dyslexia and levels of creativity, and that's where I've had huge issues with Bella because we keep saying "look tell everybody, it's really acknowledged in the acting trade, you know, it's really, really liked; in fact, people love dyslexic actors, they think it's rather trendy!"

Bella, however, found that her reading and memory problems made it difficult for her to take part in script readings and performances where she needed to learn lines. She found some tutors were supportive and helpful, providing her with strategies to overcome her reading and memory problems. Another tutor, however, opting to make reasonable adjustments to make life easier for her, took away three-quarters of her part so she did not have so much to learn. Bella felt this discriminated against her:

When we're doing presentations in our groups, I think people assign less to me, on purpose, and even though I could probably do just as much. We were doing a play last year, and everyone was sort of struggling with lines, and I had quite a big part, but everyone else was double cast, but I just had the one part to concentrate on. And my tutor took about three-quarters of my part away from me, and gave it to someone else. And then later on I asked why, and he was like "Oh, it's because of your dyslexia." But I thought I could have done a job of it. It affects my memory, but I think everyone was like struggling to know lines but more than half of my role had been taken away from me.

Interviews with Bella and her tutor revealed the importance of fairness and trust as values that underpinned the course. Actors need to trust each other to perform effectively, and any hint of unfairness can undermine this trust. Bella felt it was unfair that she had lesser parts to play, but tutors had been told by the central disability support system to make reasonable adjustments to accommodate her dyslexia. Bella was left confused about when to disclose her dyslexia; its value changed depending on whether she was a dyslexia student working within the university system or a dyslexic actor looking outward to attract the interest of outsiders and possible employment.

### Brandon: A Dyslexic Needs a Set of Tools to Help Work the System

Brandon was in his third year studying engineering, having twice repeated a year. His difficulties with reading were noticed early in his school career and he had moved through different schools, colleges, and two universities, developing a fund of independence, self-awareness, and pragmatic approaches as he found a pathway through to the next stage. He was happy to play the system, using anything that made it easier for him to study, submit assignments, or take exams.

[For this module] there was one assignment, one in-class test and one exam. Fortunately I have a friend who's very, very good at it and I'm not, so he helped me considerably. More than he should have done really. But I heard rumours that the lecturer you get in the second year is much better, and it actually gets easier in the second year which I'm pleased to say is true. So – I cheated to get through the first year! (laughs).

He used universal services (for example, for math support), disability support services, standard dyslexia assessment adjustments, help from friends, complaints procedures – all the tools available in disability support, departmental processes, and central services. His pragmatism verged on cynicism, leading him to suspect it was the dyslexic label that had got him his previous university place to help that university to show it was recruiting disabled students:

Well, I imagine it [the label disabled] might even be a benefit because I've always been under the impression they want people with the appropriate, you know, wheelchair, black and Asian and dyslexic and blind to fill in quotas.

He had a clear idea of his own strengths (visual tasks, organization, independence, perseverance) and weaknesses (reading, writing, and capacity to grasp certain concepts). These weaknesses made studying difficult, so Brandon accepted the label "disabled student" because of what it offered him to make studying easier. He sometimes revealed an undercurrent of doubt about where the dyslexia ended and limitations in his own ability began.

[The word disability] is just a convenient title. [Dyslexia] was always termed as a learning difficulty; learning disability was stretching the gate wider.... I'm not too bothered as a title, just so people have a vague idea, to where you lie, I suppose. I suppose I don't really [consider myself disabled]. I suppose I think disabled is more in physical form, then, but, I suppose I am a bit ... sort of inconvenienced. I don't think it's always because of my dyslexia, it's just my ability overall, my dyslexia will have an effect on [it] I guess. There are some subjects I know that some people just don't get, full stop, and I think I was included in that one sadly, on top of the [dyslexia].

Brandon singled out understanding and flexibility from lecturing staff and extra time in exams in a separate room as the most helpful aspects of support. He also had one-to-one support from a dyslexia support tutor and used various technology aids (microphone and mini-disc recorder), but these were much less important.

I suppose [the fact that] people know [laughs] is the simple thing [that has resulted from disclosing my dyslexia]. I mean you get the extra time, you get the sympathy if you ask for it, a bit more understanding; if you just need a couple more days on an assignment or something you generally get it, if you don't push your luck presumably.... [The academic staff have supported me] superbly. They all understand, they're all willing to flex a little bit and if you ever need help just appear at their office and they're always willing to give some help.

His pragmatic approach – scanning interlocking systems for any mechanism that might make things work better – fit very well with the values and approach of his chosen discipline, and staff members were as keen as he was to try out the tools– as long as it didn't impair the overall efficacy of the course.

Brandon was adept practically, so lecturers did not have concerns about him coping in industry and were happy to "flex a little" and tweak exam procedures, allow retakes, and advise on modules with the most suitable assessment procedures. All his tutors had recent contact with the figured world of engineering, where making things work took priority; Brandon's position as someone who struggled academically but who worked the system to get through fit into this world more successfully than it might have done in a less vocationally orientated course.

### Barry: Dyslexia Righting Past Wrongs

Barry was a mature student in his third year of an art and design course, having repeated a year because of illness. He had struggled through school, finding himself in the remedial class and had left without taking qualifications to follow a career in manufacturing, then worked in adult custodial care. He discovered his artistic ability while attending night classes and, when illness forced him out of his job, he decided to pursue this interest into university study and was on target for a first class degree.

He was assessed as dyslexic when he started his university course and by the time of the interviews eagerly accepted the label. Barry's interviews with me during the study involved him in much discursive labor as he sought to reconcile his struggles at school and his success at university. He explained passionately the effect the label "remedial" had had on him and on his feelings of self-worth, and his decision to disclose his dyslexia:

At that time they called it remedial education, so we got the label of "rem" which stuck with me for many many years – that has more of a detrimental effect on you than the lack of the education because it's such a big handle to take through school. You got into this fear factor that you didn't really want to put up your hand, so that mental problem then and that psychological, negative imprinting, plays a part now in my psyche. [Declaring dyslexia made me feel] apprehension, because obviously I'd always looked upon it as being a negative and being very much a thing I should keep under wraps, and not express to other people … and I thought "no, you've got to bite your, sorry, suppress that, and open your mouth and mention it," and I'm glad I did, because like I say, the support has just been quality.

He had a clear idea of his strengths and weaknesses, and mentioned several things at which he excels (photography, practical work), and other things he found difficult (planning, reading, organizing written work). In interviews he readily drew attention to aspects of his own learning style that corresponded with that of a dyslexic, and enthusiastically adopted the concept of dyslexia as a difference.

Dyslexia is not to do with IQ; it's purely a learning dysfunction, i.e. in a different way. You've got to approach a dyslexic in a different way, that's all.

He found working with his dyslexia support tutor beneficial, but felt his subject tutors thought this meant he did not need any other support from them. This led to problems with relationships with his tutors, which revealed his sensitivity about how he was treated and his discomfort with the power imbalance inherent in the tutor-student relationship.

I don't like being spoken down to, and there's still that element in the education system from the tutors unfortunately who tend to treat us as if we're all college leavers … they think you're lesser than them, they're putting themselves on pedestals and at the end of the day they're only tutors, they're nothing that special.

His tutors' acknowledgment of his dyslexic status meant affirmation that he was not a "rem" but a student of equal value to the others. Barry fought for this recognition, for example, by insisting on handouts printed on yellow paper.

When discussing his studies, however, it became clear it was not his dyslexia but his medical condition, which he had not declared to disability support, that constrained his attendance and submission of assignments. Health considerations dominated many aspects of how he organized his life: *I've mapped out everything round my health.* Given that he was comfortable with the label of disabled student, and not at all reluctant to offer in-depth accounts of the effect of his medical condition, it was surprising he had not declared it and sought reasonable adjustments to accommodate his enforced absences through illness and subsequent problems with submissions. However, he knew he could make adjustments to accommodate his medical condition; he spoke about it confidently and knowledgeably, with no hint that he felt it positioned him as a "lesser mortal." He had agency here, recounting all the adjustments he was making to his lifestyle to minimize the effects of his medical condition. It could be argued that the dyslexia label was much more important for him; it distanced him from his past experience as a "rem" and offered him a new identity in relation to his fellow students that was enabling him to take part in university education on an equal basis.

## Billy: Disability Supporting Participation

Billy was a mature student on a multimedia arts course. He was recovering from heroin addiction and had a prosthetic leg and reduced function in his hands. These injuries had occurred as a result of accidents during drug episodes. Billy did not see himself as disabled but accepted he was different.

He had a clear idea of his strengths (being able to talk about his addiction to others; explaining things through "parables") and weaknesses (difficulties with analytic work as opposed to creative work). He had not intended to seek support for his mobility impairments but found out that he was eligible to receive DSA and could use the money toward a computer, which meant he could work at home. However, this was of benefit to him more because of his needs as a recovering addict than because of his mobility impairment; he still found it difficult to be around people for any length of time and was easily distracted, so preferred to work at home.

When he was taking part in activities with other students, however, rather than have reasonable adjustments made for him, he preferred to be treated just like everyone else. Possibly, at this point on his trajectory as a recovering addict, the label "disabled" conflicted with his desire to be classed as normal again; declaring disability placed him "out of the ordinary" (Jacklin, 2010). Instead of being given extra facilities to overcome his mobility impairment, Billy preferred to find his own way around the problem to produce work equivalent to what had been produced by everyone else.

The thing is with me and with my disability I don't want any extra treatment or anything. If I need anything I'll ask for it and I actually get the same as what everyone gets. I think oh I'll have a go at this and if I can't do it the way people who are able bodied do it I'll find a way to do it in my own way, and the end result is the same. They make a film and I make a film. Me personally, I don't like that word [disabled] because it means that I have limits, even though I do, but so does everyone else without a disability. So therefore it's like, "well, why aren't they tagged with something?"

Billy's struggles with difference, disability, and disadvantage in relation to other people demonstrated most clearly the dialogic nature of identity. Holland and Lave report similar inner debates of individuals in contested contexts: "Identity development can often be characterized as forming around dialogues over difference between self and internalized version(s) of 'the other'" (2009, p. 9). Billy displayed considerable insight into his own identity trajectory, which he readily shared with others. Unlike the four dyslexic students, his physical impairment clearly marked him out as different from others, but it was the persona of recovered drug addict, rather than disabled student, that Billy took on, and it was from this standpoint that he talked about himself to others. His recovery was the result of immense individual effort and determination; he had acted with agency to turn his life around and escape the limitations and pressures of his environment. He displayed the same agency in response to proposed adjustments and support; if he could make changes himself to move toward the same end result as his fellow students, then he preferred this to the possibility of having changes made for him by others.

## Advantages of Ambiguity

These brief accounts from case studies of five students who declared disability underline the importance of considering the individual in context. Each student found his or her own way of coping with this new self in relation to others. But while both brain dysfunction and the characteristics of the way our society is constituted (notably a reliance on print-based media) are considered necessary conditions for dyslexia (Danermark, 2001, p. 58), I would like to suggest the ambiguity of the category dyslexia (is it a disability? a difference? is there something physically wrong with them or are dyslexics victims of ineffective teaching or over-aspirational parents?) allows students to exist in between universal and special support systems. It enables them to take part in the disability support systems without necessarily taking on the identity of "disabled student," and to adopt a student persona in which disability is not foregrounded. For example, Brandon and Ben positioned themselves in relation to the student as party animal. Brandon distanced himself from this – *It wasn't the usual student get drunk and party because I just don't do that, it's not me* – while Ben accepted going out and getting drunk as a normal part of student life: *it was standard … getting hammered…. I spent a lot of time in the pub.* For them, these were more salient possible ways of being a student than being dyslexic.

Positioning themselves on the fringes of the disability support system offers students choices about how to understand and explain their difficulties with university study. Holland and colleagues (1998) explore the benefits offered by ambiguity in Lachicotte's study of Roger, a patient whose mental health difficulties were difficult to diagnose, but who found the eventual diagnosis of borderline personality disorder allowed him to work through concerns about culpability and will (whose fault was it, and what could he do about it?).

By becoming borderline at the proper times and places, Roger empowered a sense of agency, his active self-expression, without letting go the legitimate disabilities of his illness. (Holland et al., 1998, p. 207)

This "double posturing" means individuals can call on two kinds of discursive work; having something physically wrong with me offers a release from blame, but acknowledgment of environmental effects (contextual barriers to participation) enables me to avoid the determinism of biological deficit.

## Implications for Inclusive Provision in Higher Education

Examination of the ways these five students used the tools available to them as students who had declared disability within the system of disability support, while questioning the effects of assuming the label of disabled student on their sense of self, shows the usefulness of both kinds of analysis. The original activity theory analysis led to understanding how contradictions arose in the use of tools, rules, and values in linked activity systems, while pursuing an analysis using concepts developed in Holland's work and paying particular attention to differences among participants revealed the differences in the experiences of individuals who, in terms of division of labor, occupied the same part in the system.

I suggest students like the five described here who, for a variety of reasons, are positioned at the boundaries of disability, are particularly likely to be involved in exploring the limits of systems for disability support and bringing contradictions to light. Because the ambiguity of their position blurs the line between disabled and nondisabled student, this has the potential to inform the development of inclusive provision and to promote exploration of the effects of impairment beyond unhelpful polarizations of the medical and social model of disability. The support these students required to help them overcome barriers to participation in higher education depended not only on the exact nature of their impairment, but also on their individual history of coping with that impairment, as well as the particular characteristics of their chosen course of study. Such an approach is consistent with Shakespeare's (2006) interactional model of disability, which recognizes the importance of physical impairment in the socially constructed world of the disabled individual, and Macdonald's (2009) sociological model of dyslexia, which accepts a biological ontology to learning difficulties but indicates the impact social organization/interpretation has on constructing discrimination and exclusion for these groups.

Students with impairments have been compared to canaries in the mine; the first to be affected by pedagogical practices that ultimately may affect all (Jacklin, 2010). Adjustments originally introduced to accommodate the needs of disabled students (availability of lecture notes before sessions; choice of assessment mode) have met a more widespread need that spans the current disabled/nondisabled divide. Billy's reflection on his own identity trajectory – we all have limits, so why are some limits recognized and entitled to special support (and draw discriminatory attitudes)? – extends ambiguity to the concept of disability itself. This point is taken a step further by Shakespeare to remove the distinction between disabled and nondisabled

154 Georgeson

altogether; "We believe that the claim that everyone is impaired, not just 'dis-abled people,' is a far-reaching and important insight into human experience, with major implications for medical and social intervention in the twenty-first century" (Shakespeare & Watson, 2002, p. 25). The insights shown by the individuals described here hint at ways regulated provision for disabled students could develop into inclusive provision that would benefit all.

## References

Danermark, B. (2001). Interdisciplinary research and critical realism – The example of disability research. *Paper presented at 5th Annual IACR Conference*. Roskilde University, Denmark, June 2001.

Fuller, M., Georgeson, J., Healey, M., Hurst, A., Riddell, S., Roberts. H., and Weedon, E. (2009). *Improving Disabled Student Learning in Higher Education*. London: Routledge.

Georgeson, J. M. (2009). Organisational Structures for Disability Support: Contradictions as Catalysts for Change, in M. Fuller, J. Georgeson, M. Healey, A. Hurst, S. Riddell, H., Roberts and E. Weedon (Eds.), *Improving Disabled Student Learning In Higher Education*. (pp. 146–163). London: Routledge.

Higher Education Statistics Agency (HESA). (2011). *Students and Qualifiers Data Tables* Available at http://www.hesa.ac.uk/index.php?option=com_datatables&Itemid=121&task=show_category&catdex=3#disab (accessed April 26, 2011).

Holland, D., Lachicotte, W., Skinner, D., and Cain, C. (1998). *Identity and Agency in Cultural Worlds*. Cambridge, MA: Harvard University Press.

Holland, D. W. and Lave, J. (2009). Social practice theory and the historical production of persons. *Actio: An International Journal of Human Activity Theory*, **2**, 1–15.

Jacklin, A. (2010). To be or not to be "a disabled student" in higher education: The case of a postgraduate "non-declaring" (disabled) student. *Journal of Research in Special Educational Needs*, (forthcoming: Article first published online May 19, 2010).

Macdonald, S. J. (2009). *Towards a Sociology of Dyslexia: Exploring links between dyslexia, disability and social class*. Saarbrucken, VDM Publishing House Ltd.

Mills, D. (2007). Dyslexia: A big, expensive myth. *Daily Telegraph*, January 15, 2007. Available at http://www.telegraph.co.uk/health/children_shealth/3347022/Dyslexia-a-big-expensive-myth.html (accessed April 29, 2011).

Redford, K. (2007). Disability awareness training – The big picture. *Training and Coaching Today*, **17** July. Available at http://www.personneltoday.com/articles/2007/07/17/41447/disability-awareness-training-the-big-picture.html (accessed April 26, 2011).

Shakespeare, T. (2006). *Disability Rights and Wrongs*. London: Routledge.

Shakespeare, T. and Watson, N. (2002). The social model of disability: An outdated ideology? *Research in Social Science and Disability*, **2**, 9–28.

Urrieta, L. Jr., (2007). Figured worlds and education: An introduction to the special issue. *The Urban Review*, **39** (2), 107–16.

# 10

# Internship: Navigating the Practices of an Investment Bank

## Natalie Lundsteen and Anne Edwards

The internship now replaces the starting job as the place where college students actually begin their journey into the workplace. (Gardner, 2011, p. 1)

For many college students, internships are the first places where education and work intersect; yet we know very little about what happens when students move, mid course, from sites of formal study to the workplace. Despite the lack of information, internships are popular with students, universities, and employers. Their prevalence has increased over the past two decades, with participation growing from 17 per cent of graduates having experienced them in 1992, to over 50 per cent of college students undertaking at least one internship before graduation in 2008. Many university courses now offer internships for academic credit; across higher education university career services help students find and organise personal internship experiences. The latter kind of internship is the focus of this chapter. As a university career counsellor in both the United States and the United Kingdom, Lundsteen grew increasingly aware of the unquestioned popularity of internships and the lack of preparation students received prior to undertaking them.

Their unquestioned benefits are based on linking internship with employability. Internships are therefore encouraged by universities seeking proof of the economic relevance of their courses and by students who aim at entering the job market with goods to offer potential employers. For employers, internships also often operate as auditions where talent can be spotted. These multiple yet overlapping purposes have led to a degree of conceptual confusion with strong claims made for their value and too little attention paid to how these different purposes play out in the internships students experience.

Most research on internships, funded as it is by universities and driven by a concern with graduate employability, has examined how universities prepare graduates for full-time employment. Findings from these studies have pointed to the value of gaining workplace skills or to the increased economic benefits internships provide both students and employers. These studies have generally assumed knowledge transfers between different work settings, taking the stance that college graduates should be able to move effortlessly into the world of work, using skills gained from internships.

University career counsellors therefore promote the idea of developing and recognising transferable skills such as problem solving, and encourage participation in internships as a way of honing them. However, there is little evidence that students transfer broad work-relevant skills from their time at university and internships into post-graduation workplaces. Recent research reveals a significant proportion of U.S. undergraduates demonstrate no marked improvement in their critical thinking, complex reasoning, and writing skills during their university education (Arum & Roksa, 2011). These skills form the basis of the so-called transferable skills students are meant to carry from the university to the workplace, and the implications of their absence are provocative for universities and higher education policy makers. If internships are not honing transferable skills and increasing employability, what are they doing and what is being learnt while participating in them? We suggest it is therefore timely to open up the black box of internships and examine what happens when students engage in them, what skills they use, and what they learn.

While delving into the black box, we have drawn on some of the analytic tools offered by Cultural Historical Activity Theory (CHAT). These tools have allowed us to examine the trajectories of students during internships and to study their transitions from university to a workplace as a process of navigation through practices. The use of CHAT concepts has meant interrelationships between learners and practices are highlighted, and learning is seen as an outcome of engagement in activities shaped by culture. In brief, the CHAT analytic resources we outline have been used to identify how students try to make sense of the practices they encounter, take up opportunities for particular forms of action in activities, develop ways of being, and seek out and work with the mediational means found in the workplace.

The discussion is based on a study of six university students from one elite English university who were following different degree programs. The students arranged the internships without university help, as the experience was not part of their programmes of study. The three-month summer internships were on the trading floor of an investment bank based in London. The highly competitive practices of the floor offered a particularly challenging learning environment for the students and threw into relief how cultural practices shape activities and permissible actions. The intention therefore is not to generalise from one workplace, but to identify how CHAT tools can assist in the analysis of the demands and possibilities found in internships.

The students were tracked over their three-month paid internships (Lundsteen, 2011), with data collected over three summers while each intern worked in the bank during one university vacation. Each student was interviewed prior to and after the internship and three times during his or her time in the bank. Lundsteen also spent time in the bank observing the interns' interactions at work to ground the interviews in the practices of the trading floor. The interviews were transcribed and aimed at eliciting how the students learned to interpret and engage with these practices; whether or not they were supported as learners when entering a workplace where aggressive and competitive practices were the norm; and how identities changed as students aligned their individual motives with workplace practices.

A key feature of the analysis was the identification of what the students were learning. It quickly became apparent that what they learnt consisted of first identifying what was regarded as valued behaviour in the workplace, then recognising more deeply what mattered in the practices and finally, for some, aligning their own actions and motives with what mattered in the established practices of the bank. Attention to the motives that shaped trading floor practices and the activities that comprised them together with the ability to accept and work with them marked those who were offered posts on graduation and who decided to accept them. This finding was arrived at by using CHAT concepts to examine how students navigated the landscape of the investment bank; the processes of implicit and explicit mediation they experienced; the relational support, if any, offered in the workplace; and how the trading floor provided opportunities for the students' development as potential investment bankers or as people who decided banking was not for them.

None of the interns anticipated difficulties in adjusting to the trading floor. They were all successful students in a university where competition was the norm. Yet they utterly underestimated their need for feedback which would mediate for them what mattered in these new practices. They entered an environment where they wanted to succeed: that is to at least receive an offer of a post even though they might reject it. They also recognised that for the bank, their internships were auditions rather than learning opportunities and the stakes were high. What they learnt owed very little to their university courses and very much more to their capacity to watch, analyse, and act carefully. This chapter next discusses how this fits with universities' concerns with employability and the transferability of skills from higher education.

## From Transfer to Transition

What was happening for the students was captured by the CHAT approach to transfer of learning. The CHAT line is to talk of transitions between practices and developing a capacity for sense making, rather than of transferring knowledge and skills from university courses into workplace tasks. Nonetheless, the currently entrenched view of movement from university to workplace that influences so much policy on graduate employability is, as we have already observed, rooted in the idea of knowledge transfer.

The use of the terms *transferable* and *employable* skills in relation to undergraduates implies a student's readiness to enter the workplace (Harvey & Bowers-Brown, 2003), where *employability* is defined as: 'the qualities needed to maintain employment and progress in the workplace' or 'ensuring students find jobs' (AGCAS, 2010). It can also be summarised as 'a set of achievements – skills, understandings and personal attributes – that make graduates more likely to gain employment and be successful in their chosen occupations, which benefits themselves, the workforce, the community and the economy' (Yorke & Knight, 2004, p. 3). This line of thought leads us to expect that what students have learned about substantive topics and about processes such as report writing and seeking support are transferred with ease from university to workplace.

However, we know transfer is far from easy. Pea has described knowledge transfer as 'a process of recognizing the similarities between a past situation *x* (source) and current situation *y* (target), and then using the details of one's memory of *x* to structure and elaborate one's understanding of *y* (1987, pp. 644–45). But this definition suggests transfer relies heavily on similarities between the two situations. It is therefore unsurprising that ease of transfer, or what Sfard has termed *acquisition and application* (Sfard, 1998), is increasingly questioned in the literature on learning and the workplace.

Hager locates the problem of transfer in what he sees as a limited understanding of learning and learning outcomes. 'Transfer is assumed to be unproblematic' because it is viewed in the same way as education-based learning, 'a pure learning-as-product approach' (2004, p. 5). According to Hager, 'the point of transfer is not replication'. He proposes instead looking at learning in terms of how an individual 'knows with' rather than 'knows that' (replication) or 'knows how' (application) (2004, p. 10). Here Hager points to what will be our suggestion – that having concepts with which to interrogate workplace practices may be a useful way of preparing students for understanding and acting in internship workplaces.

Despite the growing critique, transfer persists as a dominant metaphor in the employability discourse. Even Eraut, in his extensive work on professional learning (2001, 2004a, 2004b), sustains the transfer metaphor, while offering a Vygotskian twist. He sees transfer as an active process, highly mediated, where more competent others help learners reshape what they know. The emphasis on mediation here suggests he is talking about transition, rather than transfer as application of knowledge. Transfer is, from this perspective, not a simple process of knowledge application, but rather a more complex process of mediated engagement with the knowledge-laden practices that make up what Holland and her colleagues (1998) have termed the 'figured worlds' of workplaces.

Features of workplace practices, according to the perspective offered by Holland, structure the opportunities for learning as well as for work. Edwards (2009, 2010) suggests too little emphasis is placed on how others may act as resources to support action in the workplace. Drawing on Lundvall's (1996) idea of the importance of 'know-who', she has pointed to the existence of what she terms *distributed expertise* and the capacity to work with what others offer. However, the competitive structuring of the trading floor meant any distribution of expertise was highly boundaried. The strength of these boundaries was most evident in the students' fruitless seeking for mediation that might support their navigation of the bank's practices.

## The Object Motive in Practices

The study was based in the premise that practices in institutional settings are historical accumulations of interactions where 'the purposes of activities are shaped by the practices in which they are set' (Edwards, 2010, p. 6), and these purposes have the potential to sustain a dynamic which ensures practitioners engage and reengage with the knowledge that matters. In the bank the interns engaged with artefacts and in activities which appeared similar to university, such as using computer software or working in project groups. However, the purposes of the engagement were different because the motives that shaped the practices within which the activities were set were different from those of the university.

The CHAT perspective is helpful in identifying how these artefacts and activities differed between institutional practices. Leont'ev's work on the object of activity and the object motive is key here. He argued activities could be distinguished by 'the difference in their objects i.e. what was recognized as important and was being worked on. It is exactly the object of activity that gives it a determined direction ... the object of activity is its true motive' (1978, p. 17).

On the trading floor, the object motive in almost every activity was winning by making a profit. In the university, it was demonstrating a capability by solving a problem. Therefore, to operate within the practices of the bank, the interns needed to recognise and value what mattered within its socially and culturally constructed realm (Holland et al., 1998, p. 52) and adjust their actions and reactions to align with the motives of the bank's practices and the activities that comprised them.

The idea of the figured world (Holland et al., 1998) provided a lens through which we could discern how the interns recognised and navigated the practices of the workplace – those norms and expectations that were both overt and covert. The 'figured' aspects of a setting encompass individual conceptions of that setting's expectations, norms, practices, how things work, what counts as meaningful in a context, and the implicit or explicit routines that form and shape a 'world'. The interns were continuously engaged in a process of recognising the figured world created in the practices of the trading floor; making sense of what they observed; and deciding whether to participate in those practices. The trading floor of a global investment bank, an industry with many layers of behavioural standards, principles, and values was an especially rich setting for observing the sense making and subsequent actions of interns as they attempted to participate meaningfully in what mattered there.

## The Importance of Interpretation and Engagement

To succeed in a workplace, student interns found they needed to read rules, whether explicit or implicit, and to align themselves with what they saw as valued in the practices they entered. Examples of what mattered included working long hours, rigorous attention to detail, speed in accomplishing tasks, and self-sufficiency. Persistence was also important. The interns engaged in cycles of reading the practices, attempting action, rereading the situation, and trying again. In an environment where rules were never explicitly mediated, the process of first determining and then meeting or exceeding expectations took time. The interns explained:

But people aren't perhaps as easy to approach or … I'm not being checked up on as much as I anticipated. There isn't that check from my line manager "How far are you along with the project?" There hasn't been a timescale set on me, so I don't know if I'm over-performing or under-performing. And perhaps I would have expected to be kept in just a little bit more check, rather than left to my own devices quite so much.

"You've got to prove yourself, but don't annoy anyone on the trading floor."

You just have to be careful and observant basically … other people were complaining that other interns were being really rude. But … they were just having the kind of normal discussion that you would normally have at university, but it just becomes so apparent that that's just not appropriate at all … well, it's just interesting what's acceptable and what isn't acceptable.

These comments illustrate how the interns recognised that motives shaping the bank's practices were different from those in an academic setting. They recognised, for example, that to know how to align themselves with the bank's motives, they needed to work independently with very little supervision and to observe colleagues. Lachicotte explains this process of learning:

directly from more knowledgeable participants, from their responses … how to sense the framework which organizes the activity. One learns practically the "moves" one might make and the possible roles that one might play. (2009, p. 227)

All six interns struggled, with varying degrees of success, to read the practices and align their actions with what mattered within them. Variation was based on whether they had prior work experience in banking or finance and were therefore better attuned to recognising and responding to what was valued in activities on the trading floor.

## Support for Learning in the Practices

All six interns survived, completed assignments, and eventually learnt to appear to fit in. Their apparent successful engagement with the practices occurred primarily through an independent, yet continual, process of internalisation and externalisation: observing the work of colleagues on the trading floor, seeking patterns and consistencies, attempting action, failing or succeeding at those actions, eventually making sense of what they observed, and at times in limited ways contributing to the shared meaning making that comprised the public discourse of the floor. However, they had not anticipated learning in this way. They had expected much more guidance, drawing on university-based models of learning where instruction and guidance were the norm. They therefore had to quickly unlearn expectations of the support with which they were familiar at university.

The unlearning was more intense for those without prior relevant experience. The interns with some experience of banking work unsurprisingly knew how to seek and use templates for producing documents, often referencing banking industry tools such as Investopedia or Excel, and understood the right time and manner in which to ask questions of colleagues. They were also, important, able to read more complex patterns in the behaviours of other workers and to externalise these understandings and thus move themselves forward in the unwritten rules and expectations in the practices. Here is one more experienced intern describing a colleague on the trading floor.

I had him down straight away.… I could tell he was wearing an Italian made suit. Second off, I could see he had his initials on his shirt. Third I could see he was wearing a Hermes tie, fourth he had a Rolex watch, and fifth he had some amazing leather shoes. I thought, this guy likes things precise ... he's young, he's head of desk. So I thought he is quite a difficult guy to impress, you can't give him any bullshit, you've got to be kind of straight to the point with him.

The more experienced interns also recognised that opportunities for gaining support through building relationships and networks were very limited. Access to others was felt to be crucial for undertaking unfamiliar work tasks, but no guidance was given to the interns on how to develop such networks and few relationships were forthcoming. The interns who occasionally found an expert other to explain things were fortunate, because in the competitive atmosphere on the trading floor it was rare for any employee to take much interest in helping another, particularly one lower down the hierarchy. Amongst the six interns, only one female intern developed a sustained mentor-mentee relationship with expert guidance from a senior woman, and this was based on a shared cultural background.

How the interns approached their work tasks gave a clear view of the degree of their engagement with the motives in the practices of the bank. The interns with experience of work were more able to directly engage with work tasks, emphasising what mattered in a task, such as speed of response, and could more easily approach other employees and ask relevant questions. The interns without previous work experience spent a great deal of time at the start of the internship waiting for direction and trying to find purpose in activities.

Because so much of both the setting at the bank and the general knowledge of a professional workplace was new to the inexperienced interns, the internship also involved individual episodes of reflection. These illustrated processes of transition, as the interns attempted to learn about the banking industry and its purposes.

As already indicated, what mattered most in the workplace practices was an element of extreme competition, of being the best, and 'winning'. The concept of winning was not specifically linked to any contests or rewards (except, perhaps, annual bonuses), but rivalry permeated all the activities of the work system and meant the interns entered a professional discourse where knowledge was rarely shared.

The nature of work on the trading floor, marked by rapid execution and competition, meant more experienced members of staff did not have time to instruct or guide new employees, and the competitive aspects of the industry meant even colleagues could be considered rivals for closing deals or gaining bonuses. The interns were at the bottom of the trading floor hierarchy, part of a team for only a short time, and therefore not worth investing in. The competitive setting and the nature of the work on the trading floor affected each of the interns' learning trajectories at the bank. The rewards of work could be great for those able to move up the hierarchy, and the atmosphere was intense because of the risk and reward involved in the workplace activities.

At the same time, the interns also came to realise the professionals who were their superiors did not always possess vast amounts of knowledge about banking or markets, but instead operated with what could be termed a superficial level of information. The ways knowledge was mediated in the workplace were therefore important. For example, the arrangement of work groups on the trading floor into 'desks', which were not cohesive teams or units but rather sharply boundaried knowledge systems, were not always opened up to the interns. There were also harsh restrictions for interns on the use of telephones and data as workplace tools because of industry regulations. Above all, the purposely disconnected information flow, where information was guarded and not shared freely even among employees in the same work team, shaped practices so that they were not geared to knowledge sharing. Here is one first-time intern who reported colleagues on his desk all spoke Italian when he was around so that he could not follow conversations. Note his use of terminology: *studying* and *learn*. He had yet to make the transition into the bank's practices.

I am kind of left at my desk, although I have a project to do.... I just go to my desk and sort of read through pamphlets and things that turn up ... but there is no direction to what I am studying, I just don't think that can be the most efficient way to learn. I would be grateful for someone just giving me a little more direction.

If 'knowledge runs on rails laid by practice' (Brown & Duguid, 2001, p. 204), the knowledge within the investment bank's practices was like a private train the interns could not board without being accompanied by an experienced member of staff, and there was no movement between cars. Part of what allowed the bank to operate with such levels of opacity was the way so much of the knowledge within the practices was tacit, or even deliberately obscured, and as tasks were passed down the hierarchy the interns were at the very bottom of the chain, receiving the least amount of information.

Citigroup's CEO describes investment banking as an industry where 'people learn from the people above them and they copy the actions of the people above them' (Cassidy, 2010, p. 49). The mystique of the banker and the identity of the obnoxious wealthy trader are stereotypes most of the investment bank's employees were happy to perpetuate. In hindsight, it can be seen that their practices were not open to scrutiny because until 2007, the industry was too powerful to be questioned (Sorkin, 2009) and the practices encouraged concealment. Thus, getting the whole picture of work systems was deliberately made impossible. For example, one intern tried to unravel the rationale behind one of the financial products being analysed and sold on his desk and came to the conclusion they were 'bundles of nothing'. But his managers told him not to be concerned with the rationale behind such products and discouraged his attempts to learn more about them.[1]

Without access to basic knowledge for work tasks, and without understanding the figured world of the bank, the interns could find themselves paralysed while they waited vainly for guidance. In addition to waiting for direction, the novice interns were also initially concerned with working outside the hours they were expected to work and the implicit rules for clothing and physical appearance. The inexperienced interns often commented on the lack of training, or how they wished the bank would provide more or better tools to help them learn. The more experienced interns, as we have seen, moved beyond those basic concerns and gave attention to reading the intentions of their work colleagues and interpreting those intentions in the form of actions taken with work tasks.

The unwritten rules of the figured world of the investment bank in the study were probably similar to expectations in most professional workplaces: exhibit modest and appropriate behaviour, respect the knowledge of more experienced colleagues, undertake all assignments with as much intelligence and competence as possible, engage fully in the work, deliver results, build connections in the workplace, and find a mentor or guide if possible. Aspects distinctive about the trading floor relate to the specific work of financial markets, including the Chinese walls[2] that required complete confidentiality regarding certain clients or projects, the incredibly large sums of money moving around the markets and the associated risk factors, along with the high-profile clients that might include governments or global corporations. The challenges of the work on the trading floor were considerable even for the interns familiar with a banking workplace.

## Developing Identity in Practices

The interns' own identities mediated their interpretations and actions in the trading floor practices. The more closely their own motives were to those of the bank, the more clearly the interns could see their way to align with what

---

[1]   The same financial instruments, collateral debt obligations, have been referenced as significant in the collapse of many investment banks, including the site of the present study, in 2007 (Lewis, 2010; Sorkin, 2009).
[2]   Chinese wall: The ethical (not physical) barrier between different divisions of a financial (or other) institution to avoid conflict of interest (Investopedia, 2010).

mattered in the practices, and the easier it was for them to develop the identities that mediated their successful engagement.

CHAT tools were again helpful here. Learning is not just seen as acquisition of knowledge but is also evidenced in the construction of identity, for example seen in Bruner's notion of 'learning to become' (1987, p. 15). Learning therefore reflects both how a learner interprets and acts on the world and how the world recognises and responds to the learner (Brown & Duguid, 2001). In brief, identity from this perspective involves the ability to act in socially recognised ways (Gee, 2000), and therefore mediates how we interpret and act on the world.

The identities shaped during the internships were given direction by what mattered for each intern. Not all of the interns intended to work ultimately in investment banking, but all wanted successful internships. Success would be marked by an offer of full-time employment. However, a willingness to accept the offer depended on whether the intern had decided to align their motives with those of the bank.

The decision about aligning personal motives with those that shaped the bank's practices came at different points in the internships, and most interns did decide to engage. Once an intern began to see more in the practices and activities of the trading floor and attempted to align his or her own personal values with what mattered for the bank, he or she engaged in more detailed observation, internalising expectations of behaviour and following what leads they could discern in the behaviour of more experienced colleagues.

Because the interns were often invisible in the practices of the bank, their identity work was an isolated process requiring considerable persistence. Being ignored, insulted, blanked, or cut out of the knowledge and work of the team were features of both the hierarchy and the bounded knowledge communities of the trading floor desks. Therefore, the process of identity development occurred slowly.

The speed with which a banking identity could be constructed was therefore influenced in part by how easy it was for the interns to align their personal motives with those of the bank. As Edwards notes, one's identity comes from 'what matters to us' (2010, p. 10), and different things mattered for each intern. It was not enough to enter the internship with the motive of winning the offer of a post. There needed to be a more fundamental concurrence of personal motives with what mattered in the practices of the trading floor for alignment to occur.

The internships therefore provided useful opportunities for self-reflection about what was important in life. One of the interns, an excellent university athlete, began her internship with hopes of receiving a full-time offer. However, after recognising the motives of the trading floor during her internship, she concluded she did not wish to align herself with them. She was pleased to be seen as a person who could fit in there, and received an offer of work at the end of her internship, but she also came to understand she would rather be seen as a successful student and athlete than as part of investment banking.

## Concluding Points

Internships of the kind discussed in this chapter have multiple purposes: for employers, they are a selection opportunity, for students they may be auditions or may be shaped by curiosity about an employment sector. There was little evidence that the students saw themselves developing skills that would transfer to another workplace and increase their employability more generally.

The problem they faced manifested itself as a tension between the lack of receptivity in the workplace and the interns' strong desire to find a way of at least appearing to fit in. The interns in the present study were rarely seen by work colleagues as potential coworkers who might usefully contribute to work systems. They spent a great deal of time learning the norms of the workplace, while attempting to appear to be suitable potential employees. Although there was little evidence of the interns honing transferable workplace skills such as problem solving or report writing, there was a great deal of evidence of their struggling to manage unaided transitions into specific workplace practices which initially they could only grasp at a superficial level. It was also very clear that interns who had previously managed similar transitions were better placed to interpret these superficial features and to respond to them.

Investment banking may offer an extreme example of an internally competitive work environment where feedback is lacking and indeed unaided survival is seen as an asset.

Nonetheless, we suggest students could be prepared for internships by recognising that they are to undergo a transition from one practice to another very different one. To that end we suggest transfer is an unhelpful metaphor for students who expect their capacity for, for example, report writing and data analysis to be a sufficient basis for their success in organisational practices.

We therefore suggest an emphasis on personal transitions from one practice to another, together with attention to what matters in the practices in the workplace and its wider organisational setting would provide students with a strong starting point for their engagement in internships. We also suggest interns would be helped by access to intellectual tools that allow them to recognise how these purposes and values play out in the figured world of the workplace. These tools may have saved the novice interns in the present study a great deal of time and may have allowed them to engage earlier with what learning opportunities were afforded by the trading floor.

This suggestion takes us to another contribution to internships to be made by CHAT. Vygotsky's psychology was an emancipatory one where education played a key role. The role of the educator was to help the learner work with increasingly powerful ideas or conceptual tools as they operated in and on the world. The account of internship we have presented leads us to propose that the six interns would have been helped by access to some of the conceptual tools we have employed in analysing their progress in the bank.

We therefore suggest a key understanding for prospective university interns is that workplaces are structured as sets of practices comprised of different activities in which organizational motives play out. Recognising and engaging with what matters in the workplace at the level of each activity is the most basic of employability skills and, we suggest, needs greater emphasis.

Internships, if handled as a first foray into work practices upon which students are encouraged to reflect, may play an important part in preparing students for later transitions into other workplaces. We would also suggest the analytic tools offered by CHAT and discussed here may be of use to students in their reflections.

### References

Association of Graduate Careers Advisory Services (AGCAS), (2010). AGCAS website: http://www.agcas.org.uk/.

Arum, R. and Roksa, J. (2011). *Academically Adrift*. Chicago, IL: University of Chicago Press.

Brown, J. S. and Duguid, P. (2001). Knowledge and organisation: A social-practice perspective, *Organization Science*, **12**(2), 198–213.

Bruner, J. (1987). Life as narrative. *Social Research*, **54**(1), 11–32.

Cassidy, J. (2010, 29th November). What Good is Wall Street?, *The New Yorker*, 49–57.

Edwards, A. (2009). Agency and Activity Theory: From the systemic to the relational. In A. Sannino, H. Daniels and K. Gutierrez (Eds.), *Learning and Expanding with Activity Theory*. Cambridge University Press. 197–211.

(2010). *Becoming an Expert Practitioner: The relational turn in expertise*. Dordecht: Springer.

Eraut, M. (2001). *Developing Professional Knowledge and Competence*. London: RoutledgeFalmer.

(2004a). Transfer of knowledge between education and workplace settings. In H. Rainbird, A. Fuller, and A. Munro (Eds.), *Workplace Learning in Context*. (pp. 201–221). London: Routledge.

(2004b). Informal learning in the workplace, *Studies in Continuing Education*, **26** (2), 247–73.

Gardner, P. (2011). *Internships as High Stakes Events.* CERI. Michigan State University. http://www.ceri.msu.edu/wp-content/uploads/2010/01/High-Stakes-Internships.pdf.

Gee, J. (2000). Identity as an analytic lens for research in education, *Review of Research in Education,* **25**, 99–125.

Hager, P. (2004). Conceptions of learning and understanding learning at work. *Studies in Continuing Education,* **26** (1), 3–17.

Harvey, L. and Bowers-Brown, T. (2003). *The Employability of Graduates: Cross-country comparisons,* DfES Research Conference, Learning by Comparison: International Experiences in Education and Training: A Selection of Papers, Research Report: CR2003. 107–123, (Nottingham, DfES) ISBN 1844783138, available at http://www.dfes.gov.uk/research/data/uploadfiles/CR2003.pdf.

Holland, D., Lachicotte, W., Skinner, D., and Cain, C. (1998). *Identity and Agency in Cultural Worlds.* Harvard University Press.

Investopedia, (2010). www.investopedia.com/dictionary.

Lachicotte, W. (2009). Identity, agency and social practice. In H. Daniels, H. Lauder, and J. Porter (Eds.), *Educational Theories, Cultures and Learning.* (pp. 223–235). London: Routledge.

Leont'ev, A. (1978). *Activity, Consciousness, and Personality.* Englewood Cliffs, NJ: Prentice-Hall.

Lewis, M. (2010). *The Big Short.* New York: W. W. Norton & Company.

Lundsteen, N. (2011). *Learning between University and the World of Work,* Doctoral dissertation, University of Oxford. *Oxford University Research Archive:* http://ora.ox.ac.uk/objects/uuid%3Af2686c18–4133–4561–9835-ae0e3f6ab8d9.

Lundvall, B. (1996). The social dimension of the learning economy. *DRUID (Danish Research Unit for Industrial Dynamics) Working Paper* 96–1, Department of Business Studies, Aalborg University,.

Pea, R. (1987). Socializing the knowledge transfer problem. In E. De Corte (Ed.), *International Journal of Educational Research: Acquisition and transfer of knowledge and cognitive skills.* **11**, 38–62.

Sfard, A. (1998). On two Metaphors for learning and the dangers of choosing just one. *Educational Researcher,* **27**(2) 4–13.

Sorkin, A. (2009). *Too Big to Fail: The inside story of how Wall Street and Washington fought to save the financial system – and themselves.* New York: Viking.

Yorke, M. and Knight, P. T. (2004). *Embedding Employability into the Curriculum.* York: Higher Education Academy.

# 11

# Identity Change in the Context of Higher Education Institutions

## Jorge Larreamendy-Joerns

Universities, like many other human institutions, create social facts. By grant- ing diplomas at the culmination of an educational process, institutions of higher education create kinds of people: physicians, educators, psychologists, or engineers, who are socially and culturally recognized as such and who are endowed with entitlements and obligations. The social facts that universities create are professional identities. One day one is simply a student, the next day, by virtue of a graduation ceremony, a psychologist or a physician. Yet, the punctual creation of professional identities as social facts, through acts such as rituals and ceremonies and the like, tends to downplay the fact that profes- sional identity is not simply an institutional precipitate, but rather a condition negotiated and renegotiated in the course of everyday practices.

In this chapter, I draw on theoretical resources from CHAT and evidence from interviews with advanced psychology students to argue that one of the critical contributions of CHAT to our thinking about higher education is to underscore learning as a constitution of professional identities (its ontologi- cal side), and not just as the acquisition of knowledge and skills (its episte- mological side). Institutions of higher education should and usually do offer, in various forms and degrees, opportunities for students to author them- selves and provide identity resources for students to embrace in the context of the particular signified worlds that characterize disciplines and profes- sions. I use as an illustration of the mobility of students' identities in the context of higher education institutions a snapshot of a period of transition when psychology students, at the end of their undergraduate studies, have a supervised practicum and have for the first time the opportunity of con- ducting themselves as psychologists in relation to real clients. The supervised practicum, we have learned, leads students to make choices and position themselves with respect to identity models that mediate their participation in professional scenarios. It also shows the potency of higher education institutions to mobilize subjectivities by setting conditions for students to engage in authentic practices.

I refer not to just any psychology students, but to students in an undergraduate program in Latin America. Context here makes all the difference, for their experience is shaped not only by their individual choices, but also by the sociohistorical context of the institutions they inhabit. In particular, I examine the process of identity formation of a group of students at a critical historical juncture, namely, the recent attempts of teaching universities to transform themselves into research institutions. Evidence suggests such changes have had an impact on what students come to expect of themselves in terms of their emerging professional competences and, in turn, how the institution comes to "imagine" its students.

This chapter is organized as follows. First, I provide a CHAT view on the concept of identity, which subsumes that of professional identity. I focus especially on the view of identity developed by Holland and collaborators (Holland et al., 1998), which will be used as an analytical frame to address the interview data. Second, I provide a brief account of relevant features of higher education in the domain of psychology in Latin America in general and Colombia in particular. Then, an analysis of the emerging identities of advanced psychology students is presented. Finally, I draw some conclusions.

## Identity in CHAT

Professional identity is an instance of the broader concept of identity. Identity is, of course, a concept with its own scholarly history, one that has been a subject of study in many academic traditions. However, over the past decade, there has been a renewed interest in identity in the CHAT literature, fueled by the idea that learning should encompass not only how someone comes to know something, but also, and fundamentally, how learners come to be particular types of people (Boaler & Greeno, 2000; Holland & Lachicotte, 2007; Holland et al., 1998; Packer & Goicoechea, 2000; Penuel & Wertsch, 1995; Roth & Tobin, 2007a; Sfard & Prusak, 2005; Wortham, 2006).

Broadly conceived, *identity* refers to the kinds of answers someone might give to questions such as: Who am I? How do I fit into the world? And, where am I located within a particular community? As Roth and Tobin (2007b) argue, the challenge of any theory of identity is to account for the sense of constancy and permanence in how one engages in and with the world, on one hand, and for the sense of diversity and change over time, on the other, that are simultaneously part of the human experience.

In an early work, Lave and Wenger introduced the concept of identity to the learning literature. If learning is defined, as Lave and Wenger propose, as "an evolving form of membership" in a community of practice, it is apparent that learning involves a transformation of how an individual stands and acts within his or her community (1991, p. 53). Penuel and Wertsch (1995) have noted that how an individual acts and where he or she stands is a function of the cultural resources available in the community (identity models to be taken up) and the individual choices made in the context of day-by-day interactions. Thus, identity is not simply an act of will or self-convincement, but a negotiation between individual actions and the resources the context provides.

One influential, and somewhat integrative, perspective on identity in the CHAT literature has been advanced by Holland and colleagues. They draw on the work of Vygotsky, Bakhtin, and Bourdieu to propose a view of identity in practice. According to Holland, "[i]dentity is one way of naming the dense interconnections between the intimate and public venues of social practice" (Holland et al., 1998, p. 270), that is, one way to go beyond the dichotomy between the psychological and the sociological. Identities are configured in four contexts of activity. The first one is the *figured world*, a concept that refers to the relatively stable frames of meaning in which human actions are interpreted and to the "sites" in which interpretations are culturally negotiated. "Under the rubric of culturally figured worlds or figured worlds we include all those cultural realms peopled by characters from collective imaginings: academia, the factory, crime, romance, environmental activism, games of Dungeons and Dragons, the men's house among the Mehinaku of Brazil" (Holland et al., 1998, p. 51). Figured worlds provide models of identity in the sense of providing interpretations to the characters and discourses that populate them and of assigning significance to particular human acts. In that sense, figured worlds mediate behavior.

The second context of identity configuration is, according to Holland, *positionality*, a notion extensively developed in the context of Rom Harré's discursive psychology (Harré & Langenhove, 1992, 1999). The geography of figured worlds is shaped by relations of power, status, and rank, which in turn mediate the engagement of particular kinds of people in social practice. Positions are distinctive in terms of their entitlements, with some positions (such as race, gender, class, and ethnicity) more stable or structural than others. One can position others and be positioned by others, as when one presents oneself or is presented by others as independent or dependent, active or patient, hero or villain, happy or sad, advocate or detractor.

The third context in which identities in practice are configured is through the *space of authoring*, a notion Holland and collaborators borrow from

Bakhtin. People not only adopt (or alternatively, are given) positions and develop dispositions in figured worlds. They also craft *responses* and *narratives of themselves* as the basis of their agency. "People tell others who they are, but more importantly, they tell themselves and try to act like they know who they are. These understandings of ourselves, especially those with strong emotional resonance for anyone who expresses them, are what we refer to as identity" (Holland et al., 1998, p. 3). Spaces of authoring provide conditions to articulate voices or responses that engage in dialogue with the discourses that circulate in particular figured worlds. As Holland notes, in a way that resembles Giddens's (1979) ideas on structuring, the narratives of the self constitute a juncture between the personal and the public, as well as a foundation of individual agency.

Finally, identity is configured in the context of *making worlds*. Worlds of meaning are not only already figured and inhabited, but also constructed and transformed through creative, novel actions, which themselves craft new imaginaries and sites for identity. In that sense, identity can be transformative of the reality through the literal creation of new figured worlds.

In sum, the ever-changing result of the negotiation between individual commitments and cultural and symbolic resources is precisely a sense of identity. Seen this way, identity formation involves adopting (i.e., inhabiting) culturally shared worlds, establishing a positioning within such worlds, and developing a sense of agency; that is, a sense of how one can legitimately act on and within such a world (Larreamendy-Joerns, 2011).

Professional identities are no different. Professions are frames of meaning (some of them, such as psychology, rely on disciplinary frameworks), but, most important, they are repositories of socially sanctioned practices (and artifacts) often enacted in the context of institutionalized systems of activity (e.g., hospital wards, organizational settings, community organizations, educational institutions). Professional worlds are usually ordered in tiers of expertise, with complex relations of power that are the result of expert performance and positionings within particular activity systems.

## Institutional Context

Institutions of higher education are not simply a backdrop against which professional and disciplinary identities are constituted. As I have noted, higher education institutions should and often do provide identity resources that help configure the kinds of persons students may become. Higher education institutions introduce students to disciplinary and professional figured worlds and provide opportunities for them to craft their own selves in such worlds. As noted before, a revealing example of how identities are shaped in institutional contexts is the emerging professional identities of psychology students at a critical juncture of their formation process: their first supervised professional practicum. Yet the meaning of such a practicum can only be understood if one brings to the fore the scenario of higher education in Colombia and Latin America.

In Colombia, as in most Latin American countries, psychology is a professional program offered at the undergraduate level. Generally, after five to six years of study, students graduate as psychologists, and are entitled by law, with no other requirement, to provide full professional services. Although desirable, graduates do not need to pursue graduate studies, nor are they required to obtain a professional license by demonstrating their competence through examinations or other process of accreditation. A survey of representative undergraduate programs in Latin America (Peña, 2009) shows the number of course credits (one credit being one classroom contact hour with students) ranges from 127 to 270 (with a mean of 190 credits), which requires about sixty-three courses on average (about six per academic term) over the course of the entire period of undergraduate studies. Usually, the two last academic semesters (that is, on average, the fifth year of studies) are devoted to a supervised professional practicum, an experience during which students, under the tutelage of a qualified psychologist, take their first steps with actual clients, while the course workload decreases.

Compared with programs in the United States and more recently in Europe (particularly after the Bologna Declaration), psychology programs in Latin America certainly look unusually specialized for undergraduate purposes. Students are exposed not only to introductory courses in psychology, but also to courses that cover topics from basic psychological processes (e.g., emotion and motivation, human development, thinking and reasoning, perception, learning and memory) to methodological issues (e.g., quantitative methods, qualitative methods) and instrumental areas (e.g., psychometrics, psychological interviews, psychological assessment and evaluation, psychopathology). Additionally, programs regularly introduce students to professional fields, offering courses in areas such as educational psychology, clinical psychology, and organizational psychology, in addition to a number of specialized elective courses.

One may wonder why undergraduate programs in Latin America, unlike their counterparts in the United States and (currently) in Europe, are so heavily populated by courses. I conjecture that this is due to the convergence of three forms of reasoning that have historically constituted bearings for the professional and disciplinary identities of psychology graduates in the context of Latin American higher education institutions, as well as played a critical role in the definition of educational programs in the discipline: curricular encyclopaedism, curricular necessarianism, and program finalism. By *curricular encyclopaedism* I refer to the idea that undergraduate programs need to cover everything deemed significant in a discipline or a profession, an idea that runs counter to a view of the curriculum as consisting of critical steppingstones or selected domains that constitute enabling conditions for the learning of other subject matters. By *curricular necessarianism* I mean the presumption that there are fixed, unalterable routes to knowledge, that constitute the *sine qua non* conditions for access to particular competences. Thus, for example, one may think a deep knowledge of Piaget's theory is not only desirable, but absolutely necessary to the development of initial conceptual competences in psychology. The problem arises when diverse proponents defend and multiply routes of access to knowledge, making what one might consider a possible access into a necessary trajectory. Finally, by *program finalism* I refer to the belief that undergraduate programs should be the final cycle in the formation of professionals and that, as a consequence, should provide a preparation as complete as possible, not leaving space or necessity for postgraduate education. Program finalism is a belief often aligned with the appreciation that students, given their socioeconomic condition, have no real possibility of undertaking graduate study and need, therefore, to enter the job market as soon as possible. Curricular encyclopaedism, curricular necessarianism, and program finalism still constitute important aspects of the figured world of academia in Latin America and prefigure not only the practices expected from students and professionals (in terms of conceptual and practical competences), but also the institutional arrangements that should be in place to nurture such practices.

This landscape, however, has changed slowly over the past decade as many higher education institutions, traditionally conceived as teaching institutions, have adopted the profile of research institutions. To that has contributed the development in recent years, in countries such as Brazil, Chile, and Colombia, of government-based systems of science and technology, which have emphasized research and publication as the commodities by which to judge scholarly productivity, and have accelerated the creation of graduate programs in the disciplines and the professions.

Such is the case of the middle-sized university in Colombia from which our psychology students graduate. The university decided to become a research university and, accordingly, implemented a series of measures, such as the reduction in the duration of undergraduate programs from five to four years, a shift in the goals of undergraduate programs (from specialized programs to programs of general education in the professions and the disciplines), and the creation of graduate programs. These measures have had the effect of reorganizing undergraduate education as a whole and of throwing students into unchartered waters, into still-forming figured worlds, where old expectations meet new realities. In particular, some programs are now predicated upon assumptions that deviate from the three aforementioned forms of reasoning. How are the students' identities mediated through the supervised practicum? How are their professional identities changing in context of the opportunities for engagement provided by the higher education institution?

## Data

To answer these questions, a series of in-depth interviews was conducted with twenty-nine advanced psychology students, an entire cohort, a few months after the initiation of their supervised practicum and less than a year from their graduation as professional psychologists. The interview questions were previously planned, although arrangements were made to allow for additional queries in a conversational format. The interview asked participants to describe in general terms the experience of the supervised practicum, to elaborate on its most difficult aspects, to provide a sense of the most valuable things learned, and to discuss the extent to which their undergraduate studies had prepared them to deal with the supervised practicum. The interviews were transcribed and annotated for denotational content (Wortham, 2000), explicitly attempting to single out in the narratives references to identity construction, that is, discursive traces indicative of transitions in the students' frames of meaning with respect to their own professional competences, in the students' positionings within their social professional practice, and in the students' views of the higher education institution as mediating their engagement with the supervised practicum. For reliability, interviews were coded and annotated in a collective consisting of the principal investigator and a team of three graduate research assistants. For the purposes of the present analysis, I reference testimonies as exemplary cases of the kinds of trends found in the interviews as a set.

## Transitions in Students' Frames of Meaning

The interviews revealed a complex set of perspectives on the supervised practicum. The practicum is experienced as a period of transition and change, one that introduces students to a different set of meanings, to a world of a professional practice, yet anchored in the safeguards the higher education institution provides for its students. In one of the interviews, a student expressed it in the following terms. Asked to appraise the supervised practicum in general terms, the student noted (interview data originally in Spanish; translations have been made to preserve features of informal speech):

The practicum is, I say to myself, is...um, is when everything begins, like a rupture, um, between theory and practice. It is learning but inside...within the world itself. No more empty speech, but full reality. I wonder if the practicum could be located rather at the beginning, you know, like in medical school, but for us, for us...for us it's at the end, when I guess everything changes.

Notice how the student opposes theory and practice, empty speech and full reality, medical school and psychology studies. Seen in this way, the practicum introduces a new set of affordances, a new world that needs to be figured. This opposition appears even in cases where students acknowledge a smooth transition between their previous studies and the experience of the supervised practicum. For example, another student, answering the same general probe, said as follows:

I always waited for this moment, and I always believed, you know, that...that I was going to do it right, and I feel I'm doing it right. It's like, I haven't had any major difficulties, but in any case you have to relearn everything, how to behave in an alien context, with people you know nothing about, with experiences, um, that...that are simply new, things that you don't know how to do, new habits.

Notice the new beginning is not simply a learning of additional concepts, but a "relearning" that occurs in the context of fairly concrete constraints: new people, novel procedures, novel habits. It is, as the student suggests, a new way of conducting oneself in the world.

The otherness of supervised practicum, in the sense of demanding an identity shift, seems to be a function of the different web of meanings the practicum itself brings about:

I've been listening about diagnostic categories since a long time ago, when I took [the courses of] Introduction to Psychology, and then Psychopathology. For me, those words were always concepts to be learned for an exam, for the instructor's sake, for the quizzes. Now, they are for real, they apply to real persons and have consequences, so I'm much more reluctant to use them and to write them down in a clinical record or the like. Thank God I have my supervisor at times restraining what I would be tempted to do.

So, meanings change through the students' engagement in new practices that are, however, harbored by the higher education institution through the work of the supervisors. Students learn not only new procedures and courses of action, but also new ways of language use. In short, the supervised practicum is seen as a deep experience, as an eventful scenario that brings about unexpected occurrences and that is associated with new ways of being in the world. The practicum is opposed to what antecedes it and is depicted as a setting where new intersubjective relations are formed.

### Shifts in the Students' Positionings within their Social Practice

Not surprising, changes in the frames of meaning, that is in the figured worlds where the students enact themselves, are associated with changes in their positionings with respect to the community of reference. The higher education institution is making it possible for the students to "cease" to be students and to author themselves as professionals in a supervised, yet authentic, context. This authoring implies adopting positionings that are thrown out to be taken up, in the midst of social interaction.

My practicum has been in a way a life changing experience, something I always thought about, at least since I decided to study psychology, but that I never expected to be like it has been. All of a sudden, you become a psychologist, I mean, a practicing psychologist. Or, to be honest, it is not that you become, as much as that the people you are working with make you so.

Here we witness how the student implicitly construes the practicum as an unexpected experience, as something that could not be anticipated, and one that brings about a new identity via a new *status function* assigned by clients (Searle, 1995). The clients, and in general the "people you are working with," make the student a psychologist, repositioning her and attaching to her a new set of entitlements. It is the relational character of identity at its best. This is also an example of proleptic identity in the sense that a presumed, given identity anticipates the full preparedness of the student, in this particular case in a clinical situation.

### Higher Education Institution as Mediator of Students' Engagement

We asked the students whether they believed their undergraduate studies had prepared them to deal with a supervised practicum. It was a question probing how the education provided by the specific higher education institution had mediated their initial professional practices. Because they comprised the first cohort of students to go through a four-year program as opposed to the traditional five-year program, we were interested in inquiring about their position as to the extent to which the characterization of the supervised practicum as an identity-forming experience was in a way mediated by their stance with respect to the length of their undergraduate education.

All the students stated their undergraduate studies had not prepared them sufficiently for the challenges of the supervised practicum. Several students expressed a clear sense of a mismatch between what the institution expected, in terms of competences, and what they could offer based on what had been given to them. However, the students articulated two different perspectives. First, the idea that the specific curriculum they had followed (particularly its length) had not been sufficient (*contingent* insufficiency). Second, the view that *any* undergraduate education, regardless of its structure and length, would have been insufficient to anticipate the challenges of the practicum (*inherent* insufficiency). The first perspective is aligned with the following testimonies:

Would five years have made a difference? I don't know. At times, I feel as if I have been unleashed prematurely. Five years would have given me the opportunity to learn more stuff before putting everything into practice. There's a reason why psychology is five years in most universities. This is not philosophy, or the humanities. You've got to deal with mental health, and so on, so, um, you have to be ready.

The program was five years when my sister went to college. And now, for me it's only four years. That means, I guess, a reduction, a tremendous shortening. I wish I had been in a five-year career, simply because it gives you room to grow, to mature, I mean, as a person, no so much as…I mean in terms of knowledge, that doesn't matter, because knowledge is always incomplete, but being a grown up takes time, necessarily.

Here we have the students advancing the idea that longer is, by definition, better, either because more knowledge can be accumulated or because maturational processes occur in the interim. They do not seem to comprehend that a reduction in the length of the program entails a renegotiation of the goals of undergraduate education. The imaginary that *longer is better*, which runs counter to the institutional dictum that *less is more*, is also contrary to the idea that the supervised practicum is a radical experience in and of itself, an idea put forward by another group of students. Yet *longer is better* is moderated by expressions that suggest knowledge is always incomplete and that what one needs to learn is to adapt, to be ready even when one is not. These moderating claims seem to suggest the identity that is emerging rests, as this particular higher education institution claims, less on terminal competences and more on the ideal of readiness to learn when it is so necessitated.

The idea of the insufficiency of undergraduate studies as being contingent upon the duration of the formation opposes the idea of the insufficiency as inherent to any educational process. Let us see some expressions of the latter:

The practicum has been like a bridge that connects real life and my life as a quiet student. I have the sense that through the practicum I'm becoming more and more aware of my insufficiencies, my limitations. But, you know, there will always be insufficiencies, so even if we had ten years, the practicum would still be something challenging, if only because it's different.

Here we witness an entirely different perspective. It is not the institutional stance of *less is more*, nor the other students' *longer is better*, but the idea that *longer makes no difference*, at least with respect to the radicalness of the supervised practicum. These students seem to envision the supervised practicum as an experience that implies, in and of itself, an identity shift, a personal mobilization with respect to their professional profiles.

### Concluding Remarks

We have seen that the supervised practicum is a time for identity shift, a period of often dramatic transition from a plain student to a liable professional. It is a transition signified in the context of institutional changes, where students are faced with new concrete realities embodied in new ways of engaging with the world; where they assume identity models frequently in advance of their actual professional readiness; and where they position themselves and are positioned by others with respect to their own learning experiences.

Changes of this kind take place in higher education institutions that might otherwise be thought of only as sites for research and knowledge transmission. A CHAT perspective, however, suggests that what is implied in higher education is not only the development of skills and the acquisition of professional or disciplinary knowledge, but also, and fundamentally, the constitution of identities. Seen in this way, learning a profession is tantamount to inhabiting disciplinary and professional figured worlds, positioning oneself within a community, finding a voice to participate in ongoing conversations, and transforming reality by creating new meanings.

The supervised practicum is but just one site for the constitution of professional identities within higher education institutions. One might wonder how identities are forged in other scenarios, such as classrooms, student-faculty interactions, research laboratories, forums, and extracurricular activities. In any event, however, it is clear that learning involves, as Packer and Goicoechea

(2000) would say, an ontological transformation whose characteristics are deeply connected with what institutions make possible and nurture.

## References

Boaler, J. and Greeno, J. (2000). Identity, agency, and knowing in mathematics worlds. In J. Boaler (Ed.), *Multiple Perspectives on Mathematics Teaching and Learning* (pp. 171–200). Westport, CT: Ablex Publishing.

Giddens, A. (1979). *Central Problems in Social Theory: Action, structure, and contradiction in social analysis.* Berkeley: University of California Press.

Harré, R. and Van Langenhove, L. (1992). Varieties of positioning. *Journal for the Theory of Social Behaviour*, **20**, 393–407.

Harré, R. and Van Langenhove, L. (Eds.) (1999). *Positioning Theory: Moral contexts of intentional action.* Malden, MA: Blackwell.

Holland, D. and Lachicotte, W. (2007). Vygotsky, Mead and the new sociocultural studies of identity. In H. Daniels, M., Cole, and J. Wertsch (Eds.), *The Cambridge companion to Vygotsky* (pp. 101–35). Cambridge, UK: Cambridge University Press.

Holland, D., Lachicotte, W., Skinner, D., and Cain, C. (1998). *Identity and Agency in Cultural Worlds.* Cambridge, MA: Harvard University Press.

Larreamendy-Joerns, J. (2011). Aprendizaje como reconfiguración de agencia. *Revista de Estudios Sociales*, **40**, 33–43.

Lave, J. and Wenger, E. (1991). *Situated Learning: Legitimate peripheral participation.* New York: Cambridge University Press.

Packer, M. J. and Goicoechea, J. (2000). Sociocultural and constructivist theories of learning: Ontology, not just epistemology. *Educational Psychologist*, **35**, 227–41.

Peña, L. E. (2009). *Comparación de programas de pregrado en Latin America y los Estados Unidos.* Asociación Colombiana de Facultades de Psicología. Technical report. Bogotá: ASCOFAPSI.

Penuel, W. R. and Wertsch, J. V. (1995). Vygotsky and identity formation: A sociocultural approach. *Educational Psychologist*, **30** (2), 83–92.

Roth, M. and Tobin, K. (2007b). Aporias of identity in science: An introduction. In M. Roth and K. Tobin (Eds.), *Science, Learning, Identity: Sociocultural and cultural-historical perspectives* (pp. 1–14). Rotterdam. Sense Publishers.

(Eds.) (2007a). *Science, Learning, Identity: Sociocultural and cultural-historical perspectives.* Rotterdam: Sense Publishers.

Searle, J. (1995). *The Construction of Social Reality.* New York: Free Press.

Sfard, A. and Prusak, A. (2005). Telling identities: In search of an analytic tool for investigating learning as a culturally shaped activity. *Educational Researcher*, **34** (4), 14–22.

Wortham, S. (2000). Interactional positioning and narrative self-construction. *Narrative Inquiry*, **10**, 157–84.

(2006). *Learning Identity: The joint emergence of social identification and academic learning.* New York, NY: Cambridge University Press.

12

# Developing Skills for Collaborative, Relational Research in Higher Education: A Cultural Historical Analysis

## Ioanna Kinti and Geoff Hayward

### Introduction

There has been a growing trend for higher education to be seen by the state as central to national economic success (cf Barnett, 1990; Brown, Lauder, & Ashton, 2011). In the process, the state, in many countries, such as the United Kingdom, has sought to influence higher education research and there are growing demands for universities to be more accountable for addressing the concerns of contemporary society. These demands are also reflected in changing relationships between researchers and the fields they investigate, as academics respond to calls for experts, such as university researchers, to integrate what they know now with what those who are practice-based want to do in the future (Lundvall & Archibugi, 2001). There is, therefore, a growing expectation, in the social sciences as well as science, technology, engineering, and mathematics (STEM) subject areas, that university-based researchers will increasingly work in collaborative ways with external organisations, such as commercial companies or other university-based research laboratories, to generate and test new knowledge at practice boundaries with potential end users (Gibbons et al., 1999), often involving co-configuration work, a form of knowledge creation that requires continuous expert-user interaction and active user involvement in designing new products and services (Victor & Boynton, 1996).

However, such emphases set up a noticeable tension about the nature and purpose of academic research. Some university researchers react by embracing the new expectations that they collaborate across subject boundaries, becoming either more 'user oriented' (Gibbons et al., 1999; Rickinson, Sebba, & Edwards, 2011) or open to interdisciplinary work; whilst others react by pointing to the importance of preserving the right to inner dedication (Bernstein, 2000). The reality, we suspect, is that most academic researchers strive to find a balance between pure and applied research, while embracing the opportunity to communicate aspects of their work to a wider public audience and to provide advice to policy makers.

Nonetheless, research students and young researchers find themselves at the centre of this tension. For the most part, they are expected to engage in processes of developing expertise within specific subject domains, being involved in knowledge creation with experienced researchers within a single research centre or group, producing a thesis on a specific topic under the tutelage of a university-based supervisor that has to be defended via a traditional *viva voce* examination. Yet, as they develop as researchers, they will increasingly be asked to interact creatively and inventively with experts from other subject domains, university departments, agencies, or organisations, and perhaps also practitioners in their fields of study beyond the university.

This chapter focuses on how young researchers might be prepared for this wider role and research work at such boundaries, what we term collaborative, relational research work. It identifies in more detail the capabilities that participating in these kinds of research activities requires and suggests the sorts of learning experiences that might be included in research training programmes to develop necessary capabilities. In so doing, we reflect on whether the current training for postgraduate and research students in the United Kingdom, which is couched in the language of generic and transferable skills (Roberts Review, 2002), and supported, for example, by the UK Economic and Social Research Council (ESRC), is sufficient to develop the capabilities identified as crucial for the new boundary work to be undertaken by them. A Cultural Historical Activity Theory (CHAT) perspective is used to critique the generic and transferable skills approach to research training, which does not really address the capabilities needed by young researchers to engage effectively with knowledge creation at discipline, practice, and organisational boundaries.

## The Learning Challenge

Given the policy imperative, what do young researchers need to learn and how might such learning best be facilitated? Policy initiatives undertaken to improve the flow of knowledge from universities and other public research organisations to private companies have typically focussed on intellectual property rights and encouraging academic entrepreneurship, for example establishing university spin-out companies and patenting inventions so they become available for commercial exploitation by private companies (Geuna & Nesta, 2006; Haeussler & Colyvas, 2011; Mowery et al., 2004). Given this, the learning challenge might be construed as providing opportunities for young researchers to learn about technology transfer, the mechanics of patenting, and intellectual property rights while developing the business-related knowledge and skills needed to set up spin-out companies.

However, as Perkmann, Kong, and Pavelin point out:

Patenting and academic entrepreneurship... are imperfect measures of knowledge transfer and co-creation occurring during university-industry interactions. Relational forms of involvement, such as collaborative research, contract research, and consulting are more widespread and seen as more relevant by firms... relational involvement with industry may demand more faculty time and dedication than patenting, which may be a by-product of the research. Furthermore, collaboration differs from academic entrepreneurship in that it tends to be informed by research-related rationales, rather than an explicit desire to appropriate the financial returns on academic knowledge. (2011, p. 539)

How can research-training programmes best respond to the challenges of preparing people to become academic researchers confident about working at the boundaries of their disciplines, practices, and organisations to generate new knowledge that corresponds with the problems faced by contemporary societies? Some insight into the learning challenge for higher education institutions charged with developing the next generation of researchers to engage with such relational forms of university-industry collaboration can be gleaned from employer opinions about the knowledge, skills, and other attributes they seek to recruit in their research and development staff members. Employer surveys, for instance, consistently show that technical competence, including a deep conceptual understanding in their domain of subject expertise, combined with a range of so-called generic skills such as communications, team working, time management, and organisational skills, are deemed essential for young researchers working in commercial and public sector organisations (BIS, 2011, p. 160). Successive employee skills surveys (Felstead et al., 2007) also point to the growing importance of such skills as communication, writing, and problem solving.

The current educational response to the preparation of research students is largely couched in this language of generic skills. For example, Gareth Roberts's Review *SET for Success* raised concerns doctoral training was not doing enough to ensure that:

PhDs are producing people with the necessary balance of skills to conduct high quality research and development in industry, universities and the public sector. Currently, insufficient emphasis is placed on transferable skills. (HMT, 2002, p. 112)

In particular, concern was voiced that the model of research training where a PhD student was apprenticed to a supervisor, often to work in a research group, was too focussed on a narrow preparation for academic scholarship based on engagement in 'curiosity driven research' which neglected broader education and training objectives. The Review concluded:

Current arrangements do not therefore give satisfactory training in communication (including teaching), management and commercial awareness to fully equip researchers for the professional demands of modern academic life and employment in R&D. (p. 128)

Roberts's Review argued for the provision of at least two weeks of dedicated training a year, principally in transferable skills, for which additional funding should be provided and over which the student should be given some control (2003, p. 11). The outcome has been an increased focus on supplementary training programmes offered to young researchers to develop their generic skills and to raise awareness of intellectual property rights. For example, the UK's Economic and Social Research Council (ESRC), in its 2009 training guidelines, sets out the following three outcomes in addition to those normally associated with developing the skills of an academic researcher in the social sciences:

- an appreciation of the potential use and impact of their research within and beyond academia;
- an ability to engage with relevant users at all points in the research process, from devising and shaping research questions through to informing users' efforts to improve practice; and
- an ability to communicate research findings effectively to a wide range of audiences.

The same document then specifies the main components of such research training, including:

- Exploitation of Research and Intellectual Property Rights (IPR)
- Communication, Networking, and Dissemination Skills
- Leadership, Research Management, and Relationship Management Skills
- Personal and Career Development (pp. 20–21).

The ESRC guidelines also explicitly state:

The development of skills around co-production of research, public engagement and enterprise skills can play an important role in helping postgraduate students to raise their profile and to disseminate their knowledge to wider audiences. (p. 21)

We have little problem with such attempts to develop the transferable skills of beginning researchers and to raise their awareness of IPR issues and knowledge coproduction. However, this definition of the learning challenge is based on an assumption that the learning needs of beginning researchers can be read off in a rather straightforward way from employers and employees' responses to survey questions or from self-report data gleaned from interviews. When graduates and postgraduates engaged in knowledge-intensive jobs are actually observed doing their work, it emerges that they are using complex amalgams of knowledge, skills, and highly contextualised understandings to solve the problems that confront them rather than simply applying previously learnt generic skills (see Davies and Birbili, 2002; Eraut, 2007). This is recognised in feedback from employers and suggests the learning challenge of equipping inexperienced researchers for the demands of collaborative, relational research work may be greater than merely developing the generic skills of postgraduate research students:

An engineering company, for example, mentioned the challenges of today's industrial research which needs an integrated skills set that is both multi-disciplinary and multi-natured – a project could involve graduates from conception through to design, testing, manufacture, delivery and support. (BIS, 2011, p. 160)

This indicates the need to go beyond the generic skills model of additional research training for beginning researchers. However, it also requires a better understanding of the nature of research work as it takes place across organisational boundaries. Collaborative, relational research activity may be fruitfully conceptualised as involving the generation and testing of knowledge at practice boundaries. Some employers recognise the challenge of such work in calling for postgraduates who can better handle uncertainty, ambiguity, and complexity (BIS, 2011). According to Alvesson, ambiguity in contexts of knowledge creation work involves:

uncertainty, contradictions that cannot be resolved or reconciled, absence of agreement on boundaries, clear principles or solutions. (1993, p. 1002)

Generic skill training, while it may be useful, is, in our view, unlikely to help young researchers deal with the essential features of such ambiguous situations. As a theory of practice development, CHAT can be a useful resource in that respect because it provides the language and conceptual tools to enable us to reflect on processes of cognitive development across levels (individual, group, organisational system) as this takes place in complex work activity.

### A CHAT Perspective on Research as Collaborative
### Knowledge Creation Work

We hypothesise that expertise in collaborative, relational research work involves both technical competence and the ability to configure and reconfigure new affinity spaces (Gee, 2004) at disciplinary or institutional boundaries, which become new solution spaces (Hartley, 2007). Such boundary spaces or zones are places where social practices are open to negotiation and the ideas carried in established practices are exposed to new interpretations (Edwards, 2010). Such boundaries define what is and what is not valued, and who and what can be included in meaning making around work problems (Midgley, 1992) to develop new collaborative practices. Working in a boundary zone with other experts can be a source of both creativity and innovation, but also potentially risky for the actors involved as they might be requested to work outside of their normal institutional shelters and cultures, under conditions of uncertainty and ambiguity over roles and responsibilities, the rules for engagement, and the motives and values underpinning such engagement. Such situations will likely produce profound challenges to a young researcher's conception of his or her academic identity and purpose (Jain et al., 2009). The learning challenge, then, is how to prepare young researchers to meet these demands. In part, this requires a better theorisation of the nature of this type of work which we believe CHAT can provide. It is to this that we now turn.

We represent collaborative, relational research activity in Figure 12.1, employing, as a heuristic device, Engeström's diagrammatic conception of third generation activity theory. This representation is intended to convey the idea of actors coming together from their parent activity systems – here a university computer laboratory (ComLAB), a hardware manufacturer (M1), and a specialist software company (M2)    to engage in research and development collaboration. The representation could equally be applied to university-based social scientists working with policy makers and third sector organisations, for example, around finding solutions for unemployed young people in areas undergoing economic decline. The actors form what we have labelled a 'Solution project team', again represented as an activity system.

Although the example is based on a longitudinal study of collaborative work (Kinti, 2008), it is important to recognise the essentially heuristic nature of Figure 12.1. At the beginning of a relational collaborative research project, there is no central shared activity system: the activity has to be created anew as the actors work to develop a collective problem space to define the motive that will guide their collaborative work. The work practices of the

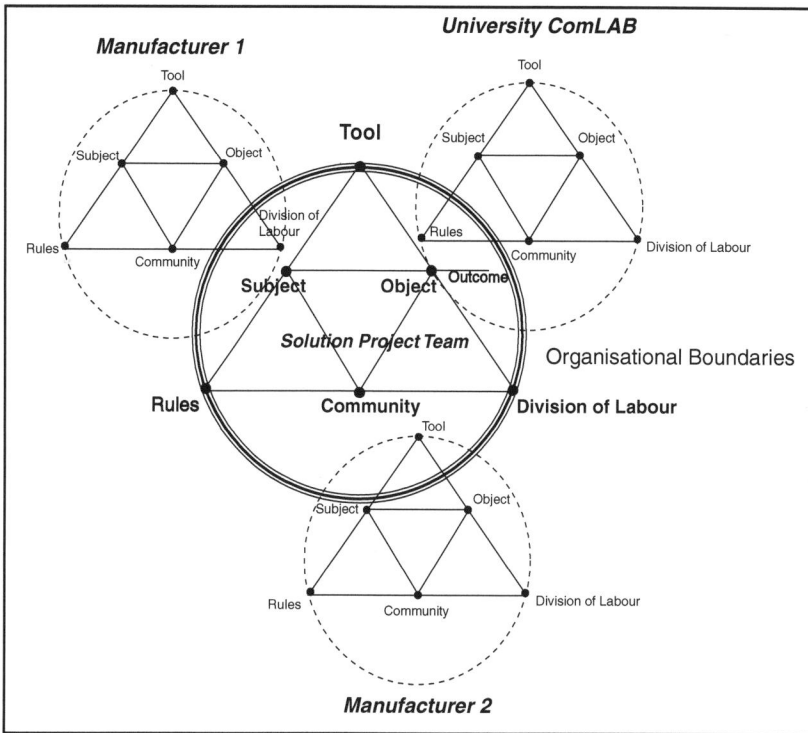

FIGURE 12.1. Relational research work between activity systems interacting across organisational boundaries.

Solution project team at the beginning of a collaborative project have to be constructed, to some extent, *de novo*, typically via a bootstrapping process utilising existing features of the practice of an actor's parent activity system. To understand the nature of this type of work it is, therefore, necessary to view it diachronically, as a developmental accomplishment. The important dimension of time, which can be imagined as an axis running perpendicular to the page, is therefore missing from Figure 12.1.

As a result, the representation in Figure 12.1 is far too static: actors do not cross into an activity system represented as the Solution project team and work there with each other. Rather they shuttle back and forth between the developing activity of the Solution project team and their parent activity systems. Further, the parent activity is never static: commercial pressures, for example, may cause shifts in the motivational imperatives driving aspects of the parent activity or changes in government may lead to significant shifts in policy. This, in turn, will affect the motivation of the actors, as what matters in their parent activity system is shifted often along with how their performance will be judged. This can cause shifts in their commitment to the activity of the Solution project team, leading to breakdowns in the work – due, a CHAT perspective suggests, to the fragility of emerging rules and the division of labour (Kinti, 2008).

In addition, while the individual actors are experts in their parent activity, that expertise has to be continually established in the Solution project team: it can never be taken for granted. As a result, actors' professional identities and their competence are open to question and challenge. This has important implications for actors' sense of worth in the emerging project solution team, the exact nature of the role they are to play in the emerging activity, and how the value of their work will be judged. Meeting the challenges presented by work breakdowns and the continual self-questioning of the contribution made to the collaborative project and its value requires considerable resilience.

A CHAT perspective that views expertise as a relational attribute of systems rather than individual mastery of well-defined tasks provides a useful lens through which to examine this developmental process. Such a perspective that construes expertise as the 'collaborative and discursive construction of tasks, solutions, visions, breakdowns and innovations' (Engeström & Middleton, 1996, p. 6) is better attuned to recognising the social systemic nature of 'skill' in this process. This is not to suggest experts should not simultaneously be viewed as individuals holding high levels of personal and propositional knowledge about specific domains (Dreyfus & Dreyfus, 2005). Rather, the issue is how such actors can combine their expertise horizontally to foster emergence of novelty and new knowledge creation at the boundaries of their professional practices.

A cultural-historical understanding of the problem suggests researchers arrive in such collaborative teams with different ontogenies developed through different histories of participation in professional practice, with all that implies: different 'definitions, tools for problem solution, and particular tactics of solution' (Rogoff, 1990, p. viii). A cultural historical understanding of human beings does not conceive of them as ahistorical selves or abstract individuals – as does conventional social network research where individuals are represented as nodes and relationships are represented as lines connecting nodes. Rather, they should be seen as persons defined by their different social, cultural, and historical circumstances which, in turn, mediate their development, for example, shaping their professional identity in the world of work.

This interpretation, however, means that to understand better the conditions for knowledge mobilisation in work and research contexts that span practice boundaries, we need to take explicit account of actors' potentially incommensurate motives not only at an individual but also at an institutional level. Such conflicting motives become more apparent as a research team navigates its course through oppositional discourses to integrate knowledge across subject domains and disciplinary boundaries (Oborn & Dawson, 2010). In cultural-historical terms, this challenge is expressed and theorised by Daniels when he discusses how discourses shape institutions and vice-versa: 'When we talk in institutions, history enters the flow of communication through the invisible or implicit mediation of institutional structures' (2009, p. 106). According to this analysis, actors arrive in a research collaboration with different ontogenies because they have been socialised into the structures and discourses of different institutional systems – such as their university departments or research laboratories or smaller research teams; other professional practice communities, such as social workers; or the political mores of civil service – and feel they need to stay accountable to what is important to those systems.

Motivation to enact expertise within a particular activity system, then, is not construed as an internal state but as a sociohistorically constructed process linked to the object of activity for this system. In this type of knowledge creation work, however, the activity is likely to be defined between actors originating in different communities of practice and arriving at the interaction driven by different objects. Engeström and colleagues, as well as scholars in the field of organisation studies, conceptualise such processes of knowledge creation work to emerge through acts of boundary crossing (Bechky, 2003; Carlile, 2004; Tuomi-Grohn et al., 2003) and the development of boundary objects (Star, 2010) between actors involved in interacting activity systems.

However, the metaphors of boundary crossing and boundary objects, we feel, fail to capture the dynamic and profound struggle and identity negotiation that an actor, such as a university researcher, undergoes and experiences whilst engaged in collaborative knowledge creation work with other, differently positioned, specialists and experts across organisational boundaries. Expert actors engaged in this mode of work experience struggle and resistance to boundary crossing (Tuomi-Grohn et al., 2003) from their parent activity system, as is evident in Antony's case, the 'ComLab' team leader of the project solution team:

M1 [the big manufacturer involved in this collaborative research project] wants to do something that just works whereas we [the 'ComLab'] want to solve some real problems and we are not given enough space to learn in this project.

Antony's statement indicates how actors will often pull back within an established organisational position to defend an existing professional identity before they can expand their identity by adopting new rules and ways of thinking across practice boundaries. This, then, shows how necessary it is for researchers and other professionals involved in this mode of work to balance their performance and contribution of expertise at practice boundaries, between the twin demands of satisfying the requirements of their parent activity systems *and* contributing creatively, effectively, and in a timely manner to the work of the collaborative solution team. It is not a question of one or the other but of both simultaneously. This requires a type of performance we would characterise as boundary balancing rather than boundary crossing, a metaphor that points to the dynamic and ongoing effort to maintain a personally and institutionally acceptable position and identity at an organisational boundary (Kinti, 2008).

From a CHAT perspective, then, this suggests that, in our study of research activity as a complex collaborative object, we need to move beyond the question of systems of 'economic exchange' to foster innovation (the perspective inherent, for example, in an emphasis on IPR and spin out formation), to explore the different 'regimes of value' (Appadurai, 1986) that research projects as complex collaborative objects encapsulate. Thus, the analytical focus needed to understand the challenges of this kind of boundary work should not only attend to the mechanisms employed to achieve knowledge creation in such projects, but also to what such processes create. We suggest, for example, that the creation of common knowledge (Edwards, 2010) or common ground (Bechky, 2003), or new work process knowledge (Boreham et al., 2002), which enables shared meaning making around ill-defined problems and motivates collaborative and creative work, needs to be recognised as an important element of boundary work, giving stability to the balancing the researchers experience. How such common understandings are created, therefore, should be given attention in research training.

### Recasting the Learning Challenge

The changes in the expectations held of researchers, which we outlined earlier in this chapter, mean becoming a researcher is not just a matter of developing a deep understanding of a particular subject domain but also involves:

a) negotiating expertise and identity in debates with knowledgeable others (Edwards & Kinti, 2009); and

b) developing collaborative working skills to get work done across disciplinary and professional boundaries, while also learning to share such skills with peers and younger researchers.

Gaining these capacities requires young researchers to be trained to become 'adept at recognizing and working with the (i) the professional resources that other practitioners bring to bear on interpreting a problem…and (ii) the resources that these practitioners use when responding to those interpretations' (Edwards & Kinti, 2009, p. 127). The skills and capabilities that ought to be included in research training programmes for young researchers to exercise *relational agency* (Edwards, 2010) and engage resourcefully in processes of knowledge creation with other researchers should, then, in CHAT terms, be seen as cultural artefacts designed flexibly enough to mediate knowledge mobilisation by taking account of actors and research teams' need of boundary working in specific historical circumstances.

So what are the skills and capabilities? We suggest, on the basis of the research we have undertaken so far, the following as indicative:

1. To act responsively, reflectively, reflexively, and responsibly.
2. To actively and rapidly read an emerging landscape of the collaborative team while simultaneously contributing to its emergence and development.
3. To understand that routines which guide practice in one context will likely be disrupted and may be dysfunctional in the context of a research collaboration with multiple experts – there will be disruptions and one's understandings of what it means to be a researcher will be challenged.
4. To be able to accommodate the needs of others to co-configure knowledge while maintaining a distinct sense of adherence to one's professional values and identity, i.e. not going native and be able to exercise agency in contested terrains; a form of performance we have more precisely conceptualised as boundary balancing (Kinti, 2008), not boundary crossing.
5. Seeing the development of expertise in such collaborations as involving both conceptual growth and a capacity to engage in the development of shared meaning.
6. Valuing ambiguity and tension in such collaborations as generative resources, and not expecting clear definitions of project aims at the outset. This requires considerable resilience and ability to cope with emotionally charged processes of negotiation.

### A Developmental Pedagogy that Supports Knowledge Creation

It is, of course, one thing to specify such a list of skills and capabilities, quite another to construct developmental curricula that will enable young researchers to develop such capabilities. Adopting a CHAT perspective, the sort of educational experiences we need to provide for young researchers can be construed essentially as a form of identity work, of expanding their professional identities to encompass both their work as research scientists and as professional collaborators with external agencies. We suggest a developmental pedagogy to achieve this has two key, interlinked components. First, engagement in learning tasks that enable active reflection on the struggle to construct meaning and identity at practice boundaries. Second, being encouraged to utilise a meta-language based on CHAT concepts to aid reflection.

CHAT emphasises the role of the object of activity as a heterogeneous and internally contradictory, yet enduring, constantly reproduced purpose of collective activity that motivates and defines the horizon of possible actions (Engeström, 1995; Leont'ev, 1978). Making such a distinction available to young researchers should serve to remind them that a key component of the learning challenge they face is to understand the importance of negotiating a common object of activity over time rather than just agreeing on short-term goals. This is an indication of how the language of CHAT can be a useful communicative resource in environments of research coproduction, such as the ones proposed by the ESRC.

A key abstraction is that negotiating a common object over time does not involve smoothing away difference but embracing multivocality. Another aspect of the learning challenge is that young researchers need to understand they ought to expect conflict and tension within such collaborative research activity; it is to be embraced as a source of potential innovation and not to be managed away. Such multivocality is linked to contradictions as the essential driving impetus of change and development in activity systems. Contradictions are 'the principles of [an activity system's] self-movement and {...} the form in which the development is cast' (Il'enkov, 1977, p. 330 quoted in Engeström, 2005, p. 150). Note that by contradiction we do not mean conflict or problems but fundamental, accumulating historical tensions. For example, the tension between undertaking academic work, on one hand, and commercialisation of that work, on the other hand, which lies at the heart of UK government policy on innovation. Working with contradictions as a source of innovation to solve ill-defined problems is at the heart of the learning challenge young researchers face whilst engaged in collaborative knowledge creation work.

In an effort to prepare young researchers for collaborative research work with other experts, this contribution has so far presented the conditions under which higher education policy and research policy in the United Kingdom remain anchored in the language of generic and transferable skills. We then proposed ways to unpack such emphasis on transferable skills by highlighting the role of relational characteristics and capabilities a young researcher should develop to engage creatively, inventively, and in a timely manner with collaborative knowledge creation work. CHAT has been a conceptual resource in that endeavour because of the particular stance it takes on the problem of expertise development and coordination across practice boundaries, but also because it argues for an understanding of the phenomenon of collaborative and relational research as a form of work, hence the example of the project solution team and its actors, to illuminate aspects of collaborative research as a form of knowledge creation work.

The analysis so far has provided a quick view of the sorts of learning experiences that could be included in research training programmes to develop necessary capabilities. In an ideal world, it might be thought that the best learning activity would include beginning researchers within experiences in collaborative projects, such as the ones outlined earlier. However, this is still a relatively uncommon form of research work. Compared to the established practice of a research team or laboratory, such work systems are unlikely to prove conducive as learning environments in the first instance, even with large amounts of mediation – the pace of engagement is very fast and politically charged. The alternative is *simulation exercises* that would at least give a flavour of such activity. Such opportunities must provide individuals with authentic learning experiences afforded by participation in ongoing collaborative activity with actors external to their usual epistemic communities. Further, there must be scope for *active reflection* on the practices of *identity expansion*, especially *when working with end users to inform them about how they can improve their practices as proposed by the ESRC*, which – we hypothesise – is essential in becoming proficient in engaging with collaborative, relational research work.

The obvious candidate for the design of such learning environments is a variant of developmental work research (DWR) (Engeström, 2007) utilised to construct a learning environment based on joint problem solving between research students drawn from different disciplines (social, physical, and biological sciences, arts and humanities) focussed around a time-limited interdisciplinary project. This would necessitate participants negotiating a common object of activity while experiencing the ambiguity and contradictions inherent in meeting alternative definitions of, and understandings of how, to solve a problem. Videoing the ongoing activity and using the normal procedures of *mirroring* and *open discussion* would facilitate reflection on what is happening and why, thereby deepening understanding of the challenges of this type of work and the capabilities needed to succeed in undertaking it. This could be supplemented by case study-based work. That still leaves the problem of transferring such learning unaddressed. For transfer to happen, we hypothesise, learners need to form a more abstract conceptualisation of what occurs as they struggle to solve a problem with those from a different academic background and tradition. We suggest this involves the internalisation and externalisation of a meta-language to guide reflection drawn from CHAT.

But this is not the end of their learning journey. Such simulations of collaborative research activity cannot effectively deliver an experience of the powerful political forces and values at play between the different researchers in the reality of such collaborations. These influences often remain at a tacit level, yet they need to be surfaced and discussed if the young researcher is to learn to read the landscape in which the project is operating and to work relationally and productively with others in often shifting and complex environments. This is where the language of CHAT could be particularly useful. Concept donation could be achieved through the active mediation of more experienced others, to the extent that they can see the usefulness of becoming familiar with the language of CHAT. Such a coaching role – by the project's manager or by more senior researchers lecturers and research fellows – would involve helping young researchers unpack the learning they had already undertaken as part of their research training. Yet it leaves in the margin research students who work in isolation. This, however, indicates the pivotal role in designing new doctoral programmes of constructing *collaborative research teams* so that all young university researchers can be included in an activity system with other researchers, at different levels in their academic development.

An additional issue that must be considered when designing such programmes is the challenge engagement with external users raises for professional academics. We see this as a legitimate activity to engage in with young research scientists, but others have voiced concern about such a move because it may negate notions of 'inwardness' and 'inner dedication', seen as central to professional identity by writers such as Bernstein (2000). While we need to take such concerns seriously we also need to emphasise that what is being proposed is not the substitution of one identity for another but an expansion of an existing identity. Such expansion, we suggest, will enable participation in a wider range of activities than has previously been considered appropriate for university-based researchers. Maintaining an identity as a university researcher then lies in ensuring there is a coherent values component to the education of young researchers so that they engage in activity with external agents from a strong ethical base.

## References

Alvesson, M. (1993). Organizations as rhetoric: Knowledge intensive firms and the struggle with ambiguity. *Journal of Management Studies*, **30**(6), 997–1015.

Appadurai, A. (1986). Introduction: Commodities and the politics of value. In A. Appadurai (Ed.), *The Social Life of Things: Commodities in cultural perspective* (pp. 3–63). Cambridge: Cambridge University Press.

Barnett, R. (1990). *The Idea of Higher Education*. Buckingham: SRHE and Open University press.

Bechky, B. (2003). Sharing meaning across occupational communities: The transformation of understanding on a production floor. *Organization Science*, **14**/3, 312–30.

Becker, G. (1993). *Human Capital: A theoretical and empirical interpretation with special reference to education*. Chicago, IL: University of Chicago Press.

Bernstein, B. (2000). *Pedagogy, Symbolic Control and Identity: Theory, research and critique*. London: Taylor and Francis.

BIS. (2011). STEM graduates in non-STEM jobs. BIS Research paper Number 30. Available online at: http://www.bis.gov.uk/assets/biscore/further-education-skills/docs/s/11-771-stem-graduates-in-non-stem-jobs.

Boreham, N., Fischer, M., and Samurcay, R. (2002). *Work Process Knowledge*. London: Routledge.

Brown, P., Green, A., and Lauder, H. (2001). *High Skills: Globalization: Competitiveness and skill formation*. Oxford: Oxford University Press.

Brown, P., Lauder, H., and Ashton, D. (2011). *The Global Auction: The broken promises of education, jobs, and income*. Oxford: Oxford University Press.

Carlile, P. (2004). Transferring, translating and transforming: An integrative framework for managing knowledge across boundaries. *Organization Science*, **15**(5), 555–68.

Daniels, H. (2009). Implicit or invisible mediation in the development of interagency work. In H. Daniels, A. Edwards, Y. Engeström, T. Gallagher, and S. Ludvigsen (Eds.), *Activity Theory in Practice: Promoting learning across boundaries and agencies* (pp. 105–25). London: Routledge.

Davidson, C. (2011). So last century. THES. 28 April 2011.

Davies, C. and Birbili, M. (2002). What do people need to know about writing in order to write in their jobs? *British Journal of Educational Studies*, **48**(4), 429–45.

DIUS. (2008). *Innovation Nation*. Norwich: TSO.

Dreyfus, H. and Dreyfus, S. (2005). Expertise in real world contexts. *Organization Studies*, **26**/5, 779–92.

Edwards, A. (2009). From the systemic to the relational: Relational agency and activity theory. In A. Sannino, H. Daniels, and C. Gutierrez (Eds.), *Learning and Expanding with Activity Theory* (pp. 197–211). Cambridge: CUP.

  (2010). *Being an Expert Professional Practitioner: A Relational Turn*. Dordrecht: Springer.

Edwards, A. and Kinti, I. (2009). Working relationally at organisational boundaries: Negotiating expertise and identity. In H. Daniels, A. Edwards, Y. Engeström, T. Gallagher, and S. Ludvigsen (Eds.), *Activity Theory in Practice: Promoting learning across boundaries and agencies* (pp. 126–39). London: Routledge.

Engeström, Y. (1995) Objects, contradictions and collaboration in medical cognition: An activity-theoretical perspective, *Artificial Intelligence in Medicine*, **7**(5): 395–412.

Engeström, Y. (2005) Development, Movement and Agency: Breaking away into mycorrhizae activities. Available online at http://lchc.ucsd.edu/mca/Mail/xmcamail.2008_12.dir/att-0247/Yrjo.dev.pdf. Last accessed April 2013.

(2007). Putting Vygotsky to work: The change laboratory as an application of double stimulation. In H. Daniels, M. Cole, and J. V. Wertsch (Eds.), *The Cambridge Companion to Vygotsky* (pp. 363–82). New York: Cambridge University Press.

Engeström, Y. and Middleton, D. (eds.) (1996). *Cognition and Communication at Work*. Cambridge: CUP.

Eraut, M. (2007). Learning from other people in the workplace. *Oxford Review of Education*, 33(4), 403–22.

Felstead, A., Gallie, D., Green, F., and Zhou, Y. (2007). *Skills at Work, 1986 to 2008*. Available online at http://www.skope.ox.ac.uk/publications/skills-work-1986–2006.

Gee, J. P. (2004). *Situated Language and Learning: A critique of traditional schooling*. London: Routledge.

Geuna, A. and Nesta, L. J. J. (2006). University patenting and its effect on academic research: The emerging European evidence. *Research Policy*, 35(16), 790–807.

Gibbons, M. (1999). Science's new social contract with society. *Nature*, 402, C81.

Gibbons, M., Limoges, C., Nowotny, H., Schwartzman Scott, P., and Trow, M. (1999). *The New Production of Knowledge*. London: Sage.

Haeussler, C. and Colyvas, J. A. (2011). Breaking the ivory tower: Academic entrepreneurship in the life sciences and UK and Germany. *Research Policy*, 40, 41–54.

Hartley, D. (2007). The emergence of distributed leadership in education: Why now? *British Journal of Educational Studies*, 55(2), 202–14.

HMT. (2002). SET for Success: The Report of Sir Gareth Robert's Review. London.

Holland, D., Lachicotte, W., Skinner, D., and Cain, C. (1998). *Identity and Agency in Cultural Worlds*. Cambridge: Harvard University Press.

Il'enkov, E. V. (1977). *Dialectical Logic: Essays in its history and theory*. Moscow: Progress.

Jain, S., George, G., and Maltarich, M. (2009). Academics or entrepreneurs? Investigating role identity modification of university scientists involved in commercialization activity. *Research Policy*, 38, 922–35.

Kinti, I. (2008). *Balancing at the Boundaries of Organizations: Knowledge co-configuration between experts in an e-Science Project*. Thesis submitted to the University of Oxford for the Degree of Doctor of Philosophy.

Knorr-Cetina, K. (1999), *Epistemic Cultures: How the sciences make knowledge*. Cambridge: Harvard University Press.

Leont'ev, A. N. (1978). *Activity, Consciousness, Personality*. Englewood Cliffs, NJ: Prentice Hall.

Lundvall, B. A. and Archibugi, D. (2001). Introduction: Europe and the Learning Economy. In D. Archibugi and B-A Lundvall (Eds.), *The Globalizing Learning Economy* (pp. 1–17). Oxford, Oxford University Press.

Midgley, G. (1992). The sacred and profane in critical systems thinking. *Systems Practice*, 5/1, 5–16.

Mowery, D., Nelson, R., Sampat B., and Ziedonis, A. (2004). *Ivory Tower and Industrial Innovation: University–industry technology transfer before and after Bayh-Dole*. Stanford, CA: Stanford University Press.

Oborn, E. and Dawson, S. (2010). Knowledge and practice in multidisciplinary teams: Struggle, accommodation and privilege. *Human Relations*, 63(12), 1835–57.

Payne, J. (1999). *All Things to All People: Changing perceptions of 'skill' among Britain's policy makers since the 1950s and their implications.* SKOPE Working paper Number 1. Available online at http://www.skope.ox.ac.uk/publications/all-things-all-people-changing-perceptions-skill-among-britains-policy-makers-1950s-and.

Perckman, M., Kong, Z., and Pavelin, S. (2011). Engaging excellence? Effects of faculty quality on university engagement with industry. *Research Policy*, 40, 539–52.

Roberts, G. (2002). *SET for Success: The supply of people with science, technology, engineering and mathematics skills.* Final Report of Sir Gareth Roberts' Review.

Rickinson, M., Sebba, J., and Edwards, A. (2011). *Improving User-Engagement in Educational Research.* London, Routledge.

Rogoff, B. (1990). *Apprenticeship in Thinking: Cognitive development in social context.* New York: Oxford University Press.

Spender, J. C. (1996). Organizational knowledge learning and memory; three concepts in search of a theory. *Journal of Organisational Change Management*, 9(1), 63–78.

Star, S. L. (2010). This is not a boundary object: Reflections on the origin of a concept. *Science, Technology & Human Values*, 35(5), 601–17.

Tuomi-Grohn, T., Engeström, Y., and Young, M. (2003). From transfer to boundary-crossing between school and work as a tool for developing vocational education: an introduction. In T. Tuomi-Grohn and Y. Engeström (Eds.), *Between Work and School: New perspectives on transfer and boundary-crossing* (pp. 1–15). London: Pergamon.

Victor, B. and Boynton, A. C. (1998). *Invented Here: Maximizing your organization's internal growth and profitability.* Boston: Harvard Business School Press.

# 13

# Teacher Education in the Public University: The Challenge of Democratising Knowledge Production

## Viv Ellis

Universities around the world are held to be in crisis, but the public university is seen as the institution most at risk, with higher education's role in the creation of the conditions for democracy under threat. Historically, the public university is a type of institution that has evolved to widen participation in postsecondary education at the same time that new kinds of publics (multiple, competing, and stratified) have, at least in part, been created through its work. The public functions of the university have included what Dewey (1927) referred to as the development of a 'collective intelligence' in society, but also the creation of the open social structures that permit the deliberative public discourse and flows of knowledge necessary for our democratic existence. Public universities can therefore be institutions of democratic education in the fullest sense (Gutmann, 1999), and the majority of institutions in North America and the United Kingdom were, until very recently, regarded as such – at least in ideal-type terms – whether the four-year colleges and research-intensive state universities in the United States or in the civic and modern universities that grew up in England through the nineteenth and twentieth centuries. Indeed, as Holmwood points out, until the last few years, the public functions of the university were explicit in higher education policy: in the United Kingdom, the Robbins Report of 1963 saw the universities as 'serving democratic citizenship by improving debate and the capacities of citizens' (Holmwood, 2011, p. 7), and the Dearing Report of 1997 argued the benefits of higher education went beyond individuals' accumulation of social and cultural capital, but that the institutions were necessary to:

sustain a culture which demands disciplined thinking, encourages curiosity, challenges existing ideas and generates new ones; [and to] be part of the conscience of a democratic society, founded on respect for the rights of the individual and the responsibilities of the individual to society as a whole. (Dearing Report 1997, para. 5; cited in Holmwood, 2011, p. 9)

The past few years have seen something of a change in concept, to say the least, as brutal funding cuts across entire systems – 25 per cent across the University of California in 2009, for example – or the complete withdrawal of state funding to undergraduate teaching in the arts, humanities, and social sciences in England from 2012 indicate. Scholars in the humanities have been extremely active in reasserting the case for the public university and arguing for the importance of the humanities. Wendy Brown, politics professor at the University of California, Berkeley, has characterised the change in higher education as a shift from 'a social and public good to...personal investment in individual futures, futures construed mainly in terms of earning capacity' (2011, p. 23). The university, in this argument, has disengaged from society, has had its public functions removed by the state and replaced by the right of government to 'represent' public interests in all spheres. The university's role in the creation of the publics has been lost. The student becomes a consumer whose choices will be guided by market rationality and, outside individuals' investment in their economic futures or the university's position in global rankings such as the Shanghai Jia Tong, there need be no relation to society. The decline of the public university coincides with the withering away of other democratising institutions. As Brown puts it:

Neoliberal rationality recognises and interpellates the subject only as a speck of human capital, making incoherent the idea of an engaged citizen, an educated public or an education for public life. (2011, p. 23)

Humanities scholars such as Brown, Lye, and Vernon (2011), Collini (2011), Gutmann (1999), and many others have been active in their reassertion of the democratising function of the public university against the challenges of neoliberalism and market rationality. In some respects, they are part of a long tradition of advocates of the liberal arts as well as of education for democracy per se. And like their predecessors they argue the current crisis is not simply a result of recession and budget deficit – not an inevitable 'product of necessity', as Lye and Vernon put it (2011, p. 5) – but a contemporary manifestation of historical contingencies that can be understood, articulated, and changed. A different future is possible.

In this chapter, I want to assert the value of teacher education in the public university in the face of the general crisis of higher education and of the crisis of professional training, in particular, where academic work can be seen as a distraction from the accumulation of classroom 'experience' (my quotation marks indicating its conventional proxy status for expertise) and the enactment of policy priorities. My argument has two parts and is informed by sociocultural and cultural-historical theories, theories useful in helping us to recognise the situation as well as to act on it. My first claim is that teacher education is almost uniquely situated as an activity of the public university that has a democratising function. Teacher education lives through its necessary relationships with other parts of the university (the arts and humanities, social and natural sciences, technology) as well as to the whole education system outside the university (the nursery or kindergarten, school, college, etc.) and to the differentiated public sphere more generally – whether the local community immediately around the institution or wider and more distributed communities concerned with the arts and culture, politics, science and technology, business, and religion. Teacher education is therefore – actually and even more so in its potential – an intellectual project that reaches both deep into the university and outside of it and has a democratic function that while not always realised is nonetheless important in its articulation.

The second part of my argument arises from the first and proposes teacher education as a good example of a democratic and powerful mode of knowledge production that grows out of hybrid practices (academic and professional, instrumental and reflexive, personal and political) and out of dialogue between researchers and research subjects and research end users. In working in the hybrid spaces between universities, schools, and communities, teacher education can bring together diverse actors with varying interests and expertise to create knowledge that can meet multiple tests of rigour in intersecting networks of practice. Conceptualising teacher education as hybrid knowledge-creating practices or as an activity rich with potential for a more democratic mode of knowledge production also requires us to think through the power differentials in bringing people together – teachers and professors, children and students, parents, members of communities. The implication is therefore one of struggle – of competing interests – in which there is something for everyone to give up as well as for a collective, democratic gain.

After making these arguments at a theoretical level, I then briefly discuss an empirical study in the teacher education setting (designed using cultural-historical methodologies) that has helped me identify the barriers to the realisation of my theoretical arguments about teacher education's potential while also trying to realise that potential in joint work with participants. In concluding, I suggest cultural-historical theories offer interesting ways of understanding teacher education as a democratic and democratising form of higher education – but also of developing it. And an essential preliminary to this potential is a critical consciousness of the current situation among the leaders of the profession. I do not underestimate the difficulty of attaining even this first base.

## Four Types of Knowledge and the Pivotal Position of
## Teacher Education

In his proposal for an alternative framing of the functions of the public university, sociologist Michael Burawoy places a knowledge problem at its centre. Universities, says Burawoy, have been dealing with twin governmental tendencies: the *commodification* of knowledge and the *regulation* of knowledge production: 'If commodification raises the question of knowledge for whom, regulation raises the question of knowledge for what?' (2011, p. 31). In response, Burawoy categorises four types of knowledge under two broad headings – instrumental and reflexive – and contends the public university must attend to all four types of knowledge even while the balance between the four may vary from discipline to discipline. The instrumental types of knowledge are those that allow certain kinds of work to be accomplished; instrumental knowledge is about 'orienting means to ends' (2011, p. 31). Reflexive types of knowledge are those that require dialogue about values and purposes underlying the development of necessary instrumentalities towards broader social goals. Although Burawoy claims reflexive knowledge is at greater risk in relation to contemporary emphases on the instrumental, he nonetheless accepts the importance of instrumental types of knowledge. Thus, *professional* knowledge (defined as that produced in research and scholarly activity) he sees 'at the heart of the public university' (2011, p. 32). But the autonomy of *professional* knowledge is only possible if there is a community of scholarly practice to examine it critically and to do so from a moral and ethical (i.e. value-laden) perspective. It is this *critical* knowledge that is the 'conscience' of the academic community. These dimensions – *professional* and *critical* – exist primarily in academic discourse communities, but they have heteronymous relationships with the kinds of knowledge Burawoy calls *policy* and *public*. *Professional* knowledge can be transformed (and transformative) in the realm of *policy*, but the two types of knowledge are interdependent. Similarly, the reflexive *critical* knowledge of the academic discourse community has an interdependent relationship with *public* knowledge about ends, purposes, and consequences for society. Just as the development of *professional* knowledge cannot be 'short-circuited' in the service of *policy* knowledge, *critical* knowledge is not shared with wider publics at the risk of damage to the development of *public* knowledge and to the development of the *critical* knowledge that is the 'collective conscience' of the university (2011, pp. 32–33). Burawoy asserts:

the public university gives weight to each of the four types of knowledge, requires them to be in dialogue with each other and recognises their interdependence *even as they are in an antagonistic relation*. Each knowledge depends on the other three. (2011, p. 33; my emphasis)

TABLE 13.1.  *The Functions of Teacher Education in the Public University*

|  | AUTONOMY<br>Academic audience | HETERONOMY<br>Extra-academic audience |
|---|---|---|
| Instrumental<br>knowledge | PROFESSIONAL<br>Knowledge arising out of<br>research designed to develop<br>educational practice (however<br>conceptualised), such as<br>effective teaching | POLICY<br>Knowledge associated with<br>the application of research<br>designed to improve<br>educational practice in<br>achieving governmental<br>functions and political<br>aims for society |
| Reflexive<br>knowledge | CRITICAL<br>Knowledge associated with the<br>critical evaluation of research<br>and traditions of research that<br>seek to develop educational<br>practice, knowledge that<br>situates this research in wider<br>intellectual contexts | PUBLIC<br>Knowledge associated<br>with the deliberation<br>of critical knowledge<br>about the development<br>of educational practice<br>in the public sphere that<br>enables the creation of<br>multiple publics |

*Source*:  Adapted from Burawoy (2011, p. 32).

In Table 13.1, after Burawoy, I provide a framework for understanding these types of knowledge in relation to the functions of teacher education in the public university.

Burawoy states that the university, if it is to have the democratising functions associated with the public university, must address all four types of knowledge in the balance of its activities. He does not present this integrative balance as easy or permanent, but as something that must be continually remade. For Burawoy, it is the social sciences that 'form the pivot around which the four knowledges revolve' (2011, p. 33), but I argue it is the social science we call teacher education that is that pivot and that teacher education is therefore an activity essential to the work of the public university. Teacher education, in different ways and at different times, involves the preparation of teachers *as citizens* (Grumet, 2010) who in turn have some responsibility to society for preparing new generations of the citizenry.

The professional knowledge (in Burawoy's definition) of teacher education arises out of a variety of disciplinary activities that might also take place in the school setting. It is instrumental in its orientation towards the improvement of educational practice – but is nonetheless deliberative, systematic, and subject to the community's rituals of verification. Professional knowledge that does not seek a relationship with policy knowledge will, as Burawoy puts it, 'wither away'. If teacher education does not seek to inform the development of policy for institutions such as schooling, then it removes itself from society and becomes a circular game of individual, academic *embourgoisement* (c.f. Guillory, 1994). Similarly, if the realm of policy tries to co-opt professional knowledge on its own terms, selectively and in ideologically driven ways, or if policy seeks to buy professional knowledge through narrowing research priorities, then both professional and policy knowledge are devalued. The only option is that of continuing and difficult dialogue. And these types of knowledge also require the reflexivity provided by critical examination within and outside the academic community. Instrumental forms of knowledge associated with the development of educational practice (such as effective teaching) must be situated within the historical intellectual contexts in which such activities evolve as well as in deliberations over the direction of society and the extra-academic moral and ethical interests of the publics. In its work across the university, into the realm of policy, and deep into the community, teacher education can (and, just occasionally, does) promote just the sort of 'critical engagement and deliberative democracy' Burawoy has been arguing for the public university as a whole.

Drawing on Cultural Historical Activity Theory, Ken Zeichner has been explicitly arguing for a similar shift in the existing practices of teacher education in the United States. Recognising the actual and potential distinctive strengths of university coursework in preservice programmes – the development of student teachers who are more able to exercise judgement in classrooms through their exposure to research-based knowledge, for example – he nonetheless makes a broader argument for the profound reconfiguration of the practices of teacher education:

[T]he preparation of teachers for democratic societies should be based on an epistemology that is itself democratic and includes a respect for and interaction among practitioner, academic and community-based knowledge. (Zeichner, Payne, & Brayko, 2012, p. 5)

So, for Zeichner, this is also in part a knowledge problem where the professional knowledge of university education professors has been deployed in 'nonegalitarian' ways with school teacher partners (along the lines of 'research has "lessons" for teachers'), but it is also a problem of the university's relation to society. In their arguments for a more democratic teacher education, Zeichner and colleagues use the concept of 'hybrid spaces' – designed social environments that bring actors from different fields of practice together to work on a potentially shared problem or, in activity theory terms, object (Engeström,

Miettinen, &Punamäki, 1999). In these 'third' spaces, new knowledge and value-laden practices can emerge from the dialogic sharing of expertise by the various partners. It is in these new practices that distributed knowledge of different types can actively work on the development of teacher education practice – work that is more democratically organised as well as democratising (challenging achievement gaps related to cultural and class background, for example). The difference between Zeichner's position and the one I have argued thus far is that I am proposing that the integration of professional, policy, critical, and public knowledge is the responsibility of the public university *as a whole institution* and that, while new spaces may well be necessary, the democratising functions of knowledge work in teacher education should place it at the heart of this type of university.

These arguments are challenging for many within the university teacher education community as they might be regarded as going against the direction of much of the work of disciplining teacher education (giving the field some perceived intellectual rigour) over the last thirty years or more. Teacher education has sought to professionalise itself, to justify its activities on what it sees as the criteria of other social science disciplines to raise its institutional status and ensure its security. Many powerful advocates for this sort of professionalising activity may see the kind of integration Burawoy is arguing for generally – and I am arguing for particularly – as a step down the disciplinary ladder. But the argument I am making is neither for ill-disciplined activity nor for dismantling the professional, disciplinary goals of teacher education, but rather that teacher education as an intellectual project models a kind of integrative balance between different types of knowledge that exemplifies the democratic mission of the public university as whole.

## Hybrid Practices and Mode 2 Knowledge Production

Traditions of research in teacher education have long included what we might call exceptional arguments about knowledge in and for teaching (c.f. Ellis, 2007). Concepts such as 'craft' knowledge (Tom 1984) or 'pedagogical content knowledge' (Shulman 1987) have been advanced as exceptional categories of teachers' professional knowledge that resist codification and are, to various degrees, tacit, embodied, and situated. This exceptionality – that there is a special kind of wisdom unique to effective teachers and teaching – was part of a wider claim for the professional status of the profession as well as justifications of the kind of work that went on in universities' teacher preparation programmes. In this chapter, I am making a very different argument: the kind of hybrid social practices that characterise teacher education programmes align very closely with the mode of knowledge production identified by Gibbons and colleagues (1994) as Mode 2. Although Gibbons and his colleagues' research arises out of the sociology of science rather than cultural-historical theory, the work is highly relevant as it emphasises the complex social mediations necessary for the growth of scientific concepts.

Gibbons and his colleagues argued that the traditional (Mode 1) ways knowledge is produced (experimental science being their key example) have responded in complex ways to demographic and technological change as well as economic globalisation to the extent that a new modality of knowledge production is identifiable. Mode 1 knowledge production is determined by academic interests, 'primarily cognitive' in orientation (Gibbons et al., 1994, p. 1), with a hierarchical, 'homogenous' social organisation that prizes autonomy. By contrast, Mode 2 is characterised by heterogeneity, transdisciplinarity, social accountability, and reflexivity in hybrid social practices that are at the same time academic and nonacademic, instrumental and critical, personal and political. So rather than being unusual or exceptional in the ways it produces knowledge, teacher education is a potentially good example of a highly networked, participatory, diverse, and distributed mode of knowledge production. In its intentions, at least, it offers a more democratic alternative.

As Nowotny, Scott, and Gibbons later reflected in 'Mode 2 Revisited', their idea was taken up rather differently across fields, with those with 'most to gain...struggling to wiggle out from under the condescension of more established...disciplines' (2003, p. 179), sometimes espousing Mode 2 in rather ill-informed and uncritical ways. Similarly, as they acknowledge, many appropriations of Mode 2 erased the economic context of the idea and the commercialisation of the research 'business', the knowledge outcome – or 'product' – determined at least in part by the interests of global capital (whether in public or private research funding infrastructures). Nonetheless, Mode 2 does offer a useful metaphor for a shift in the ways knowledge is produced across the professional, policy, critical, and public functions of the university. At its core is a fundamental cultural-historical idea: a 'dialogical process, an intense (and perhaps endless) "conversation" between research actors and research subjects' (2003, p. 187) and, we might add, users. This blurring of identifications of investigators, subjects, users, and 'scientific peers' also blurs the categorisations of basic or pure and applied research as well as traditional linear chronologies of 'projects' (from data collection through to dissemination). As such, Mode 2 offers a challenge as much as it is a realistic description.

The nature of the challenge is indicated by Nowotny's use of *agora* to represent the hybrid spaces, forums, and communities of the original Mode 2 theorisation (Gibbons et al., 1994). *Agora* is used to indicate marketplace as well as meeting point and is therefore a somewhat controversial archaism that seeks to account for different kinds of capital. Originally, Gibbons used hybrid space, for example, to describe the 'meeting point of a range of diverse actors, frequently in public controversies' (1994, p. 167). The correspondence here was with the third Mode 2 principle of 'organisational diversity'. In the later Nowotny, Scott, and Gibbons reflections, the *agora* has become a more explicitly political as well as commercial zone of proximal development – literally a social market that is simultaneously a space for conceptual growth:

> The *agora* is the problem-generating and problem-solving environment in which the contextualisation of knowledge production takes place. It is populated not only by arrays of competing 'experts', and the organisations and institutions through which knowledge is generated and traded, but also by variously jostling 'publics'. It is not simply a political or commercial arena in which research priorities are identified and funded, nor an arena in which research findings are disseminated, traded and used. The *agora* is a domain of primary knowledge production – through which people enter the research process, and where 'Mode 2' knowledge is embodied in people and projects. (2003, p. 192)

The teacher education partnerships between schools, universities, and, potentially, communities constitute one such difficult and antagonistic *agora*. In structural terms, at least, the connections and communication channels exist and, in England, have been mandated for twenty years even though their potential as complex and distributed zones of proximal development has not been systematically realised. Zeichner, Payne, and Brayko use the concept of 'horizontal expertise' from Cultural Historical Activity Theory to speculate on the possibilities for more egalitarian and democratising teacher education practices, where partners' 'different interests, values and practices' can be socially mediated and a new and potentially transformative shared object might emerge (2012, p. 7). Zeichner also draws on Engeström's (2008) concept of 'knot-working' to suggest the participation of multiple actors with diverse expertise (academic, policy, community, etc.) needs to be more fluid and object oriented than conventional institutional structures allow. 'Knots' signal difficult, collaborative work on an object that is shared across institutional boundaries and it is in this joint work on transforming the object of activity that new knowledge is produced through innovative practices. Again, this presents a challenge (perhaps especially to academics) as a different kind of knowledge is prioritised – knowledge from the *agora* rather than knowledge from the *acropolis* – and means there is something to give up for all partners in shared aspirations for a collective, democratic gain. Judged individually, knowledge that emerges from such hybrid practices can appear weak – attribution is fragmented and individual capitalisation more difficult. Seen more collectively – and understanding hybridity etymologically – hybrid practices of knowledge production are stronger, more socially accountable and reflexive, and more generative of the kind of democratic flourishing that is the mission of the public university.

### Cultural-Historical Theories at Work in the Analysis and Development of Teacher Education Practices

Teacher education partnerships of various kinds exist all around the world with universities playing more or less significant roles. In this chapter, I am particularly focussed on teacher education in relation to universities in England and the United States where different responsibilities in interinstitutional relationships have evolved historically. I have been arguing that such partnerships in their potential can already support the democratic modes of knowledge production and the democratising functions of knowledge I have been discussing. Currently, they often do so in ad hoc or serendipitous ways; occasionally they work more systematically towards these ends. But my argument is that the full potential of such hybrid spaces has not been realised and to do so we need to more fully embrace the sense of crisis in higher education and align our motives with those of the public university as an ideal. Next, I briefly reflect on one example of an empirical project that addresses these issues.

#### Developing English Teaching and Internship Learning (DETAIL)
Between 2005 and 2008, I engaged in a formative intervention in the teacher education setting that adapted the developmental work research (DWR) methodology of Engeström (2007) to create new spaces for learning within an established teacher education partnership (e.g. Ellis, 2010, 2011a). Working with four high school English departments, four mentor teachers, and sixteen student teachers, I planned and implemented a year-long series of Change Laboratories – participatory data analysis workshops in which the teachers, student teachers, and I analysed data from their practice settings using the conceptual tools of activity theory. The data had been generated by a research assistant, the student teachers (as part of their coursework), and myself in response to each school department's selection of a 'problem of practice', something concerned with the teaching and learning of English (as a school subject) that they wished to improve. As is usual in these circumstances, the identification of the problem of practice formed a large part of the research

(in addition to a year of relationship building in advance) in that the teachers, student teachers, and I needed to understand the existing practices of the English departments at a conscious and articulated level before we could begin to think about change.

In one of the English departments, the problem of practice was identified as the teaching of writing, particularly around the use of writing frames, resources strongly recommended in literacy education policy in England at the time (c.f. Ellis, 2011b). Writing frames provide students with the text-level structure of the written genre the teacher has selected for instruction (e.g. providing sentence starters and discourse markers). In the dialogic space of the Change Laboratory, our collective understandings of the problem were mediated by the activity theory tools so that the functions of writing frames in the activity systems of the English classrooms were examined. Rather than functioning coherently as pedagogical tools – scaffolding young writers into new or unfamiliar genres (i.e. mediating their writing activity) – the writing frames were functioning as rules, in activity theory terms, a determining characteristic of the social organisation of the classrooms. For the teachers and student teachers, this realisation initially turned on their understandings of genre as a concept and how this concept was appropriated in their pedagogical activities. Genre was understood as a 'tick list' of conventions ('A-grade texts have these linguistic features') rather than as a recognisable pattern of social interaction. For myself as researcher, the realisation turned on how the social organisation of the particular classrooms, the English department and school more generally, and the political economy of English teaching in England determined the object of the pedagogical activity. Genre was appropriated relatively superficially in these English classrooms because the object of activity had become success in performance management systems where teachers (and the head of the English department particularly) were held accountable and potentially rewarded for the test results of their students. Writing frames, although potentially tools that might scaffold learners' participation in new genres, were used as rules of compliance within a very different division of labour in which students become data for measuring teacher performance rather than their learning becoming the concrete object of teachers' activity.

The DWR Change Laboratories of the DETAIL project can be seen as hybrid social spaces where different kinds of expertise were brought together to work on a shared object. Albeit in a limited way, the Change Laboratories brought together the *professional* (academic and school teaching) knowledge of the participants in relation to the *policy* knowledge required of schoolteachers and teacher educators (the coercive power of policy to recommend writing frames as the 'solution' to poor-quality student writing) and also knowledge from the wider disciplinary communities of sociology and politics that is *critical* of naïve associations between an individual's competence in a written genre and that individual's economic prosperity (e.g. Luke, 1998). A weakness of the DETAIL project – as with so many of teacher education's activities – was that it did not achieve wider public conversations about the direction of literacy education policy in England nor did it engage with community knowledge of literacy practices. That said, if the publics includes the school teaching profession outside the specific local community of the research, then one could argue public deliberation was stimulated. In one sense, of course, it does not matter if the problems of practice in the DETAIL schools were 'solved' through the application of the DWR methodology, as any expectation of 'solving' is probably indicative of a poor understanding of 'a practice'. The conscious articulation of the problem, stimulated and made possible in the rebalancing of the professional, policy, critical, and public functions of knowledge, was a worthwhile outcome in itself. But it is undoubtedly true that until that rebalancing coincides with the greater semiotic freedom of participants to reconfigure the social organisation of the problematic activities – and the material conditions in which they are situated and shaped – sustainable change in practices is inevitably limited.

Without wishing to advance cultural-historical theories or methodologies as *panacea*, it does seem reasonable to claim they offer a distinctive and useful means of working on the democratisation of knowledge production. Rejecting dualistic understandings of mind and behaviour, cultural-historical theories require us to attend to the materiality and social organisation of human activity to understand the development of higher psychological functions. So in teacher education activity, the division of labour (between schools and universities but also *within* universities and beyond to communities) matters for the kinds of knowledge that is possible both to access and to develop in prospective teachers as well as in mentor or supervisory colleagues and university faculty members. Cultural-historical research also offers us the tools of a radical and interventionist tradition with a formative or developmental purpose; it works from an interested and progressive standpoint. But it is also underpinned by the Vygotskian emphasis on dialectics, the relationship between spontaneous and scientific concepts, historical continuity, and revolutionary change. A cultural-historical approach therefore necessarily challenges ahistorical or immaterial interpretations or the studied disinterestedness of universities that want to sit outside of the world. So a researcher in the cultural-historical tradition does not seek to lesson schoolteachers, for example, through the delivery of 'findings' to 'end-users'. As Engeström points out in his comments on the design experiment methodology, such a linear view of knowledge *transfer* 'ignores what sociologists teach us about interventions as contested terrains that are full of resistance, reinterpretation, and surprise' (2007, p. 369). Rather, cultural-historical researchers recognise the expertise of others as well as their own and resist the position of final arbiter in the process of knowledge production. Unlike some other perspectives – such as recent iterations of citizen science, for example – cultural-historical researchers do not simply include the publics to increase the validity of their data collection (c.f. Cohn, 2008). Cultural-historical researchers have a different object to those from other traditions in that they seek the formation of '*critical design agency* among all the parties: researchers, teachers, and students or, respectively, researchers, managers, workers, and clients' (Engeström, 2007, p. 370; emphasis in the original). In terms of the current relationships between university education faculty members and schoolteachers, this aspiration for the collaborative exercise of different agencies presents a formidable challenge, not the least of which is a risk associated with the general approach which Engeström describes as 'paternalistic manipulation' (Engeström, 2007, p. 382). But the challenge also extends to schoolteachers who must also be willing to give up their rugged or 'heroic' individualism and the tacit wisdom of the 'craft' to gain greater control over their own activities and their development through an active engagement in the production of new knowledge.

From the perspective of higher education, cultural-historical theories can support the development of pedagogy and the design of learning environments at practical and organisational levels. Formative interventions in the Engeström tradition are one example of a powerful methodology. But they cannot be successfully co-opted in service of the status quo, layering a sociocultural veneer over business as usual. A cultural-historical perspective demands the creative disturbance of existing practices so that they might be reconfigured, a change process that has to be desired by willing participants. Such a desirable reconfiguration implies a transformation of sense making. And transformation is necessarily disruptive. How far we will allow our practices to be disrupted and how willing we are to be surprised are important questions for all those interested in realising the potential of a cultural-historical approach to the development of teacher education in the public university.

## Disenthralling Ourselves: Embracing the Crisis

In her collection *Dream of a Common Language*, poet Adrienne Rich (1993) writes about a time of personal crisis around her decision, during the 1970s, to live as a lesbian. The crisis, as she expresses it in the poem 'Transcendental

Etude', is as much a crisis of knowing as it is of identity; a transformation of one way of being in the world to another way of being requiring her to know the world differently. The poem has often spoken to educators at their own times of crisis, notably during the presidency of George W. Bush when Maxine Greene (2008) quoted from it as a call to action, to resist antidemocratic tendencies as well as specific education policies such as 'No Child Left Behind'. At one level, the poem is a recognition of the power of crisis to stimulate difficult but transformative change – an idea entirely consistent with the Vygotskian understanding of development as revolutionary rather than evolutionary. But the poem is also a powerful expression of the loss involved in transformation and development, an expression of what we have to give up when we change who we are and the way we know the world. The desire to produce a new kind of knowledge is coupled in Rich's poem with the requirement to 'pull back from the incantations/rhythms we have moved to thoughtlessly'; to know differently involves a disruption and disturbance of comforting routines. So at a time of crisis when we have to desire rather than merely accept change, we have to 'disenthrall ourselves' of those routines and ways of being and 'cleanse' ourselves of 'oratory, formulas, choruses, laments, static/crowding the wires' (Rich, 1993).

In this chapter, I have made an argument about teacher education as an activity of the type of university that I, after many others, am referring to as the public university. Given the aim of this book, I have inevitably focussed on the relationships between the public university and the schools and the people who work in those institutions and the flows of knowledge between them and more widely into the world. My discussion of communities (i.e. both specific communities and the noneducation professional publics) has been limited. Nevertheless, it strikes me that these relationships between types of institution and types of worker as well as our conceptualisation of the public university as a whole are key to questions about doing higher education better (as well as teacher education better), by which I mean enabling more democratic and democratising modes of knowledge production. My argument has not been made on the basis of an exception for education as a discipline or teacher education as a disciplinary activity. I have not argued teacher education is a special case in the public university, but that it is one of its core activities and could even more strongly exemplify the public university's democratising integration of different types of knowledge at work in the world as well as more strongly exemplifying a more democratic mode of knowledge production. In making this argument, I have pointed to the structural constraints embedded in the social organisation of teacher education as an institutional activity and suggested that

transformation of existing arrangements into more democratic and powerful alternatives means embracing the crisis and accepting loss as part of the
change process. In terms of university teacher education personnel and a
commitment to the ideals of the public university, the challenge is considerable and necessarily one of leadership, as Wendy Brown concludes:

> Faculty interpellated by neoliberal rationality are generally unable to grasp,
> let alone resist, what is happening to postsecondary education. Distinguished
> faculty who enjoy the privileges of the top end of privatised publics tend to be
> focused on their own research, publications, invitations, prizes, fellowships,
> rankings, offers, and counter-offers. Younger faculty relentlessly socialised by
> neoliberal careerism are frequently unaware that there were or could be alter-
> native academic purposes and practices to those organised by a neoliberal table
> of values. All have grown accustomed to the saturation of university life by the
> rationales, metrics and economies of capital. (2011, p. 34)

During a teach-in at UC Berkeley to protest budget cuts across the University of
California system in 2009, former U.S. Secretary of Labor and Berkeley professor
Robert Reich said that, during the Bush presidency, it was easy to get car-driving
faculty to honk to a 'Out of Iraq' placard: 'everybody honks!' (Reich, 2009). It's
easy to get people like you to agree with you and it's comfortable to blame the
other side. Instead, he argued, it is people like us who must take responsibility
for the urgency and depth of the crisis; we are guilty of 'denial, escapism, scape-
goating, cynicism' in refusing to address the problem. It is not clear from Reich's
speech just how much responsibility he apportions to agoraphobic academics
and the institutionalising power of the tenure track and professorial ladder, but
he clearly identifies a failure of leadership. In teacher education, such leadership
will be difficult to exercise, but it is a kind of leadership that must look outside
the academy into schools but also far beyond and aspire to the kind of rebalancing of knowledge functions typified by the public university as an ideal.

## References

Brown, W. (2011). The end of educated democracy. *Representations*, **116**, 1, 19–41.
Burawoy, M. (2011). Redefining the public university: Global and national contexts. In
    J. Holmwood, (Ed.), *A Manifesto for the Public University* (pp. 27–41). London and
    New York: Bloomsbury Academic.
Cohn, J. P. (2008). Citizen science: can volunteers do real research? *BioScience*,
    **58**(3), 192–97.
Collini, S. (2011). From Robbins to McKinsey. *London Review of Books*, **33**(16) (August
    2011), 9–14.
Dewey, John. (1927). *The Public and its Problems*. New York: Holt.

Ellis, V. (2007). *Subject Knowledge and Teacher Education: The development of beginning teachers' thinking*. London & New York: Continuum.

(2010). Impoverishing experience: The problem of teacher education in England. *Journal of Education for Teaching*, **36**(1), 105–20.

(2011a). Re-energising professional creativity from a CHAT perspective: Seeing knowledge and history in practice. *Mind, Culture and Activity: An International Journal*, **18**(2), 181–93.

(2011b). What happened to teachers' knowledge when they played 'The Literacy Game?' In A. Goodwyn and C. Fuller (Eds.), *The Great Literacy Debate: A critical response to the literacy strategy and the framework for teaching English* (pp. 27–44). London and New York: Routledge.

Engeström, Y. (2007). Putting activity theory to work: The change laboratory as an application of double stimulation. In H. Daniels, M. Cole, and J. V. Wertsch (Eds.). *The Cambridge Companion to Vygotsky* (pp. 363–82). Cambridge and New York: Cambridge University Press.

(2008). From Teams to Knots: Activity-theoretical studies of collaboration and learning at work. Cambridge: Cambridge University Press.

Engeström, Y., Miettinen, R., and Punamäki, R. L. (eds.) (1999). *Perspectives on Activity Theory*, Cambridge: Cambridge University Press.

Gibbons, M., Limoges, C., Nowotny, H., Schawrtzman, S., Scott, P., and Trow, M. (1994). *The New Production of Knowledge: The dynamics of science and research in contemporary societies*. London: Sage.

Greene, M. (2008). Art, imagination, and school renewal: Towards a common language. In B. Z Presseisen (Ed.). *Teaching for Intelligence*. 2nd ed. (pp. 45–60). Thousand Oaks, CA: Corwin Press.

Grumet, M. R. (2010). The public expression of citizen teachers. *Journal of Teacher Education*, **61**(1–2), 66–76.

Guillory, J. (1994). Literary critics as intellectuals: Class analysis and the crisis of the humanities. In W.-C. Dimock and M. T. Gilmore (Eds.), *Rethinking Class: Literary studies and social formations* (pp. 107–149). New York: Columbia University Press.

Gutmann, A. (1999). *Democratic Education*. Revised Edition. Princeton, NJ: Princeton University Press.

Holmwood, J. (ed.). (2011). *A Manifesto for the Public University*. London and New York: Bloomsbury Academic.

Luke, A. (1998). Genres of power. Literacy education and the production of capital. In R. Hasan and G. Williams (Eds.), *Literacy in Society* (pp. 308–38). New York: Longman.

Lye, C. and Vernon, J. (2011). The Humanities and the Crisis of the Public University. In The Newsletter of the Townsend Center for the Humanities at the University of California Berkeley (February/March 2011). Retrieved from http://townsendcenter. berkeley.edu/pubs/TC_Newsletter_FebMarch_2011.pdf.

Nowotny, H., Scott, P., and Gibbons, M. (2003). 'Mode 2' revisited: The new production of knowledge. *Minerva*, **41**, 179–94.

Reich, R. (2009). Save the university: Robert Reich. Part 5 [Video file]. Posted to http://www.youtube.com/watch?v=NrHQZNIX9jA.

Rich, A. (1993). *The Dream of a Common Language: Poems 1974–1977*. New edition. New York: W. W. Norton & Co.

Shulman, L.S. (1987). 'Knowledge and Teaching: Foundations of the new reform', *Harvard Educational Review*, **57** (1): 1–22.

Tom, A. (1984). *Teaching as a Moral Craft*. New York, NY: Longman.

Zeichner, K., Payne, K., and Brayko, K. (2012). *Democratising Knowledge in University Teacher Education through Practice-Based Methods Teaching and Mediated Field Experiences in Schools and Communities*. Issue Paper 12–1: University of Washington Center for the Study of Learning to Teach in Practice. Seattle, WA: University of Washington.

# 14

# What Does "Transformation of Participation" Mean in a University Classroom? Exploring University Pedagogy with the Tools of Cultural Historical Theory

Holli A. Tonyan and Glenn Auld

One of the prerequisites of professional programs is that the world of work is brought into contact with powerful concepts that help practitioners interpret and act on problems of practice in usefully informed ways. When university-based teachers engage with practitioners from worlds with which they are also familiar, they aim at achieving an interplay between the field of practice and useful concepts through evidence-based conversations. These conversations can ratchet up conceptualizations of the field and allow informed scrutiny of everyday responses to problems of practice. However, when the field of practice is poorly understood, achieving a productive interplay is more difficult. In this chapter, we identify such a problem, in this case arising when teaching a course in a national culture we did not know. We then discuss how ideas from Cultural Historical Activity Theory (CHAT) helped us build a basis of shared knowledge with students that could act as a springboard for their learning.

As teachers in higher educational settings, our concern is to help students on professional courses transform their participation in the activities of their academic and professional communities (Rogoff, 1995, 2003; Rogoff, Mistry, Göncü, & Mosier, 1993; Rogoff et al., 2007). The analytic resources of CHAT concepts have allowed a systematic reflection on our work. They have led to some suggestions for making relevant professional courses, so that local practices may connect with or raise questions about the global, where the global is represented by the powerful explanatory concepts offered by the course. In this concern we were mindful of the need to avoid intellectual colonialism. Instead, we wanted to create learning spaces where concepts could be tested as potentially useful tools in detailed examinations of local conditions.

The teaching context was a unit of study as part of a Masters of education in early childhood. It had previously been offered on campus at an Australian university and was being launched in distance mode in Singapore, a country neither of us knew well. The unit was one of three specialized early childhood units offered in combination with units focused on educational leadership. On this occasion, it was the first unit in which the students enrolled as part of their course. The course was designed in thirteen-week terms with four to five weeks of independent study, four days of intensive face-to-face interaction, and then four to five weeks of continued independent study. The readings for this unit asked students to consider tensions between local and global contexts of childhood and the ways adults' conceptions or images of children affect opportunities for learning, including the type and organization of activities through which children learn. The unit assignments asked students to present images of children and childhood found in some domain of children's lives in their local context and then to research the kinds of activities in which children participate with adults in that context. During the research they were to employ CHAT-based concepts from the unit.

Students read about learning as transformation and about how the images of children and childhood that adults hold may have different affordances for early childhood educational practice (Dahlberg, Moss, & Pence, 1999). They were also introduced to historical analysis and provided with concepts to help them examine how childhood was constructed in different historical eras. At a conceptual level the unit required students to analyze learning and development employing concepts such as mediation and tool use across multiple, interrelated levels (e.g., historical contexts, institutional settings and contexts, interpersonal relations, and individual understandings, actions, and characteristics). They were also helped to see learning and development as a dynamic process of transformation as individuals become increasingly capable of using and transforming the tools and material resources of their cultural community that they initially see others use (Rogoff, 2003).

The unit of study represented some of the tensions between local and global interests in higher education, not least because the four students following it were paying a high tuition fee for an international product offered through a Singaporean school of business and management, which was selling the intellectual property we had generated in a faculty of education in Australia. For example, the management school recruited students by marketing the degree on the grounds of the status we conferred as international scholars. However, our very status as scholars from outside Singapore meant we were not familiar with local contexts.

We interpreted the challenge of making what we brought to Singapore relevant to local circumstances through the analytic tools of CHAT. The topic of the unit was "contexts of childhood," and because of the way the course had been developed in Australia, the initial frame of reference offered to the students in Singapore was derived from content local to Australia. We gathered examples of children interacting in everyday contexts in the region of Australia where we were working and compiled a CD-ROM that presented the local examples together with quotations from the readings and questions to guide their reflections.

Examples included video clips of children engaged in preparing food with an adult or sorting through groceries to put them in their proper places in the pantry. These clips provided concrete examples from which to discuss the different ways adults structure learning interactions, ranging from task-oriented language (such as language focused on how to get the roti the right shape for dinner rather than on teaching about shapes as concepts) to directed, language-rich instructional discourse (such as "what shapes are these cookies?" Or asking how a child knew where to put groceries).

The students were then asked to research and present parallel examples of the theoretical concepts in use in early childhood settings from their own local contexts. As a consequence we taught each other about our different environments using unifying conceptual tools to bridge across the contexts and constructing a more global understanding through a shared theoretical frame.

The students drew on the knowledge they brought to the unit to create a shared fund of knowledge as a resource for staff members and students. For example, one student with a professional background in advertising used the images of childhood we had discussed to analyze advertisements from the past and from different magazines with different target audiences to explore how children were represented. She brought her prior experiences of analyzing advertisements for gender bias to examining images of children in advertising while still incorporating the intellectual tools of discourse, historical setting, and so on. In presenting her analysis to the class, she taught the authors about the local Singaporean context, and drawing on her understanding of advertising, she helped her peers reinterpret their local contexts using the common language of course concepts combined with expertise developed in her prior professional work.

The unit of study also represented a time of transition at the personal, professional, institutional, and national levels for us, for the students, and for the host institution. As relatively new and probationary faculty, we were making the transition from graduate student to professor and at the same time learning to teach in an unfamiliar context. The students, we soon learned, were not predominantly early childhood professionals, as we had expected. Three were moving on from previous occupations as homemakers or business professionals (marketing and engineering), and only one was working in early childhood settings. At the institutional level, this was a new unit of study and part of an emerging collaboration between the business school and the university in which we worked in Australia.

The two nations were also in transition in the field of early education – with Singapore enthusiastically seeking to develop a higher education-based infrastructure in early childhood education at the same time as Australia was severely cutting back on investment in its own early years higher educational infrastructure. As a result of all these transitions and multiple layers of context, there were often competing discourses that made learning both complex and potentially rich.

In analyzing the situation we begin by describing how the CHAT concepts of guided participation, activity, and community (Rogoff, 1995) were useful to us in planning for and understanding the interpersonal dynamics of learning in the environments we have described. We then explain how the concepts of common knowledge and relational expertise (Edwards, 2010) provided analytic tools for understanding the changes we saw in ourselves and the students. We finally reflect on our experiences overall and the impact they have had on developing an ethical approach to teaching and learning that made the global relevant to the local through a sensitivity to the purposes and priorities of cultures inhabited by the students.

## Guided Participation

In considering how to be mediators of what matters in society across a distance and without direct access to the society in which the students would be working, we found Rogoff's writing about guided participation particularly useful. It occurs as:

[t]he events of everyday life as individuals engage with others and with materials and arrangements collaboratively managed by themselves and others. It includes direct interaction with others as well as engaging in or avoiding activities assigned, made possible, or constrained by others, *whether or not they are in each other's presence* or even know of each other's existence. Guided participation may be tacit or explicit, *face-to-face or distal*, involved in shared endeavors with specific familiar people or distant unknown individuals or groups – peers as well as experts, neighbors as well as distant heroes, siblings as well as ancestors.... Participation requires engagement in some aspect of the meaning of shared endeavors, but not *necessarily in symmetrical or even joint action*. (1995, p. 147, emphases added)

This way of describing learning activity encouraged us to look for (a) how individuals contribute to understanding each other, which Rogoff terms *mutual bridging of meanings* and Edwards describes as the *building of common knowledge* (Edwards, 2010); (b) how individuals coordinate their activity in participating together, which Rogoff calls *mutual structuring of participation* and Edwards terms *the exercise of relational expertise*; and (c) the purposes of activities from the perspectives of all the participants, remembering that "activity is directed, not random or without a purpose" (Rogoff, 1995, p. 148).

## Activity

According to CHAT approaches, learning and development are best understood in the context of meaningful joint activity. In this view, we can misrepresent and misunderstand if we attempt to examine components of activity without regard for the intertwining of contexts, public meaning, and personal sense making. Rogoff explains:

The use of "activity" or "event" as the unit of analysis – with active and dynamic contributions from individuals, their social partners, and historical traditions and materials and their transformations – allows a reformulation of the relation between individual and social and cultural environment in which each is inherently involved in the others' definition. (1995, p. 110)

For example, although reading could be seen as an individual or solitary activity, Rogoff's approach suggests that during reading a student engages with the author as well as historical traditions mediated by the educator through direct and indirect means. Consequently, the reader is actively involved in making personal sense of public understandings. We used these ideas to design a multimodal resource that supported the students' learning.

We designed an electronic study guide that directed students to excerpts from the readings and asked them to relate the ideas they contained to their own experiences and contexts. This was important because few of the readings examined the particular contexts of childhood in Singapore. Nonetheless, they contained theoretical constructs for analyzing how specific features of childhood in one context might relate to features of childhood in others, that is, to bring into dual focus the local and the global. We prompted students to reflect on their own experiences in relation to the extracts. In this way, we directed their sense making by highlighting particular elements; while also leaving possibilities for students to engage with the questions raised elsewhere in the readings. The study guide required students to create reports of their responses to the extracts and to the prompts given to guide their reading. The intention was that they would bring the reports to face-to-face meetings, when the authors were in Singapore, as texts for discussion and/or post them to the relevant web-based discussion forum prior to the meetings.

Another way educators in higher education contribute to mutual bridging of meanings in the activity of reading is by sharing examples of data to
complement ideas in the readings. Many of the readings for the unit referred
to patterns of interaction between children and between adults and children
that were difficult to imagine when working solely from textual descriptions; but few commercially produced videos exist to illustrate the patterns
of interaction described. We, therefore, included video examples from our
research in Australia and provided prompts to help students relate the video
examples to their readings and local contexts. The video clips presented
examples of children's everyday experiences across diverse Australian settings. Prompts included directing students to identify components of the
activity, based on theoretical constructs from the readings, and asking them
to reflect on the kinds of activities children in Singapore might experience
and how those activities might compare with the activities portrayed in the
video examples.

The study guide and the prompted data sharing provided students with
strategies for making sense of complex material, while learning at a distance from the providing university. In addition, the intention was to create
opportunities for students to exercise their personal agency in deciding how
to structure their participation in the activities provided. We asked students
to keep a log of their thoughts about the material and to share the log with
classmates and with us as they saw fit. We had also hoped the students would
be able to contribute to and adjust the design of the technology in a process
of co-construction. However, flexible technology that could be used easily
in dynamic ways across a distance was not available to us at that time. We
were therefore restricted to CD-ROM technology (Auld & Tonyan, 2006)
to distribute the electronic study guide. Nonetheless, we hoped the study
guide could be redesigned during face-to-face sessions *with* students, using
examples they identified themselves for their assignments. Unfortunately, the
students were not interested in redesigning the technology; but instead chose
to structure their participation by presenting their ideas and examples in the
form of technology they all knew well already: PowerPoint presentations.

Persistently, we continued with our intention of redressing what we saw
as the imbalance of a knowledge flow predominantly from faculty members
to course participants. We therefore structured the face-to-face sessions to
achieve a shift from more expert-guided to more student-guided interactions.
Sessions early in the unit were designed around guided joint exploration of
the texts, whereas later sessions involved students bringing the extracts and
images they had been selecting and gathering to create a new set of examples
they would organize and structure themselves. The final face-to-face session

involved the students presenting drafts of what would be their presentation assignment where students and faculty were the audience.

Mutual structuring of participation was also incorporated into assessments by our designing tasks that focused on students examining teaching and learning processes. The assignment guidelines and marking criteria privileged critique and deconstruction of the contexts and activities that adults designed for children. The guidelines and criteria also indicated some of the theoretical concepts to be used in the analysis of contexts and activities. The students decided how to use those concepts in the context of their chosen topic, with assistance provided during face-to-face sessions. This structured support appeared useful in setting expectations, as all the students were able to use ideas from the unit to analyze and understand aspects of their own local contexts by the time they completed their final assignment.

## Communities

From the beginning of the program we did not profess to be creating a community of practice. Nonetheless, we had anticipated entering a professional community when we planned the Singapore experience. We drew on Rogoff's view of communities as "groups of people who have some common and continuing organization, values, and understanding, history, and practices" (2003, p. 80). In Melbourne, all Australian students enrolled in the course were practicing early childhood professionals, with only a few students enrolling to change from one profession to another. Therefore, we expected the enduring Singapore community from which the relatively temporary groups of students would be drawn would be an overarching early childhood community (Fleer et al., 2006). We understood the early childhood community in any cultural environment to involve professionals trying to accomplish the care and education of young children. These communities would be marked by: some stability of involvement as regulated by government bodies and professional organizations; attention to the ways they relate to each other in terms of government regulations and professional standards; and traditions that transcend individuals as curricula are adopted and changed. In most countries, training is provided by institutions; governments or regulating bodies manage accreditation; and certification is required for participation.

However, we soon found that the model we have just outlined was not matched by what we found in this case. In Singapore, the students did not see themselves as participating in a community of early childhood educators. Instead, they saw themselves as *planning* to participate in the community of early childhood practitioners, mostly in the role of directors of early childhood centers. Their resistance to our intentions to engage them in the wider community obliged us to broaden our sense of what participation in communities meant and raised questions about how to maintain the focus on learning to engage in practices with historical legacies and meanings that might link individuals together into meaningful groups or communities.

Although we did not recognize it at the time, we had created a space where "common knowledge" (Edwards, 2010) could be exercised. Edwards argues that when people from different practices come together to work on a shared problem, their interactions are mediated by knowledge held in common and that knowledge consists of "what matters," that is, the motives that give shape to action in activities in those practices, in each of the contributing practices. In the unit we are discussing, common knowledge was built by revealing what mattered in the different practices that informed it by applying the analytic resources of CHAT to local Singaporean practices and to the practices in the Australian video clips. Our reflections on how we met the challenges of bringing local practices into broad conceptualizations of practice suggest we created what Edwards has called "emergent, flexible configurations of practices" (2010, p. 29).

Conceptualizing the unit in this way has the potential to offer a vision more generally for professional courses in higher education. In the context of the temporary, but potentially "emergent, flexible" groups of people who find themselves together in higher education courses, educators can work toward first establishing shared understanding of conceptual tools and then engage in working with and on them. These shared tools subsequently become the means to understand the practices participants have come from and those they are hoping to either enter or inform once the course ends.

### Research Projects as a Way of Practicing Expertise

We also reflected on the reconfiguring of understanding that arose for ourselves and the students during processes of sense making. Following the CHAT line taken by Edwards (2010), we see learning as involving working on problems using concepts that allow us to enhance our understanding of the problem and how we might respond to it. Edwards has used the terminology of activity theory, which sees an "object of activity" as a problem space at which energy is directed. She has explained learning as follows: "transforming the object of activity through acting on it and seeing it differently," for example, "revealing more of the meanings inherent in a task" (Edwards & D'Arcy, 2004, p. 148). The call for pedagogy as "enhancing [students'] disposition to engage with and transform features of their worlds" (Edwards & D'Arcy, 2004, p. 147) resonated with us and the goals we had set forth in the digital study guide and assignments for students.

The assignments for the unit provided evidence that students were seeing increased complexity and transforming features of their worlds. The digital study guide we produced and the organization of the face-to-face sessions were planned to help students learn about the intellectual tools, internalize them, and begin to act with them on unit tasks. The first assignment asked them to formally externalize their understandings of those tools by finding images of children and childhood in their local context, analyzing them using the intellectual tools that were the topic of the unit, and presenting the analyzed images to us during the face-to-face sessions. The second assignment asked students to research a local context designed for children, interview key stakeholders, and use concepts from the course to understand the evidence generated. Both assignments, originally developed by our colleague Marilyn Fleer, encouraged the development of students' ability to see a new complexity in previously unremarkable aspects of their local environment (e.g., advertisements, the organization of parks or spaces, the design of clothing). The common knowledge built over the unit brought together students' prior expertise, their interpretations of local contexts, evidence from Australia, and conceptual tools from CHAT. That knowledge then became a resource for the whole group and for us as educators to be used to expand understanding of previously taken for granted phenomena.

A CHAT approach to learning also highlights the dialectic of individual internalization and externalization. The assignments, for example, aimed at capturing the students' externalization of course concepts in the worlds in which they were to be working. To find local images of children and childhood, which they saw as historically and culturally situated representations embedded in local practices, the students had to internalize a set of intellectual tools. Subsequently presenting their analyses of images to us and to each other involved externalizing their analyses using these tools. Each presentation involved matching examples of the ideas from the assigned readings with their own interpretations and relating these to local examples. In the resulting PowerPoint presentations they worked with globally recognized theoretical ideas to understand local conditions and practices and then related the local back to the global to understand the implications for theory and practice.

Face-to-face sessions provided the first steps in what we now see as encouraging students to build common knowledge which, in turn, we were able to connect to global analyses of early childhood education and care. For example, one student examined advertisements for early childhood programs in Singapore specifically to understand how the programs positioned children in the advertisements. In response to his presentation, the class discussed the intellectual and cultural origin of the programs. The discussion considered the extent to which Singapore programs highlighted Western philosophies and curricula (e.g., Montessori or a U.S.-based model called Developmentally Appropriate Practice) with little attention to local cultural heritage or practices.

Another example of a growing understanding of links between local and global occurred when one student examined provision for children at four different religious institutions. He interviewed the staff members responsible for organizing the activities about the goals of the activities and how the activities were organized. He then analyzed the activities using intellectual tools from the course to identify how the activities varied across sites in, for example, what was mediated and how the mediation occurred and how children were positioned as learners at each site. He was able to critique the activities and suggest ways the activities could more effectively recognize and encourage children to be seen as active agents able to begin to take some responsibility for their own learning trajectories. Coursework encouraged him to look for new ways of conceptualizing children and childhood in his own local context with respect to a problem he identified – how adults inadvertently restrict opportunities children have to participate in the practices of their religious institutions.

The final assignment also provided students with opportunities to demonstrate their developing capacity to work alongside others on a shared problem. The "relational" form of expertise needed for that kind of activity is described by Edwards as "being able to make what matters for you as a professional visible; and being able to negotiate interpretations and responses to complex problems which incorporate what others can offer" (2010, p. 21).

The assignment asked students to identify experts and work alongside them on a locally meaningful project, interview them, and analyze their interpretations of and responses to the problem using the intellectual tools of the course. In doing so, the students were encouraged to take the stand point of the other professional and recognize the expertise being brought to bear on the problem. Edwards has argued that the ability to recognize the expertise and intentions of others is an important component of work with children as, so often, early childhood workers need to collaborate with other professionals and of course parents in supporting children's well-being and development. She terms such a capacity to align different interpretations of problems and the responses to them as the exercise of "relational expertise" (Edwards, 2010).

By working together as a group to first analyze local images familiar to them and explain the meaning of those local images to us as outsiders, the students learned to communicate and work together as preparation for subsequently talking to other professionals in the course of their research projects. The face-to-face sessions helped them exercise a growing capacity for working relationally with others as they helped each other use the intellectual tools to understand the local context they were all beginning to see with new complexity. The more relational approach to expertise was also important to us because it allowed us to legitimately place ourselves as learners keen to remedy a lack of knowledge about their local context and were genuinely interested in their interpretations of practices.

## Conclusion

Designing the technology, teaching the unit in a context for which it had not been designed, and reflecting on our work using CHAT, have provided us with a renewed sense of "becoming" as educators. As Morson has identified, the process of becoming in interactions with others populates our minds with a complexity of voices and provides opportunities for us to think with these voices, test ideas and experiences, and "shape convictions that are innerly persuasive in response" (2004, p. 330).

CHAT concepts for learning in activities in social worlds help us articulate how we were able to get beyond our naïve notions of professional courses as inevitable communities of practice. For example, our focus on building common knowledge enabled us to recognize and overcome the lack of shared background knowledge among participants in the unit and to create and mobilize a resource that could help everyone accomplish course aims. Instead of organizing the unit around mastering content, the content – knowledge of local practices brought by students and CHAT intellectual tools – formed the basis for common knowledge we could use to work together on problems of local practice.

For us as educators, the concepts of guided participation as students undertook activities helped us recognize we were working together with the students on a shared object of activity as a problem space: structuring environments for children's learning and development. Consequently we were able to create a temporary community in the short span of four days and organize activity meaningful to that temporary community in the form of research projects the student members then completed on their own.

Subsequent reflection has led us to suggest that the rather cumbersome CD-ROM technology we used limited the building of common knowledge. Had the technology created opportunities for continuous interactions between meetings, the knowledge sharing might have been enhanced. Baguley, Pullen, and Short (2009) suggest there is a move toward a collaborative approach to learning where there is rapid change in technology. Bigum (2002) identifies that successful learning around technology happens where there is an emphasis placed on the relationships between the learners and the teachers rather than the information provided by the teachers. Feenberg similarly suggests "the social values placed on the design, not just use, of technological systems" (2002, p. 14) will be a measure of how much new technological practices empower people.

Wiki environments in which learners can extend their participation between each other in both face-to-face and online environments as they co-construct a series of hyperlinked texts appropriate to their needs offer exciting possibilities. Our experiences with the digital study guide suggest attention to the community, shared activity, and the role of technology within the interpersonal dynamics of guided participation will be important assets when engaging with unfamiliar teaching contexts using these technologies.

The course was also an unfamiliar site for the students. Higher education can represent a boundary or transitional space for students seeking a new career or a career change, as was the case for three of our students. Indeed, if an object of education is to facilitate the adoption of new practices, we must acknowledge the risks involved for at least some students. Edwards uses language of "safety" and describes the difficulties professionals may face when they work in boundary spaces and "need to negotiate task accomplishment with others in activities where their expertise is not shored up by a historically accumulated set of practices which they can expertly navigate and manipulate" (2010, p. 26). Building common knowledge as a resource to be used in the work of the course as a boundary space was clearly helpful.

### References

Auld, G. and Tonyan, H. A. (2006). *Reconsidering Study Guides for Distance Education: A methological framework for digitising study guides*. Paper presented at the Australian Educational Research Association, Adelaide, Australia.

Baguley, M., Pullen, A., and Short, M. (2009). Multiliteracies and the new world order. In D. R. Cole and D. L. Pullen (Eds.), *Multiliteracies and Technology Enhanced Education: Social practice and the global classroom*, (pp. 1–17). Hershey, PA: Information Science Reference.

Bigum, C. (2002). Design sensibilities, schools and the new computing and communication technologies. In I. Snyder (Ed.), *Silicon Literacies: Communication, innovation and education in the electronic age*, (pp. 130–40). London: Routledge.

Dahlberg, G., Moss, P., and Pence, A. (1999). *Beyond Quality in Early Childhood Education and Care: Postmodern perspectives*. London, UK: Falmer Press.

Edwards, A. (2010). *Being an Expert Professional Practitioner: The relational turn in expertise.* Dordrecht, Springer.

Edwards, A. and D'Arcy, C. (2004). Relational agency and disposition in sociocultural accounts of learning to teach. *Educational Review,* **56** (2), 147–55.

Feenberg, A. (2002). *Transforming Technology: A critical theory revisited* (Rev. ed.). Oxford; New York: Oxford University Press.

Fleer, M., Tonyan, H. A., Mantilla, A. C., and Rivalland, C. M. P. (2006, January). *Is 'the play the thing'? Play as guided participation across cultural-historical contexts.* Paper presented at the Australian Research in Early Childhood Education, Melbourne, Australia.

Morson, G. S. (2004). The process of ideological becoming. In S. W. Freedman and A. F. Ball (Eds.), *Bakhtinian Perspectives on Language, Literacy, and Learning,* (pp. 317–31). New York: Cambridge University Press.

Rogoff, B. (1995). Observing sociocultural activity on three planes: Participatory appropriation, guided participation, and apprenticeship. In J. V. Wertsch, A. Alvarez, and P. del Rio (Eds.), *Sociocultural Studies of Mind,* (pp. 139–64). New York: Cambridge University Press.

   (2003). *The Cultural Nature of Human Development.* New York: Oxford University Press,

Rogoff, B., Mistry, J., Göncü, A., and Mosier, C. E. (1993). Guided participation in cultural activity by toddlers and caregivers. *Monographs of the Society for Research in Child Development,* **58** (serial No. 236).

Rogoff, B., Moore, L., Najafi, B., Dexter, A., Correa-Chávez, M., and Solís, J. (2007). Children's development of cultural repertoires through participation in everyday routines and practices. In J. Grusec and P. Hastings (Eds.), *Handbook of Socialization,* (pp. 490–515). New York, NY: Guilford.

# 15

# Gentle Partnerships: Learning from the Fifth Dimension

## Honorine Nocon and Monica E. Nilsson

University-community partnerships provide opportunities to increase the relevance of higher education for local communities and university researchers. Service learning and civic engagement provide opportunities for higher education students and faculty members to test theory in practice and to bring a critical and practical lens to theory development, while providing resources, including labor, information, and a critical lens, to community organizations and institutions. Joint activity that includes university and community actors has the potential to contribute to reciprocal development of both the community and the university. Partnership, however, is not without problems. Sustaining partnerships takes time and money. Rewarding investment in service to the community contradicts higher education's traditional emphasis on research and teaching, unless research and/or teaching are integral to the partnership. Experiential and service learning projects involve teaching, but rarely include research or a partnership design that includes the development of new and generalizable knowledge. University-community partnerships that blend service, teaching, and research are uncommon. The Fifth Dimension, 5D, is an example of such a partnership.

## The Fifth Dimension, 5D, Model

5D began in the early 1980s as an experiment in creating model learning environments, or activity systems, with which to "study simultaneously development on several interacting levels or 'genetic domains' over time" (Cole, 1995b, p. 5). The domains included those of the individual, the individual in interaction with others, the designed activity system itself, and the activity system in interaction with its community-based institutional host. The original design was research oriented and theory driven, employing a Vygotskian framework to link research, teaching, and service in the interest of advancing learning and the development of all participants as well as the partnering university and community institutions. Cole described 5D as a form of "design experiment" after Brown's (1992) method of designing complex interventions that were placed in classroom settings. However, the earliest 5Ds were placed in nonschool settings. This choice was made because earlier work by Cole and colleagues indicated that the lack of success in school, in the case of children with no physical barriers, was due, at least in part, to the culture of schooling (Cole, 1996; LCHC, 1982). The original 5D was characterized by a triangular physical arrangement of child-computer-adult learner that operationalized the zone of proximal development (Vygotsky, 1978) in an offline play world of possibilities in which sorting and ranking had no place (Griffin & Cole, 1984, 1987; Nicolopoulou & Cole, 1993).

Based loosely on the original research model, versions of the 5D have proliferated over time and geographic space (Cole & Distributed Literacy Consortium, 2006). In spite of local variation, several key elements of the 5D model have been maintained. First, 5D program settings are consciously alternative to traditional mainstream classrooms to support flexibility in teaching and learning roles. In these less formal educational settings, grade levels and ages are mixed, learners' movement is not discouraged, and cross-talk between participants is encouraged. Second, learners are not defined by their failures. Third, the incorporation of local culture as well as traditional and emergent academic cultures in 5Ds is accommodated by the model's flexible and open structure.

Most 5Ds are after-school activities that take place in *community institutions*, often with a good number of computers. The physical arrangement is organized around a structuring device, the *maze*, which is frequently represented as a three-dimensional game board. The maze contains (or represents) a number of rooms (often twenty or so). Each room contains the names of one to three software *games* and sometimes a board game. Completing a game or task at a more challenging level is rewarded by more choices about where to move next in the maze. An important component of 5D is the participation of *undergraduate students* from a local college or university who participate on a regular basis, often for a semester. Finally, at each 5D site there is a *site coordinator* responsible for running and managing the site. Most often someone from the host community institution takes on the role.

The original 5D programs in southern California were funded as part of a research study of individual development in relation to the development of a teaching/learning culture (see Cole, 1995a; Nicolopoulou & Cole, 1993). Interest in 5D expanded and, in 1990, new 5D programs opened at universities in the United States, Russia, and Mexico, as well as other parts of California. Funding for these programs included support for development of an electronically mediated research group composed of university and community researchers and implementers from the distributed program sites. This global network of locally initiated sites continues in 2012 and has expanded and contracted as 5D sites have opened and closed.

Each locally adapted 5D program is unique, a reflection of local culture, local control, and locally negotiated partnership goals, and yet recognizable as a 5D. Despite the variability, all 5Ds are governed by three principles: (1) to be sustained, educational innovations require significant changes in the social context into which they are introduced; (2) barring biological impediments, all children can learn with guidance, and (3) local cultures (both institutional and those of the individuals participating) and mainstream academic culture can be combined to create productive learning contexts.

Decades before the current impetus toward university-community partnerships, the 5D model linked higher education research, teaching, and outreach/service to local community interests. University and community participants often had different social, ethnic, economic, professional, and cultural backgrounds and different motivations for their participation. Often, there was no single, robustly shared goal (e.g., profit, learning for learning's sake) organizing participation in the 5D activity, but diverse goals of the different participants coordinated.

Since 1990, 5D has expanded in the Americas and Europe. In 2008–2009, there were thirty-five 5Ds or 5D-inspired program sites in primarily low-income communities in California. There were also programs in Florida, North Carolina, Delaware, and Pennsylvania in the United States, and in other nations such as Mexico, Spain, Brazil, Finland, Sweden, Turkey, and Canada. The numbers and places have changed as 5D sites have opened and closed, most frequently because of the departure of key researchers, whose time and research funding supported 5D sites and partnerships. In the sections that follow, we first describe 5D projects, or cases, in which we have participated. Analysis of the cases follows and suggests a pedagogic model based on Vygotskian principles and aspects of 5D can support both the creation of new knowledge and productive partnership. Implementing and sustaining such models, however, is complicated by contradictory and often competing objectives of the partnering institutions and the participants who enact partnership. We argue that attention to those contradictions in an approach that uses elements of the 5D model, what we call gentle partnership, informed by Vygotskian theories, can lead to productive university-community partnership.

## Our Roles Past and Current

The authors participated in a number of 5Ds as doctoral students and later as postdoctoral researchers and instructors. Both were researchers in one of the original 5Ds in Solana Beach, CA, and other sites in and around San Diego. Both also participated in sites in Ronneby, Sweden. Our most recent collaboration was in the European Commission research and development project: "The Fifth Dimension – Local Learning Communities in a Global World," within the framework "Information, Society, and Technology (IST), School of Tomorrow," which linked 5D sites in Sweden, Denmark, and Spain (Nilsson & Nocon, 2005). Additionally, we collaborated with colleagues in Colorado, North Carolina, California, and Denmark, Finland, and Spain in an international exchange of researchers and university students working with 5Ds funded by the European Commission and the U.S. Department of Education's Fund for Improvement of Post-Secondary Education.

## Swedish Cases

These 5Ds broadly followed the model described earlier, but with expansions that further link the cases to university missions of teaching, research, and outreach.

*The Fifth Dimension in Sweden: Education as research and developmental work.*

This series of related 5D projects developed in the mid-90s as a collaboration between the Blekinge Institute of Technology (BTH) and local actors including the public library, municipality schools, and software design companies. 5D was perceived as a tool for addressing a government initiative that Swedish universities take on the "third mission" of community development (Nilsson & Sutter, 2002) and received financial support from the university and the municipality.

Undergraduate students, mainly studying human-computer interaction, were hosts and assistants in several 5D projects located in the college's media center/library. Their participation was aimed at learning about human-computer interaction and software design, but it was also meant to support and guide children and teenagers in their use of different computer games. Since this was also a research initiative, the students obtained hands-on experience in research work. After each session, students wrote field notes and so contributed with data and simultaneously reflected on their own learning.

In the early Swedish 5D projects, different groups of researchers ran separate programs for two to four hours in the late afternoon in the same space.

The space and equipment were shared, but the program content and clientele differed. The separate programs focused on technology use, English language practice, Web page design, construction and programming of computerized robots, and digital storytelling. These programs continued in various forms and university-connected locations through 2000. After 2000, the Swedish 5D moved to an elementary school. That collaboration ran for over ten years (Nilsson, 2008). It started as an after-school activity, but became a permanent school-hour activity, with participation from undergraduates, researchers, and schoolteachers. 5D became part of the regular activity in the school and, according to the principal, was there to stay: "it has become a part of our activity here" (MN 16/11/99).

The principal liked the 5D model because it offered children the possibility of making choices based on individual goals and interests, while offering teachers the opportunity to direct and influence the children's work. Additionally, the principal appreciated that the design of the maze offered an overview of software available for the activity. He wanted 5D to be part of the curriculum of all six grade levels in the school. However, because of the shortage of undergraduates, students from the local high school, particularly students studying child development, became involved, very much to the children's joy. For the undergraduates involved this meant interactions and collaboration with a diverse set of participants, implying learning in a real-world setting with all its complexity.

In 2001, the BTH 5D researchers received a European Union grant together with two other European universities and a Swedish software company. The Swedish 5D projects became part of an international research and development partnership experimenting with intersite collaboration and different kinds of technology-based activities (Nilsson & Nocon, 2005). One such was codevelopment of a virtual 5D programmed in Active Worlds, produced collaboratively with children in Denmark (Jensen, Jensen, & Jack, 2005). As a consequence, the technology teacher at the Ronneby school, already active in 5D, was hired by the municipality as a technology and media pedagogue/coach serving all local schools.

### The "Education as Research" Project

The second Swedish case was a hybrid activity between research and teaching, which was influenced by 5D. The "education as research" project was a distance-learning course in social science (scientific methods in pedagogy), with undergraduate students located across Sweden. The course was implemented through a web-based learning platform. The idea was to frame the course as a research project with the aim of investigating the pedagogical climate in Swedish elementary schools. The students were seen as "research assistants," and the teachers as research managers. The students pursued their research in partnership with educators and children at schools in their home-towns, in three steps: observation of interaction in a classroom (recorded in field notes), interviews of pupils or teachers, and analysis of the field notes and the interviews. The data were uploaded on the learning platform, accessible to course instructors and the university students. The undergraduate students used the collective body of data for their analysis and final research reports.

The course instructors found the data, particularly the field notes, useful for research purposes. The conclusion was that the university students were able to act as researchers, producing relevant and useful empirical data in a proj-ect collectively conducted through multiple, local short-term partnerships. Students learned from being involved in a knowledge creation process.

## U.S. Cases

Two of the following cases adhered closely to the original 5D model. The third case is implicated in an expansion beyond the 5D model, which is being implemented in partnerships at the University of Colorado.

### *Magical Dimension and Explorers Dimension*
In 1996, Nocon opened the Magical Dimension in the elementary school across the street from one of the original 5Ds. This program, linked to the University of California, San Diego (UCSD), was designed for multilingual children from the school, including children with special needs. Community partners were the school and the elementary school district. Additional part-ners included two local 5D research teams and the nearby Boys and Girls Club. These formed a Community Coalition, which still exists. When the Magical Dimension closed in 1999, in part because of the lack of adults from the school and university, the partners developed a Homework Club, which ran at the Boys and Girls Club and coordinated with the original 5D program, which ran until 2009.

Soon after the Magical Dimension closed, Nocon and others opened the Explorers Dimension. The Explorers Dimension, too, was a collaboration of the university and the regional Boys and Girls Club. Additional partners included UCSD's Human Development Program, the San Diego Housing Commission, and two elementary schools. Homework emerged as a major concern of both the schools and the Housing Commission. The 5D play ele-ment was separated temporally from homework time and academic game time, much like a recess period, both at the schools after school and at the community center in the housing project. This program operated for two years, at which point Nocon left for an academic position in another state. A different iteration continued fitfully for another year, in partnership with the regional Boys and Girls Club.

### El Águila and the Urban Community Teacher Education Program

Nocon opened *El club del Águila* in 2003 as a collaboration between the University of Colorado and a local school. The club ran before and after school in a school's library/media center. This 5D was codesigned with the school's literacy coaches. The adults who worked with the children were pre-service teachers and doctoral students in education. One goal was for the preservice teachers to get to know the children outside the classroom, in a more playful learning environment mediated by technology. Another goal was to conduct research on innovative uses of technology for learning in a codesigned after-school club. Each semester, the club design was modified with significant input from teachers, school leaders, and new and returning preservice teachers. Over four years, writing remained the focus.

El Águila's Club, while supported by the school, was not an easy fit for the preservice teacher candidates. There were many demands on their time and their goal was to become teachers, not researchers. The school's teachers and administrators valued the program and its impact on children and staff members, but there was constant tension between having the teacher candidates spend time in the 5D, where they learned about children and technology as a tool, and having them in the classroom where they supported clinical teachers and learned the routines and art of formal instruction (see Nocon, 2008). As the teacher candidates neared the end of their licensure program, this tension was exacerbated.

During 2005–2006, the last year of El Águila's Club, Nocon and another professor initiated a different program in response to concern about teacher candidates' limited understanding of their students' lives. In this program, "Teaching outside the Box" (Nocon & Sands, 2007), the academics organized readings, discussions, and a series of home and community visits, through which the teacher candidates learned about their students and their communities and developed understanding of schooling as part of an ecology of human development. The approach was Vygotskian, informed by the "funds of knowledge" research (Moll et al., 1992). While this project and El Águila's Club were presented to the university's faculty, it was the teaching outside the box approach to building connections with the school's larger community that was later integrated into the teacher education program. In May 2006, Nocon left the school and El Águila's Club ceased operating.

## Analysis and Discussion

Our experience of 5D provides evidence of the value and the complications of university-community partnerships. Contradictory goals or objectives of institutions and participants constrained the sustainability of the 5D programs and the partnerships that supported them. We use two concepts from Cultural Historical Activity Theory (CHAT) to analyze 5D and 5D-inspired partnerships in which we have participated.

### *The Objects and Contradictions of Joint Human Activity*

The interinstitutional partnerships framed by 5D reveal tensions and contradictions on several levels. To understand them, we use the concept of object/motive found in CHAT (Engeström, 1987). As they worked together on 5D, the diverse partners interpreted the activity differently, in ways that reflected the different motives that were often contradictory. The university's motives or objects of research and teaching, and the more contested object of outreach or service represent another contradiction. The 5D partnership connected institutions and people, but their relationships to 5D and the partnership reflected their participation in very different activities within the partnership.

In CHAT terms, an *activity* may occur whenever a (collective) human need takes shape as an object of activity, which we can think of as an emerging motive or problem space toward which action is directed. This object then continues to motivate action, which in turn serves to satisfy needs. According to activity theory, the *object* of an activity is not exactly identical, but certainly closely connected to the *motive* of the activity (Leont'ev, 1978). In the case of higher education, we have to ask what kinds of needs are involved. Are students studying to get credentials or a degree, or because they want to learn for the sake of becoming more skilled and knowledgeable? Are these different needs incompatible or can they exist simultaneously? The concepts of use value and exchange value in the object of activity suggests they may be both. Nilsson and Wihlborg (2011) propose the concepts of *exchange-value* and *use-value* – concepts once developed by Marx (1990) in his theory of commodity production – to critically examine and assess possible consequences of tensions in higher education. The term *use-value* refers to the capacity of a product to satisfy human needs, while the term *exchange-value* refers to the price of a product on the market – that is, when it is marketed in competition with other alternative products. As Engeström (1987) points out, all human activity in contemporary Western capitalist societies involves primary contradictions between use-value and exchange-value. This naturally includes educational activities.

*Contradictions in 5D*

5D originated as research. It quickly evolved to include a teaching motive as well because, more than technology or particular games, 5D depended on the participation of more experienced adult learners, originally undergraduates at research universities, to work with less experienced learners in multiple and dynamic zones of proximal development. The choice to locate 5Ds in community settings was made prior to the development of a context for higher education favoring community outreach, circa 1980.

As it turns out, the university participants, researchers, graduate students, and undergraduate students who enacted 5D partnerships often did provide university outreach and service to communities, but there was ongoing tension between the service and research motives of the university participants, and the motives or objects of the community partners. One example from the original 5D, which ran for more than twenty years at the Boys and Girls Club in Solana Beach, was the characterization of 5D by the community partner as a service project and the undergraduates and graduate researchers as volunteers. This often led to their being tasked to fill youth worker roles in other parts of the facility (Cole et al., 2006; Nicolopoulou & Cole, 1993).

There were similar contradictions across the cases. The motives that shaped 5D in Sweden were teaching, community outreach, and research. The engagement of undergraduate students in research was part of a pedagogical motive that assumed undergraduates' learning about technology integration and software design would be enhanced by participating in research on learning in a technology-mediated learning environment. The partnering community members and their institutions were motivated by community service, including the enhancement of learning, in particular the learning of technology. The earliest Swedish 5D programs opened and closed based on short-term partnerships that responded to university participants' research and teaching needs and to the general needs of the community to learn more about technology. The associated university-community partnership changed over time and eventually linked back to the university-based 5D project. The success of the elementary school 5D was due largely to resolving contradictions between the competing objects of research and school teaching, as well as university teaching and school teaching.

When Nilsson initiated the elementary school 5D, the administrators enthused about using computers to enhance learning. They shared Nilsson's perception that traditional teaching needed changing. The teachers, however, were unconvinced; what was perceived as a tool for productive change by the researcher and school leaders they perceived as a threat. Another contradiction arose when administrators saw opportunities (additional adults, the development of technological competence) that coordinated with the researcher's wish for pedagogical change. However, they also wanted the resources that came with the 5D partnership to fit into their ongoing activity. This demand directly contradicts a basic principle of 5D: to be sustained, educational innovations require significant changes in the social context into which they are introduced. This tension was exacerbated when, because of university constraints, the number of university students participating in 5D was significantly reduced, and high school students and their teachers became partners. Their goals did not include fundamental change to the model of formal schooling.

Nilsson responded to these contradictions by deviating from the 5D model and allowing undergraduates to introduce their own activities into the 5D framework at the school. The freedom to choose a project topic that was not preordained by the research project was more appealing to undergraduates and consistent with university pedagogical norms. Resolving this contradiction turned out to be a key point of growth and development for the researchers. The researchers, consistent with a broader research motive of the distributed, international 5D research community, had introduced Activeworlds Eduverse as a platform on which children at the school would co-construct a virtual 5D world with students in Denmark. This technology was complex and remote from the schoolteachers' practice. The teachers found learning Activeworlds too time-consuming. In comparison, the teachers (and children) embraced Lego Mindstorms, originally used at the university 5Ds and introduced at the school by undergraduates. Lego Mindstorms allowed learners, undergraduates, and teachers to engage together physically in ways that enhanced learning and instruction.

Similar contradictions also emerged in the United States at the Magical and the Explorers Dimensions. Both partnerships were familiar with other local 5Ds, but did not embrace the Vygotskian concept that play and learning were related (Vygotsky, 1978), a fundamental aspect of the 5D sites and one of the underlying assumptions governing the choice to locate 5Ds outside formal schooling. The community partners in both the Magical and the Explorer's Dimensions lobbied strongly for organizing 5D programs into scholastic-like periods in which play was separated from homework, which, for the community partners, was a primary goal and indicator of learning, something it was not for the researchers. In these cases, researcher fears that school culture would shape the 5Ds came to pass, and ultimately undermined the 5Ds.

These contradictions between the objects or motives of the university and those of community partners suggest work must be done to elucidate and coordinate the motives of collaborating institutions for entering into partnership.

This further suggests the model for research in university-community partnerships cannot be that of a fixed experimental design or even a fixed structure. The implied emergent nature of the research design carries its own contradictions with university research requirements (e.g., fixed protocols for institutional review boards) and the specifications required by research funding agents.

Just as the research motive of 5D suggests a basic contradiction between research activity and a truly collaborative, emergent co-constructed partnership, there are contradictions between the divergent personal goals and collective objects of individual participants in these partnerships. For example, the research activities at the Swedish elementary school and at El Águila were organized by complex objects of service, teaching, and research. The activity shaped by the object of research has the use value of creating knowledge and potentially improving schooling and has exchange value as the commodity required to obtain a doctorate or tenure. That basic contradiction is often evident in 5Ds, where research is the primary motive of university researchers and doctoral students. It was apparent in the tension between the motives of the principals at the Colorado elementary school, for whom literacy was the object of partnership, and the researchers' intention to explore learning mediated by technology and play. While this tension persisted, the 5D goal of providing access to technology to children who did not have computers suggested the partnership had shared use value in addressing what was jointly acknowledged as a societal need.

The discussion of the undergraduates who brought Lego Mindstorms to the Swedish school points to another tension for students in university-community partnerships. For these students, we can surmise the use value of learning about computerized robotics in schooling excited their intellectual curiosity. This use value was more important to them than the exchange value of doing what was prescribed in a class to get a grade. They wished to be involved in knowledge creation of interest to them.

One of the emergent goals of 5D has been to engage university students in knowledge and culture creation. At research universities, this has been a successful model. In San Diego, for example, students often take continuations of UCSD courses that allow them to learn and play in 5Ds while they grow as researchers and increase their knowledge of child development. The Swedish "education as research" project was influenced by this element of 5D. It successfully used distance learning to engage students in research on teaching as the basis of its pedagogical design. The researcher/instructors employed this pedagogy to advance the goal of guiding their students to perceive and privilege the use value of higher education.

Nocon, in contrast, was confronted squarely with the exchange value of higher education for students when teacher candidates, engaged in preparation for professional licensure, resisted participation in the 5D. As they moved toward licensure, their dominant activity and object was to practice the techniques of formal teaching in the classroom. The use value of learning about child development was acknowledged, but deferred. This points to an aspect of 5D to be negotiated when adult learners from the university are not engaged in research apprenticeships. The emphasis on the exchange value of training for professional credentials in higher education contradicts the use value of knowledge creation for its own sake and the sake of society. In the case of El Águila, attention to this contradiction for preservice licensure students provoked a move from research on development, to inquiry directed at supporting teaching and the development of local knowledge to support the teacher candidates' learning about their students' lives. This type of very applied inquiry for local use in problems of practice is not traditionally considered research in higher education, but it has use value for teacher candidates and for the community partners.

## Contradictions in Higher Education

That contradictory demands and conditions affect students and teachers in higher education is nothing new. However, such tensions are currently accentuated to such an extent that they occupy a central position, with tangible effects. A common example of fundamental oppositions in higher education is the conflict students sometimes experience between wishing to complete their education with top marks and desiring to develop deep understanding of the subject matter. The necessity of having to choose between "learning" and "succeeding" has consequences for the manner in which students approach their studies and the type of knowledge they acquire. In CHAT terms these fundamental tensions are conceptualized as a conflict between exchange value and use value. We believe lessons can be learned from the 5D partnership model about addressing this contradiction in ways that can lead to learning and development for higher education and communities.

### Gentle Partnership: Learning from 5D

The cases in this chapter illustrate a model of university-community partnership that has seen actual partnerships form, grow, diminish, and close. In spite of this history, the 5D model has persisted over time and space. We believe this is due to the perceived value of its guiding principles and its model for integrating research, teaching, and service in university-community partnerships. New 5Ds have operated as new sites of learning, and even as they close, elements from the 5D partnership inform new designs for higher education partnerships and new important pedagogical issues to be addressed. Community and university needs are discovered through participating in the process of partnership. In the quest for relevance, being outside the university in ways that make sense to both the university and community is essential. Integrating commitment to the use value of joint knowledge creation as well as the exchange value of partnering is also essential. Successful university-community research partnerships require commitment to locally relevant research that is itself a service of the university and the basis of ongoing opportunity to develop new knowledge with the community.

If we return to the 5D-inspired "education as research" online learning in the Swedish cases, we see that this new model links distance learning/technology, that is, intersite communication, long a goal of 5D researchers, with work with social actors in schools around locally perceived needs. That is a major shift away from the original design experiment 5D research model to a pedagogical model based more directly on codesign. It requires openness about inquiry that is not consistent with the experimental model, but has the promise of being more relevant to communities. This openness to research and inquiry on community-based problems is one aspect of what we refer to as gentle partnership.

We suggest this openness may provide a potential solution to the demise of programs and partnerships when researchers and their funding leave. The traditional model of research in higher education is too dependent on individual researchers, their personal research agendas, and research grant funding. Partnership in the interest of local and societal change requires that higher education, particularly in the social sciences, engage collectively with community practitioners in all aspects of the research and teaching process, something particularly urgent in the field of education and currently endorsed by the U.S. Department of Education's Institute of Educational Studies. Structural supports for productive partnership have to be codesigned to endure beyond the departure of individuals.

Another aspect of 5D that is a precondition of productive university-community partnership is identification of a shared object of activity that has the potential to link the activities of the partners and be of benefit to all parties. An example from our cases is the object of providing access to technology to low-income children. This object of activity linked the different, but compatible goals of community members and individual researchers. This suggests to us that gentle partnership does not require that all motives be fully shared, but rather that they be made explicit to determine compatibility, and then coordinated actively by the partners.

Finally, our work in 5D has taught us that the representation of participation, or what partners perceive as active engagement, is not incidental to partnership. We have learned that funding and e-mail communication are not enough. Physical presence in support of partnership is essential, and it is expensive (Nocon, 2000). Service is traditionally the least valued object/ motive in higher education. University-community partnership requires time, effort, support, and a long-term view. This suggests the need for policy changes in higher education that reward and support partnership work.

## Conclusions and Implications

How should we as educators design the activities of higher education to strengthen its use value to researchers, teachers, students, and community members? Three conclusions can be drawn from the cases outlined in this chapter. First, learning and teaching need not be confined to classrooms and textbooks but can involve developmental work together with local societal actors. This developmental work can productively combine research and teaching with community outreach and service in ways relevant to local communities. However, expanding education in this way requires dedication from students, researchers, teachers, and, not incidentally, university administrators (Nocon, Nilsson, & Cole, 2004). Second, it is often the case that the university partners are the weak link in sustaining the collaboration. Lack of flexibility in the university research model, the different timescales of researchers, students, and practitioners, and the need to attend to nurturing the partnerships as individual actors depart, research agendas and funding sources change, and new problems of practice emerge require that the partners, including higher education partners, engage in the process of partnership beyond the signing of memos of understanding. The relationship between partners needs to be part of the ongoing work of individuals in the partnering institutions. Nilsson (2008) describes the relationship as a "thin string" strong enough to sustain the collaboration despite occasional hardships, a connection that is flexible but also tenuous. Partnership requires attention. Third, university researchers operating under the principles that are the foundation of 5D have demonstrated that diverse partners with different, but compatible, motives can engage in joint activity that coordinates compatible goals. This shared engagement can foster a spirit of community, participation, and collaborative work, what we have called here gentle partnership. The process of engaging in gentle partnership has the potential to influence the organization and structures of higher education, and should do so, if we want students to be reflective producers of relevant knowledge and societal change.

We suggest gentle partnership based on aspects of the 5D model can advance the development of higher education. Learning in 5D is not only about individual achievement in terms of exams and grades, but about shared learning that is co-constructed through engagement, care, and participation in a collaborative activity. Approaching university-community partnership gently, for its potential for reciprocal university-community learning, contradicts the image of the university as ivory tower and privileged producer of the knowledge that really counts. It has the potential for increasing the relevance of higher education.

## References

Brown, A. (1992). Design experiments: Theoretical and methodological challenges in creating complex interventions in classroom settings. *Journal of the Learning Sciences*, **2**, 141–68.

Cole, M. (1995a). Cultural-historical psychology: A meso-genetic approach. In L. Martin, K. Nelson, and E. Tobach (Eds.), *Sociocultural Psychology*, (pp. 168–204). Cambridge, UK: Cambridge University Press.

(1995b). Socio-cultural-historical psychology: Some general remarks and a proposal for a new kind of cultural-genetic methodology. In J.V. Wertsch, P. Del Rio, and A. Alvarez (Eds.), *Sociocultural Studies of Mind*, (pp. 187–214). Cambridge, UK: Cambridge University Press.

(1996). *Cultural Psychology: A once and future discipline*. Cambridge, MA: Belknap–Harvard University Press.

Cole, M. and The Distributed Literacy Consortium. (2006). *The Fifth Dimension: An after-school program built on diversity*. New York, NY: Russell Sage.

Engeström, Y. (1987). *Learning by expanding*. Helsinki: Orienta – Konsultit Oy.

Griffin, P. and Cole, M. (1984). Current activity for the future: The Zo-ped. In B. Roggoff and J. Wertsch (Eds.), *Children's Learning in the "Zone of Proximal Development,"* (pp. 45–63). New Directions for Child Development, 23. San Francisco, CA: Jossey-Bass.

(1987). New technologies, basic skills and the underside of education: What's to be done? In J. A. Langer (Ed.), *Language, Literacy, and Culture: Issue of society and schooling*, (pp. 110–31). Norwood, NJ: Ablex.

Jensen, T., Jensen, K., and Jack, M. (2005). Learning in virtual and physical communities. In M. Nilsson and H. Nocon (Eds.), *Teaching and Technology in Local and Global Communities*, (pp. 87–130). Oxford, UK: Peter Lang.

LCHC (Laboratory of Comparative Human Cognition). (1982). A model system for the study of learning difficulties. *Quarterly Newsletter of the Laboratory of Comparative Human Cognition*, **4**, 39–66.

Leont'ev, A. N. (1978). *Activity, Consciousness and Personality*. Englewood Cliffs, NJ: Prentice-Hall.

Marx, K. (1990). *Capital* (Vol. 1). London: Penguin Books.

Moll, L. C., Amanti, C., Neff, D., and González, N. (1992). Funds of knowledge for teaching: Using a qualitative approach to connect homes and classrooms. *Theory into Practice*, **31** (2), 132–41.

Nicolopoulou, A. and Cole, M. (1993). The Fifth Dimension, its play world, and its instructional contexts: The generation and transmission of shared knowledge in the culture of collaborative learning. In N. Minnick and E. Forman (Eds.), *The Institutional and Social Context of Mind: New directions in Vygotskian theory and research*, (pp. 283–314). New York, NY: Oxford University Press.

Nilsson, M. (2008). School development based on complementary needs: A case study of long-term university-school collaboration. *Journal of Educational Change*, 9(4), 349–56.

Nilsson, M. and Nocon, H. (2005). *Teaching and Technology in Local and Global Communities*. Oxford, UK: Peter Lang.

Nilsson, M. and Sutter, B. (2002). Femte Dimensionen: En lärmodell som förenar forskning, utbildning och "tredje uppgiften. I. L. Svensson, G., Brulin, and P. E. Ellström och Ö. Widegren (Eds.), *Interaktiv forskning – för utveckling av teori och praktik*. Stockholm: Vetenskaplig skriftserie från Arbetslivsinstitutet.

Nilsson, M. and Wihlborg, M. (2011). Higher education as commodity or space for learning: Modelling contradictions in educational practices. *Power & Education*, 3(2), 104–16.

Nocon, H. (2000). Developing hybridized social capital: Communication, coalition, and volunteering in non-traditional communities. Unpublished Ph.D. dissertation, Department of Communication, University of California, San Diego.

(2008). Contradictions of time in collaborative school research. *Journal of Educational Change*, 9 (4), 339–47.

Nocon, H., Nilsson M., and Cole, M. (2004). Spiders, firesouls, and little fingers: Necessary magic in university-community collaboration. *Anthropology and Education Quarterly*, 35 (3), 368–85.

Nocon, H. and Sands, D. (2007). *Teaching outside the box: Engaging the community in teacher education*. Paper presented at the American Educational Research Association. AERA, Annual Meeting, Chicago. April 11.

Vygotsky, L. S. (1978). *Mind in Society: The development of higher psychological processes*. Cambridge, MA: Harvard University Press.

# Index

Marcia. 21
Masterman, L. 107, 108
Masterman, L., Lee, S., with Francis, R. 121
Mazur, E. 45, 58, 59
McCarthy. 75, 87
McDermott, L. C., Shaffer, P. S., and PEG. 59
McVay, G. J. 115
McVay, G. J., Snyder, K. D., and Graetz, K. A. 121
mediational means. 109, 125
Mehan. 51, 59
mentor. 13, 123, 132, 133, 135, 136, 137, 162
mentored research. 124
metalanguage. 192, 194
Midgley. 186
Midgley, G. 196
Miller. 75
*mirroring*. 193
Mode 1. 205
Mode 2. 204, 205, 206
Moll, L. C., Amanti, Neff, and Gonzalez. 234
Moll, L., C., Tapia, J., and Whitmore, K. F. 121
Morozov, E. 121
Morson, G. S. 227
Moschkovich, J. 138
motive. 9, 12, 78, 81, 97, 98, 113, 140, 157, 159, 165, 186, 235, 236, 237, 238, 241
Mowery. 182
multimodal resource. 219
Muukkonen, H. 107
mycorrhizae. 115, 116

Nardi, B. A. 121
narratives of the self. 172
Nerland, M. and Jensen, K. 103
Nicol, D. J. 90, 94
Nicol, D. J. and Macfarlane-Dick, D. 103
Nicolopolou, A., and Cole, M. 243
Nijhuis, G. G., and Collis, B. 121
Nilsson, M. 16, 231, 232, 235, 236, 237
Nilsson, M., and Nocon, H. 243
Nilsson, M., and Sutter, B. 243
Nilsson, M., and Wihlborg, M. 243
Nocon, H. 16, 231, 232, 233, 234, 239, 241
Nocon, H., and Sands, D. 243
Nocon, H., Nilsson M., and Cole, M. 243
Nowotny, H. 205
Nowotny, H., Scott, P. and Gibbons, M. 213

O'Connor, M. C., and Michaels, S. 59
object/motive. *See* motive
Oborn and Dawson. 189

Oborn, E. and . Dawson, S. 197
Olson, D. R and Bruner, J. S. 65
Otero, V., Finkelstein, N. D., McCray, R., and Pollock, S. J. 59

Packer, M. J., and Goicoechea, J. 180
Paradis et al. 81
Paradis, J., Dobrin, D., and Miller, R. 87
Paré, A., D. Starke-Meyerrin, and McAlpine, L. 87
partnership. 235
patterns of participation. 85
Payne, J. 197
Pea, R. 168
peer instruction (PI). 12, 45, 46
peer interactions. 44
Peña, L. E. 180
Penuel, W. R., and Wertsch, J. V. 180
Perckman, M., Kong, Z. and Pavelin, S. 197
Piaget, J. 8, 22, 63, 72, 110, 174
Poleman. 117, 121
Pollock, S. J., and Finkelstein, N. D. 59
Ponti, M. 116, 121
positional roles. 124, 133, 135
*positionality*. 171
Postigo, H. 121
practicum. 15, 23, 31, 169, 173, 175, 176, 177, 178, 179
Prensky, M. 121
Prior, P. A. 47, 83, 87
problem solving. 52, 53, 70, 95, 96, 130, 131, 193
problem space. 186, 222, 225, 235
problem-solving. 44, 65, 156
professional education. 80, 89, 91, 92, 94, 96, 97, 98, 100, 101
program finalism. 174
public university. 15, 78, 198, 199, 201, 202, 203, 204, 207, 210, 211, 212

Redford, K. 154
Redish, E. F. 44, 59
reflection. 24, 41
Reich, R. 213
relational agency. 94, 99, 191
relational expertise. 218, 219, 224
relational research. 182, 185, 186, 193
Rensfeldt, A. B. 121
Resnick and Resnick. 93
Resnick, L. B. and Resnick, D. P. 104
Rheingold, H. 121
Rich, A. 214

17115686R00143

Printed in Great Britain
by Amazon